The *Bulletin of the Egyptological Seminar* (*BES*), produced by the Egyptological Seminar of New York, is a scholarly journal devoted to all aspects of ancient Egyptian culture, from predynastic times until the Byzantine Empire. Submissions are welcome from established scholars, students, and others active in the study of ancient Egypt. The Editorial Committee reviews all submissions for suitability and may also refer them to outside opinion for the same purpose.

Articles accepted for publication are proofread for spelling and punctuation and are typeset in BES format; matters of style and scholarly accuracy are the responsibility of the author. When preparing a manuscript for submission, authors should observe the following guidelines:

- Articles should be no longer than 5,000 words, including footnotes, and must be accompanied by an abstract of 50–100 words for use by the Annual Egyptological Bibliography.
- Use footnotes rather than endnotes. A separate bibliography may be included at the end of the article. If there is no separate bibliography, include full bibliographic material in the first footnote citation and use the short title format thereafter. Examples:

  Books. First citation: K. Sethe, *Dramatische Texte zu altaegyptischen Mysterienspielen,* UGAÄ 10 (Leipzig, 1928), 114–119. Subsequent citations: Sethe, *Dramatische Texte*, 115.

  Journal articles: First citation: A. Scharff, "Briefe aus Illahun," *ZÄS* 59 (1924), 28–30. Subsequent citations: A. Scharff, *ZÄS* 59 (1924), 28–30.

  Articles with a separate bibliography should use the short title format in all footnotes.
- Acronyms may be substituted for the titles of journals and series according to the list in *Lexikon der Ägyptologie* VII, xiv-xix. Acronyms that do not appear in that list must be defined at their first appearance in the footnotes or in a separate bibliography at the end of the article. Use short titles rather than acronyms for books: for example, Breasted, *Ancient Records*, rather than B*AR*.
- As a courtesy to readers, use numbers rather than "f." and "ff." in citations of more than one page or plate. Example: *ZÄS* 59 (1924), 28–30, rather than *ZÄS* 59 (1924), 28 ff.
- For other questions of style, consult the current edition of *The Chicago Manual of Style*.

Manuscripts prepared by computer should be submitted on diskette or CD, or via email as an attachment, as well as one copy in print form. For questions of format and compatibility, consult the Editor. If the manuscript includes hieroglyphs, illustrations, or plates, include one separate set of these. Do not send original photos or artwork until the article has been accepted for publication.

Each contributor will receive a CD with a PDF file of the article as it appears in the journal and one copy of the journal.

Subscriptions:

A complimentary copy of *BES* is provided to members in good standing of the Egyptological Seminar of New York. Yearly dues are $40 for individuals. Non-member copies and back issues of *BES* can be ordered from the David Brown Book Co., P.O. Box 511, Oakville, CT 06779; tel. no. 860-945-9329; e-mail: queries@dbbconline.com or www.oxbowbooks.com. Information about the Egyptological Seminar can be obtained at **www.esny-bes.org**.

Correspondence regarding membership, change of address, non-member copies and back issues of *BES* should be addressed to:

Stewart Driller, Treasurer
The Egyptological Seminar of New York (ESNY)
P.O. Box 1451
Cooper Station
New York, NY 10276
ESNY@nyc.rr.com

This volume was edited by James P. Allen, Ogden Goelet, and Deborah Vischak

BULLETIN
OF THE
EGYPTOLOGICAL SEMINAR
(*BES*)

VOLUME 18 2009

Bulletin of the Egyptological Seminar
(*BES*)

VOLUME 18 (2009)

Contents

Diane Bergman and Dag Bergman

Abbreviations in Egyptology 1–82

John Gee

Fronted Adverbials 83–90

Dieter Arnold

Pyramid Shapes of the Twelfth Dynasty 91–101

Abbreviations in Egyptology

by Diane and Dag Bergman
Edited by James P. Allen

The purpose of this publication, "Abbreviations in Egyptology" (AiE), is to provide scholars in the field of Egyptology with a comprehensive abbreviations tool in English to assist their research and publishing. The more than 5200 records include as many abbreviations used within Egyptology as possible. By request from scholars, AiE also includes abbreviations related to biblical research.

Abbreviation	Citation	Abbreviation alternatives
5000 Jahre Ägypten	J. Assmann and G. Burkard, eds., *Fünf Tausend Jahre Ägypten: Genese und Permanenz pharaonischer Kunst*	
A	*Codex Alexandrinus*	
Ä&L	*Ägypten und Levante*	ÄgLev
AA	*Archäologischer Anzeiger*	ArAnz; ArchAnz
ÄA	*Ägyptologische Abhandlungen*	ÄgAbh
AAA	*Annals of Archaeology and Anthropology* (Liverpool)	AAALiv; LAAA; Liv.Ann.
AAA	*Archaiologika analekta ex Athenon*	
AÄA	*Archiv für ägyptische Archäologie*	
AAAB	*Annales de l'Académie d'archéologie de Belgique*	
AAAb	*Acta Academiae aboensis*	
AAAdr	*Antichità Altoadriatiche*	
AAALiv	*Annals of Archaeology and Anthropology* (Liverpool)	AAA; LAAA; Liv.Ann.
AAASH	*Acta Archaeologica Academiae Scientiarum Hungaricae* (Budapest)	AcArch (B)
AAASyr	*Annales archéologiques arabes syriennes: Revue d'archéologie et d'histoire*	
AABSél	*Annuaire des Amis de la Bibliothèque de Sélestat*	
AAD	*Afroasiatic Dialects*	
AAEC	*Annuario dell'Accademia etrusca di Cortona*	
AAÉG	*Annuaire de l'Association pour l'encouragement des études grecques en France*	
AäG	E. Edel, *Altägyptische Grammatik*	
AAI	*Annali dell'Africa ltaliana*	
AAL	*Afroasiatic Linguistics*	
AAL	*Asien, Afrika, Lateinamerika*	
AAM	*L'Afrique et l'Asie modernes*	
AAN	*Annuaire de l'Afrique du Nord*	
AANLM	*Atti dell'Accademia Nazionale dei Lincei, Memorie*	
AANLR	*Atti dell'Accademia Nazionale dei Lincei, Rendiconti*	
AAR	*African Archaeological Review*	
AARAS	*American Academy of Religion Academy Series*	
AARASR	*American Academy of Religion Aids for the Study of Religion*	
AARCRS	*American Academy of Religion Classics in Religious Studies*	
AARP	*Art and Archaeology Research Papers* (London)	
AARSR	*American Academy of Religion Studies in Religion*	
AARTT	*American Academy of Religion Texts and Translations*	
AAS	*Asian and African Studies*	
AASA	*Annals of the American School of Athens*	ASA
AASF	*Annales Academiae scientiarum fenicae*	
AASOR	*Annual of the American Schools of Oriental Research*	
AASR	*Annales de l'Académie des sciences de Russie*	
ÄAT	*Ägypten und Altes Testament*	ÄuAT
AAW	*Anzeiger für Altertumswissenschaft*	AnzA
AAWB	*Abhandlungen der Preußischen Akademie der Wissenschaften* (Berlin) [From 1945: ADAW]	Abh Berl Ak; APAW
AAWG	*Abhandlungen der Akademie der Wissenschaften in Göttingen*	
AAWL	*Abhandlungen der Akademie der Wissenschaften in Leiden*	AAWLeid
AAWL	*Abhandlungen der Sächsischen Akademie der Wissenschaften zu Leipzig* [To 1919: ASGW]	ASAW
AAWLeid	*Abhandlungen der Akademie der Wissenschaften in Leiden*	AAL
AAWLM	*Abhandlungen der Akademie der Wissenschaften und der Literatur in Mainz*	AAWMainz; AMAW
AAWMainz	*Abhandlungen der Akademie der Wissenschaften und der Literatur in Mainz*	AAWLM; AMAW
AAWMun	*Abhandlungen der Bayerischen (Königlich) Akademie der Wissenschaften* (Munich)	ABAW
AAWWien	*Anzeiger der Österreichischen Akademie der Wissenschaften* (Vienna) [To 1946: AnzAWW]	AnzÖAW; AÖAW
AB	*Africana Bulletin*	

Abbreviation	Citation	Abbreviation alternatives
AB	*Anchor Bible*	
ABA	*Académie des Beaux-Arts: Bulletin semestriel* (Paris)	
ABAW	*Abhandlungen der Bayerischen (Königlich) Akademie der Wissenschaften* (Munich)	AAWMun
AbB	F.R. Kraus, ed., *Altbabylonische Briefe in Umschrift und Ubersetzung*	AbB
ABD	*Anchor Bible Dictionary*	ABD
ABG	*Archiv für Begriffsgeschichte*	ABG
Abh Berl Ak	*Abhandlungen der Preußischen Akademie der Wissenschaften* (Berlin) [From 1945: ADAW]	AAWB; APAW
AbIr	*Abstracta iranica* [Supplement to StudIr]	
AbIsl	*Abstracta islamica: Bibliographie sélective des études islamiques*	
ABIUSJH	*Annual of Bar-Ilan University Studies in Judaica and the Humanities*	
ABK	*Amtliche Berichte aus den Königlichen Kunstsammlungen* (Berlin)	Amtliche Berichte; BerBerlin
ABL	R.F. Harper, ed., *Assyrian and Babylonian Letters*	
ABLA	M. Noth and H.W. Wolff, eds., *Aufsätze zur biblischen Landes- und Altertumskunde*	
ABMH	*Archeion ton byzantinon mnemeion tes Hellados*	
Abod.Zar.	*Aboda Zara*	
Abot R.Nat.	*Abot de Rabbi Nathan*	
Abou-Roasch	F. Bisson de la Roque, *Rapport sur les fouilles d'Abou-Roasch, 1922-23, 1924* (FIFAO 1, pt. 3 and 2, pt. 1)	
ABPO	*Annales de Bretagne et des Pays de l'Ouest* [See also NAArm]	
ABR	*Australian Biblical Review*	AusBR
Abr	Philo, *De Abrahamo*	
ABRMW	H. Reventlow (Graf) and J. Bowden (trans.), *Authority of the Bible and the Rise of the Modern World*	
AbrN	*Abr-Nahrain: An Annual Published by the Department of Middle Eastern Studies* (University of Melbourne)	Abr-Nahrain
ABS	*Acta Baltico-Slavica: archaeologia, historia, etnographia, et linguarum scientia*	
ABSA	*Annual of the British School of Athens*	
Abyd Mar	A. Mariette, *Abydos*	
Abydos	E. Amélineau, *Les nouvelles fouilles d'Abydos*; also W.M.F. Petrie, *Abydos* (EEF 22, 24-25)	

Abbreviation	Citation	Abbreviation alternatives
AC	*L'Antiquité Classique*	AntCl; AntClass
ACAM	*Annales du Cercle archéologique de Mons*	
AcAnt	*Acta Antiqua Academiae Scientiarum Hungaricae* (Budapest)	AcAnt (B)
AcApos	*Acta Apostolorum Apocrypha*	
AcAr	*Acta Archaeologica* (Copenhagen)	AcArch (C)
AcArch (B)	*Acta Archaeologica Academiae Scientiarum Hungaricae* (Budapest)	AAASH
AcArch (C)	*Acta Archaeologica* (Copenhagen)	AcAr
AcArch (Lj)	*Acta archaeologica* (Ljubljana)	
AcArch (Lo)	*Acta archaeologica lovaniensia*	
AcArch (O)	*Acta ad archaeologiam et artium historiam pertinentia* (Oslo)	
AcArch (S)	*Acta antiqua et archaeologica* (Szeged)	
AcCITA	*Actes et mémoires du Congrès international de toponymie et d'anthroponymie*	
AcClass (CT)	*Acta classica: Proceedings of the Classical Association of South Africa* (Cape Town)	
AcClass (D)	*Acta classica Universitatis scientiarum debreceniensis*	
AcComm	*Acta et commentationes Universitatis dorpatensis*	
ACÉR	*Annales du Centre d'études des religions*	
ACF	*Annuaire du Collège de France*	
AcHist (B)	*Acta historica* (Budapest)	
AcHist (L)	*Acta historica neerlandica* (Leiden)	
AcHist (S)	*Acta historica* (Szeged)	
AcHyp	*Acta Hyperborea: Danish Studies in Classical Archaeology*	
AcIr	*Acta Iranica: Encyclopédie permanente des études iraniennes*	
AcLing (B)	*Acta linguistica* (Budapest)	
AcLing (C)	*Acta linguistica* (Copenhagen)	
ACM	*Anuarul comisiunii monumentelor istorice*	
ACNAC	*Ancient Coins in North American Collections*	
ACNT	*Augsburg Commentary on the New Testament*	
AcNum	*Acta numismatica*	
AcOr	*Acta Orientalia* (Societates Orientalis Batava, Danica, Fennica, Norvegica, Suecica), Leiden and Copenhagen	AcOr (C); AcOr (K); AcOr (L); Acta Or.; AO
AcOr (B)	*Acta Orientalia Academiae Scientiarum Hungaricae* (Budapest)	AcOrASH; AOASH
AcPhil	*Acta philologica*	
ACR	*American Classical Review*	

Abbreviation	Citation	Abbreviation alternatives
AcSum	*Acta Sumerologica*	
Acta Or.	*Acta Orientalia* (Societates Orientalis Batava, Danica, Fennica, Norvegica, Suecica), Leiden and Copenhagen	AcOr; AcOr (C); AcOr (K); AcOr (L); AO
Acts Andr.	*Acts of Andrew*	
Acts Andr.Mth.	*Acts of Andrew and Matthias*	
Acts Andr.Paul	*Acts of Andrew and Paul*	
Acts Barn.	*Acts of Barnabas*	
Acts Jas.	*Acts of James the Great*	
Acts John	*Acts of John*	
Acts John Pro.	*Acts of John* (by Prochorus)	
Acts Paul	*Acts of Paul*	
Acts Pet.	*Acts of Peter*	
Acts Pet.(Slav.)	*Acts of Peter* (Slavonic)	
Acts Pet.12 Apost.	*Acts of Peter and the Twelve Apostles* (NHC VI,1)	
Acts Pet.Andr.	*Acts of Peter and Andrew*	
Acts Pet.Paul	*Acts of Peter and Paul*	
Acts Phil.	*Acts of Philip*	
Acts Phil.(Syr.)	*Acts of Philip* (Syriac)	
Acts Pil.	*Acts of Pilate*	
Acts Thad.	*Acts of Thaddaeus*	
Acts Thom.	*Acts of Thomas*	
ActSS	*Acta Sanctorum*	
AcUniv (L)	*Acta Universitatis lundensis*	
AcUniv (R)	*Acta Universitatis latvensis* (Riga)	
ACW	*Ancient Christian Writers*	
ADA	*Anzeiger für deutsches Altertum*	
ADAIK	*Abhandlungen des Deutschen Archäologischen Instituts, Kairo*	ADIK
ADAJ	*Annual of the Department of Antiquities of Jordan*	
ADAW	*Abhandlungen der Deutschen Akademie der Wissenschaften zu Berlin* [To 1944: APAW]	
Add Dan	*Additions to Daniel*	
Add Esth	*Additions to Esther*	
ADFF	*Annali del Dipartimento di filosofia* (Florence)	
ADFU	*Ausgrabungen der Deutschen Forschungsgemeinschaft in Uruk-Warka*	
ADIK	*Abhandlungen des Deutschen Archäologischen Instituts, Kairo*	ADAIK
Admonitions	A.H. Gardiner, *The Admonitions of an Egyptian Sage*	
ADOG	*Abhandlungen der Deutschen Orient Gesellschaft*	
ADOI	M. Civil et al., eds., *Assyrian Dictionary of the Oriental Institute of the University of Chicago*	Assyrian Dictionary; CAD
ADPV	*Abhandlungen des Deutschen Palästina-Vereins*	
ADRS	*Archivio della Deputazione romana di storia patria* [Continues ASRS]	
ÄDS	*Ägyptische Denkmäler aus der Schweiz*	
ADSV	*Anticnaja drevnost'i srednije veka*	
AE	*Ancient Egypt (and the East)*	Anc.Eg.; AncEg
AÉ	*L'Année épigraphique*	AnÉp
AEArq	*Archivo español de arqueología*	
AEArt	*Archivo español de arte*	
AEArtArq	*Archivo español de arte y arqueología*	
AEASH	*Acta Ethnographica Academiae Scientiarum Hungaricae*	
AEB	*Annual Egyptological Bibliography*	
AECO	*Archivum Europae Centro-Orientalis*	
Aeg	*Aegyptus: Rivista Italiana di Egittologia e di Papirologia*	
AegAnt	*Aegyptus Antiquus/Antiqua*	
AegHelv	*Aegyptiaca Helvetica*	AH
AegInschr	G. Roeder, *Aegyptische Inschriften aus den königlichen Museen zu Berlin*	
AegMon	*Aegyptiaca Monasteriensia*	
AegMon	*Aegyptische Monumenten van het Nederlandsche Museum van Oudheden*	AeML
AegTrev	*Aegyptiaca Treverensia: Trierer Studien zum Griechisch-Römischen Ägypten*	
AÉHÉ IV	*Annuaire de l'École pratique des Hautes Études, IVe section: Section des sciences historiques et philologiques*	
AÉHÉ V	*Annuaire d'École pratique des hautes études, Ve section: Sciences religieuses*	ÉPHÉ
AÉHÉG	*Annales de l'École des hautes études de Gand*	
AEHL	A. Negev, ed., *Archaeological Excavations in the Holy Land*	
AEL	M. Lichtheim, *Ancient Egyptian Literature*	
AeML	*Aegyptische Monumenten van het Nederlandsche Museum van Oudheden*	AegMon
AEMÖ	*Archäologisch-epigraphische Mitteilungen aus Österreich (-Ungarn)*	
AEO	A.H. Gardiner, *Ancient Egyptian Onomastica*	
AÉPHÉ	*Annuaire de l'École pratique des hautes études*	
AER	*American Ecclesiastical Review*	

Abbreviation	Citation	Abbreviation alternatives
AESH	B. Trigger et al., *Ancient Egypt: A Social History*	
Aet	Philo, *De aeternitate mundi*	
Aev	*Aevum: Rassegna di scienze storiche linguistiche e filologiche*	Aevum
AevAnt	*Aevum antiquum*	
ÄF	*Ägyptologische Forschungen*	ÄgFo; ÄgForsch
AFA	*Annals of the Faculty of Arts* (Aïn Shams University), Cairo	
AfA	*Archiv für Anthropologie*	ArAnthr
AFC	*Anales de filología clásica* (Universidad de Buenos Aires) [Continues AILC]	
AFER	*African Ecclesiastical Review*	
AFGG	*Annali della Facoltà di giurisprudenza* (Università di Genova)	
AfL	*Archiv für Liturgiewissenschaft*	
AFLAix	*Annales de la Faculté des lettres et sciences humaines* (Gap)	
AFLBari	*Annali della Facoltà di lettere e filosofia* (Università di Bari)	
AFLBord	*Annales de la Faculté des lettres* (Université de Bordeaux) [Continued by RUM]	
AFLCag	*Annali della Facoltà di lettere e filosofia* (Università di Cagliari)	
AFLDak	*Annales de la Faculté des lettres et sciences humaines* (University of Dakar)	
AFLLecce	*Annali della Facoltà di lettere* (Università di Lecce)	
AFLMac	*Annali della Facoltà di lettere e filosofia* (Università di Macerata)	
AFLNap	*Annali della Facoltà di lettere e filosofia* (Università di Napoli)	
AFLNice	*Annales de la Faculté des lettres et sciences humaines* (Université de Nice)	
AFLPer	*Annali della Facoltà di lettere e filosofia* (Università di Perugia)	
AFLSiène	*Annali della Facoltà di lettere e filosofia* (Università di Siena)	
AFLToul	*Annales de la Faculté des lettres* (Toulouse)	
AFLTri	*Annali della Facoltà di lettere e filosofia* (Università di Trieste)	
AFMBar	*Annali della Facoltà di Magistero* (Università di Bari)	
AFMCag	*Annali della Facoltà di Magistero* (Università di Cagliari)	
AFMLecce	*Annali della Facoltà di Magistero* (Università di Lecce)	
AFMPal	*Annali della Facoltà di Magistero* (Università di Palermo)	
AFNW	*Arbeitsgemeinschaft für Forschung des Landes Nordrhein-Westfalen*	
AfO	*Archiv für Orientforschung*	AOF
AFOB	*Archaeological Fieldwork Opportunities Bulletin* (AIA)	
AfP	*Archiv für Papyrusforschung*	APF
AfR	*Archiv für Religionswissenschaft*	ARW
AfrBull	*Africana Bulletin*	AB
Africa (L)	*Africa* (London)	
Africa (M)	*Africa* (Madrid)	
Africa (R)	*Africa: rivista trimestrale di studi e documentazione dell' Istituto Italo-Africano* (Rome)	
Africa (T)	*Africa: fouilles, monuments et collections archéologiques en Tunisie*	
AfrIt	*Africa Italiana*	
Afr-Praehist	*Africa praehistorica*	
AfrTJ	*Africa Theological Journal*	
AfrÜb	*Afrika und Übersee: Sprachen, Kulturen*	
AfV	*Archiv für Völkerkunde*	
Ag.Ber.	*Aggadat Beresit*	
ÄgAbh	*Ägyptologische Abhandlungen*	ÄA
AgAp	Josephus, *Contra Apionem = Against Apion*	
ÄgFo	*Ägyptologische Forschungen*	ÄF; ÄgForsch
AGI	*Archivio glottologico italiano*	
ÄgInschr	*Ägyptische Inschriften aus den Königlichen Museen zu Berlin*	ÄIB; Berl.Inschr.
AGJU	*Arbeiten zur Geschichte des antiken Judentums und des Urchristentums*	
AGLC	*Annuario del Ginnasio Liceo A. Volta di Como*	
ÄgLev	*Ägypten und Levante*	Ä&L
AGM	*Archiv für Geschichte der Medizin*	
AGMNT	*Archiv für Geschichte der Mathematik, der Naturwissenschaften und der Technik*	
AGNT	*Archiv für Geschichte der Naturwissenschaften und der Technik*	
Agora	*Athenian Agora: Results of Excavations Conducted by the American School of Classical Studies at Athens*	
Agora-PB	*Athenian Agora: Picture Book*	
AGP	*Archiv für Geschichte der Philosophie*	
AGR	*Akten der Gesellschaft für griechische und hellenistische Rechtsgeschichte*	
Agr	Philo, *De agricultura*	
AGSE	*Annals of the Geological Survey of Egypt*	
AGSU	*Arbeiten zur Geschichte des Spätjudentums und Urchristentums*	
AGWG	*Abhandlungen der Gesellschaft der Wissenschaften zu Göttingen*	

Abbreviation	Citation	Abbreviation alternatives
AH	*Aegyptiaca Helvetica*	AegHelv
AH	F. Rosenthal, ed., *Aramaic Handbook*	
Ah.	*Ahiqar*	
AHAM	*Anales de historia antigua y medieval*	
AHAW	*Abhandlungen der Heidelberger Akademie der Wissenschaften*	
AHB	*Ancient History Bulletin*	
AHChr	*Annales d'histoire du christianisme*	
AHConc	*Annuarium Historiae Conciliorum*	
AHDE	*Anuario de historia del derecho español*	
AHDO	*Archives d'histoire du droit oriental* [Merged with RIDA]	
AHÉ	*Annales d'histoire économique* [Continued by AHS]	
AHES	*Archive for History of Exact Sciences*	
AHG	B. Albrektson, *History and the Gods*	
ÄHG	J. Assmann, *Ägyptische Hymnen und Gebete*	
AHMA	*Archives d'histoire doctrinale et littéraire du Moyen Age*	
AHR	*American Historical Review*	
AHS	*Annales d'histoire sociale* [Continues AHÉ]	
AHW	W. von Soden, *Akkadisches Handwörterbuch*	AkkHwb
AI	Y. Aharoni, ed., *Arad Inscriptions*	
AIA	Archaeological Institute of America	
AIAL	*Annales de l'Institut archéologique du Luxembourg*	
ÄIB	*Ägyptische Inschriften aus den Königlichen Museen zu Berlin*	ÄgInschr; Berl.Inschr.
AICA	*Annali dell'Istituto di Corrispondenza Archeologica*	
AiE	D. Bergman and D. Bergman, *Abbreviations in Egyptology*	
AIEC	*Annali del Institut d'estudis catalans*	
AIÉO	*Annales de l'Institut d'études orientales*	
AIGC	*Annuario dell'Istituto giapponese di cultura in Roma*	
AIHS	*Archives internationales d'histoire des sciences*	
AIIN	*Annali dell'Istituto italiano di numismatica*	
AIIS	*Annali dell'Istituto italiano per gli studi storici*	
AILC	*Anales del Instituto de Literaturas Clásicas* (Buenos Aires) [Continued by AFC]	
AIM	*Annali dell'istruzione media*	

Abbreviation	Citation	Abbreviation alternatives
AIN	*Annuario italiano per i numismatici e raccogliatori di monete e medaglie*	
AInstOr	*Annuaire de l'Institut de philologie et d'histoire orientales et slaves* (Brussels)	AIP; AIPHO(S); AnnBrux
AION	*Annali dell'Istituto orientali di Napoli*	
AIP	*Annales de l'Institut de philosophie*	
AIP	*Annuaire de l'Institut de philologie et d'histoire orientales et slaves* (Brussels)	AinstOr; AIPHO(S); AnnBrux
AIR	P.D. Miller et al., eds., *Ancient Israelite Religion: Essays in Honor of Frank Moore Cross*	
AIRF	*Acta Instituti romani finlandiae*	
AIS	*Annali dell'Istituto di storia*	
AIS	I. Finkelstein, *The Archaeology of the Israelite Settlement*	
AISA	*Anzeiger für indogermanische Sprach- und Altertumskunde* [Supplement to IGF]	
AISC	*Anuarul Institului de studii clasice*	
AIUON	*Annali: Istituto Universitario Orientale/Istituto Orientale di Napoli*	
AIW	*Arts and the Islamic World*	
AJ	*Antiquaries Journal: Journal of the Society of Antiquaries of London*	AntJourn
AJA	*American Journal of Archaeology* (AIA)	
AJAH	*American Journal of Ancient History*	
AJAS	*American Journal of Arabic Studies*	
AJBA	*Australian Journal of Biblical Archaeology*	
AJBI	*Annual of the Japanese Biblical Institute*	
AJN	*American Journal of Numismatics*	
AJP	*American Journal of Philology*	
AJPA	*American Journal of Physical Anthropology*	
AJSL	*American Journal of Semitic Languages and Literatures*	
AJSS	*The Arab Journal of the Social Sciences*	
AJT	*American Journal of Theology*	
AKB	*Archäologisches Korrespondenzblatt*	
AKF	*Archiv für Keilschriftforschung*	
AKG	*Archiv für Kulturgeschichte*	
AKM	*Abhandlungen für die Kunde des Morgenlandes*	
AL	G. R. Driver and J.C. Miles, eds., *Assyrian Laws*	

Abbreviation	Citation	Abbreviation alternatives
al-Andalus (A)	*al-Andalus: Revue de l'Occident musulman et de la Méditerranée* (Aix-en-Provence) [See also ROMM]	
al-Andalus (M)	*al-Andalus: revista de las Escuelas de Estudios Árabes de Madrid y Granada*	
ALBO	*Analecta lovaniensia biblica et orientalia*	
AlbReg	*Alba Regia: Annales Musei Stephani Regis*	
ALex	D. Meeks, *Année lexicographique*	AnLex
ALGHJ	*Arbeiten zur Literatur und Geschichte des hellenistischen Judentums*	
ALGP	*Annali del Liceo classico G. Garibaldi* (Palermo)	
ALL	*Archiv für lateinische Lexikologie*	
ALMA	*Annales Latini Medii Aevi: Bulletin du Cange*	
ALMArv	*Annales Latini Montium Arvernorum: Bulletin du Groupe d'études latines de l'Université de Clermont*	
AlMat	*Alma Mater: revue universitaire de la suisse romande*	
ALOS	*Annual of Leeds University Oriental Society*	ALUOS
ALOS-Suppl.	*Supplement to Annual of Leeds University Oriental Society* [Supplement to ALOS]	
AltOr	*Der Alte Orient*	AO
AltorForsch	*Altorientalische Forschungen*	AoF
AltPerg	*Altertümer von Pergamon*	
AltStadt	*Die Alte Stadt: Zeitschrift für Stadtgeschichte, Stadtsoziologie und Denkmalpflege*	
ALUB	*Annales littéraires de l'Université de Besançon*	
ALUOS	*Annual of Leeds University Oriental Society*	ALOS
AM	Ashmolean Museum	
AM	*Mitteilungen des Deutschen Archäologischen Institutes, Athenische Abteilung*	MDAIA
Am	*America* (New York)	
Amada	H. Gauthier, *Le temple d'Amada* (TemplImm.)	
AmAn	*American Annals*	
AmAnthr	*The American Anthropologist*	
Amarna	N. de G. Davies, *The rock tombs of el Amarna* (ASE 13-18)	
AMAW	*Abhandlungen der Akademie der Wissenschaften und der Literatur in Mainz*	AAWLM; AAWMainz
AmBenR	*American Benedictine Review*	
Amenemhet	A. Volten, *Zwei altägyptische politische Schriften: Die Lehre für Merikarê (Papyrus Carlsberg VI) und Die Lehre des König Amenemhet* (AnAe 4); also A.H. Gardiner, "The earliest manuscripts of the Instructions of Amenemmes I,"MIFAO 66 (1935), 479–96	
Amenemope	H.O. Lange, *Das Weisheitsbuch des Amenemope*	
AMG	*Annales du musée Guimet*	AnnMusGuimet
AMGS	*Antike Münzen und geschnittene Steine*	
AMHR	*Annuaire du Musée d'histoire de la religion et de l'athéisme*	
AMI	*Archäologische Mitteilungen aus Iran*	
AMMY	*Anadolu medeniyetleri müzesi yilligi*	
AMN	*Acta Musei Napocensis*	
AMP	*Annuaire du Musée national archéologique de Plovdiv*	
AMSL	*Archives des missions scientifiques et littéraires*	AMSL
AMT	R.C. Thompson, *Assyrian Medical Texts*	AMT
AMW	*Archiv für Musikwissenschaft*	
AN	*Archaeological Newsletter* (London)	
AN	J.J. Stamm, *Die akkadische Namengebung* (MVÄG 44)	
An	*Antiquity: A Quarterly Review of Archaeology* (Cambridge)	Antiquity; Antiquity (C)
AnadArast	*Anadolu arastirmalari: Jahrbuch für Kleinasiatische Forschung* [Continues JKAF]	
Anadolu	*Anatolia: Revue annuelle d'archéologie*	Anatolia
AnAe	*Analecta Aegyptiaca*	AnAeg
AnArch	*Annales archéologiques*	
AnatAnt	*Anatolia antiqua: Eski anadolu*	
AnatStud	*Anatolian Studies*	AnSt
AnBib	*Analecta Biblica*	An.Bibl.
AnBo	*Analecta Bollandiana*	AnBoll
Anc.Eg.	*Ancient Egypt (and the East)*	AE; AncEg
AncHist	*Ancient History: Resources for Teachers*	
AncIsr	R. de Vaux, *Ancient Israel: Its Life and Institutions*	
AncPh	*Ancient Philosophy*	
AncSoc	*Ancient Society*	
AncWorld	*The Ancient World*	AW
AndIsl	*Andaloucia islamica: textos y estudios*	
AnDobr	*Analele Dobrogei*	
ANE	*Ancient Near East: Discussion List For the Study of the Ancient Near East* (OI), Chicago	

Abbreviation	Citation	Abbreviation alternatives
ANEP	J.B. Pritchard, ed., *Ancient Near East in Pictures Relating to the Old Testament*	
AnÉp	*L'Année épigraphique*	AÉ
AnEst	*Annales de l'Est*	
ANET	J.B. Pritchard, ed., *Ancient Near Eastern Texts Relating to the Old Testament*	
AnÉth	*Annales d'Éthiopie*	
ANF	*Arkiv för nordisk filologi*	
ANF	*The Ante-Nicene Fathers*	
AnFil	*Anuario de filología* (Barcelona)	Anuario
AnFr	*Analecta franciscana*	
Ang	*Angelicum*	
AnGéo	*Annales de géographie*	
AnHist	*Anais de história*	
ANHMW	*Annalen des Naturhistorische Museum in Wien*	
Anim	Philo, *De animalibus*	
AnInst	*Annales Institutorum quae in Urbe erecta sunt*	
AnIsl	*Annales islamologiques* [Continues MélIsl, See also BCAI]	
AnIsl-Suppl.	*Suppléments aux Annales islamologiques* [Supplement to AnIsl]	
AnLex	D. Meeks, *Année lexicographique*	ALex; Alex
AnLing	*L'Année linguistique*	
ANM	*Archéologie du Nil Moyen*	
AnMal	*Analecta malacitana*	
AnMid	*Annales du Midi: Revue de la France méridionale*	
AnnBrux	*Annuaire de l'Institut de philologie et d'histoire orientales et slaves* (Brussels)	AInstOr; AIP; AIPHO; AIPHOS
AnnMusGuimet	*Annales du musée Guimet*	AMG
AnNorm	*Annales de Normandie*	AnNorm
AnnServ	*Annales du Service des Antiquités de l'Égypte* [See also CASAÉ]	ASAE
ANOC	W.K. Simpson, *Abydos North Offering Chapels: The Terrace of the Great God at Abydos*	
ANOH	*Aarbøger for Nordisk Oldkyndighed og Historie*	
Anon.Sam.	*Anonymous Samaritan Text*	
AnOr	*Analecta orientalia*	
AnPap	*Analecta papyrologica*	
AnPh (B)	*Annales de philosophie* (Beirut)	
AnPh (P)	*L'Année philosophique* (Paris)	
AnPhil	*L'Année philologique*	AP; APh
ANQ	*Andover Newton Quarterly*	
ANRW	H. Tempoini and W. Haase, eds., *Aufstieg und Niedergang der römischen Welt*	
ANS	*American Numismatic Society Museum Notes*	
AnSt	*Anatolian Studies*	AnatStud
Ant	Josephus, *Antiquitates Judaicae = Jewish Antiquities*	
AntAbend	*Antike und Abendland: Beiträge zum Verständnis der Griechen und Römer und ihres Nachlebens*	
AntAfr	*Antiquités africaines*	
AntArkh	*Anticnyj mir i arkheologija*	
AntAS	*Antike: Alte Sprachen und deutsche Bildung*	
AntChr	*Antike und Christentum*	
AntCl	*L'Antiquité Classique*	AC; AntClass
AntDenk	*Antike Denkmäler*	
ANTF	*Arbeiten zur neutestamentlichen Textforschung*	
AnTh	*L'Année théologique* [Continued by ATAug]	
AnthrAnz	*Anthropologischer Anzeiger*	
AnthrLing	*Anthropological Linguistics*	
Anthropos (F)	*Anthropos: International review of ethnology and linguistics* (Freiburg, Switzerland)	
Anthropos (V)	*Anthropos: Internationale Zeitschrift für Völker- und Sprachenkunde* (Vienna)	
AnthrQuart	*Anthropological Quarterly*	
AntHung	*Antiquitas Hungarica*	
ANTJ	*Arbeiten zum Neuen Testament und Judentum*	
AntJourn	*Antiquaries Journal: Journal of the Society of Antiquaries of London*	
AntKunst	*Antike Kunst*	
AntKunst-B	*Antike Kunst, Beiheft*	
Anton	*Antonianum*	
AntPis	*Antichità pisane: Rivista di archeologia e di topografia storica*	
AntPlast	*Antike Plastik*	
AntRev	*Antioch Review*	
AnTri	*Annali triestini*	
AntRunds	*Antiquitäten-Rundschau*	
AntSurv	*Antiquity and Survival: An International Review of Traditional Art and Culture*	
AntWelt	*Antike Welt: Zeitschrift für Archäologie und Kulturgeschichte*	AW
Anuario	*Anuario de filología* (Barcelona)	AnFil
AnVal	*Annales Valaisianes*	
ANVAO	*Avhandlinger utgitt av det Norske Videnskaps-Akademi i Oslo*	
ANW	*Alte und Neue Welt*	
AnzA	*Anzeiger für Altertumswissenschaft*	AAW
AnzAWW	*Anzeiger der Akademie der Wissenschaften in Wien* [From 1947: AnzÖAW]	AnzWien

Abbreviation	Citation	Abbreviation alternatives
AnzÖAW	*Anzeiger der Österreichischen Akademie der Wissenschaften* (Vienna) [To 1946: AnzAWW]	AAWWien; AÖAW
AnzWien	*Anzeiger der Akademie der Wissenschaften in Wien* [From 1947: AnzÖAW]	AnzAWW
AO	*Acta Orientalia* (Societates Orientalis Batava, Danica, Fennica, Norvegica, Suecica) (Leiden and Copenhagen)	AcOr; AcOr (C); AcOr (K); AcOr (L); Acta Or.
AO	*Der Alte Orient*	AltOr
AOASH	*Acta Orientalia Academiae Scientiarum Hungaricae* (Budapest)	AcOr (B); AcOrASH
AOAT	*Alter Orient und Altes Testament*	
AOATS	*Alter Orient und Altes Testament Sonderreihe*	
AÖAW	*Anzeiger der Österreichischen Akademie der Wissenschaften* Vienna [To 1946: AnzAWW]	AAWWien; AnzÖAW
AOB	*Analecta orientalia belgica*	
AOB	H. Gressman, ed., *Altorientalische Bilder zum Alten Testament*	
AOBib	*Altorientalische Bibliothek*	
AOF	*Archiv für Orientforschung*	AfO
AoF	*Altorientalische Forschungen*	AltorForsch
AOP	*Archivum Orientale Pragense*	
AOS	*American Oriental Series*	
AOSTS	*American Oriental Society Translation Series*	
AP	*L'Année philologique*	AnPhil; APh
APA	*Acta Praehistorica et Archaeologica*	
APA	*American Philological Association*	
APAACS	*American Philological Association American Classical Studies*	
APAM	*Anales de prehistoria y archeologia* (Murcie)	
APAPM	*American Philological Association Philological Monographs*	
APAT	E. Kautzsch, ed., *Die Apokryphen und Pseudepigraphen des Alten Testaments*	
APAW	*Abhandlungen der Preußischen Akademie der Wissenschaften* (Berlin) [From 1945: ADAW]	AAWB; Abh Berl Ak
APD	*Archives de philosophie du droit*	
APEF	*Annual of the Palestine Exploration Fund*	
Ap.Ezek.	*Apocryphon of Ezekiel*	
APF	*Archiv für Papyrusforschung*	AfP
APh	*L'Année philologique*	AnPhil; AP
APhC	*Annales de philosophie chrétienne*	
APIS	*Advanced Papyrological Information System*	
Ap.Jas.	*Apocryphon of James* (NHC I,2)	

Abbreviation	Citation	Abbreviation alternatives
Ap.John	*Apocryphon of John* (NHC II,1: III,1; IV,1)	
APL	*Archivo de prehistoria levantina*	
APM	*Anuario de prehistoria madrileña*	
APNM	H.B. Hoffman, *Amorite Personal Names in the Mari Texts*	
Apoc.Ab.	*Apocalypse of Abraham*	
Apoc.Adam	*Apocalypse of Adam* (NHC V,5)	
Apoc.Dan.	*Apocalypse of Daniel*	
Apoc.Dosith.	*Apocalypse of Dositheus*	
Apoc.El.	*Apocalypse of Elijah*	
Apoc.Ezek.	*Apocalypse of Ezekiel*	
Apoc.Messos	*Apocalypse of Messos*	
Apoc.Mos.	*Apocalypse of Moses*	
Apoc.Paul	*Apocalypse of Paul* (NHC V,2)	
Apoc.Pet.	*Apocalypse of Peter* (NHC VII,3)	
Apoc.Sedr.	*Apocalypse of Sedrach*	
Apoc.Thom.	*Apocalypse of Thomas*	
Apoc.Vir.	*Apocalypses of the Virgin*	
Apoc.Zeph.	*Apocalypse of Zephaniah*	
Apoc.Zos.	*Apocalypse of Zosimus*	
Apol Jud	Philo, *Apologia pro Iudaeis*	
Apos.Con.	*Apostolic Constitutions and Canons*	
APOT	R.H. Charles, ed., *Apocrypha and Pseudepigrapha of the Old Testament*	
APQ	*American Philosophical Quarterly*	
AquilNostr	*Aquileia Nostra: Rivista dell' Associazione nazionale per Aquileia*	
AR	Altes Reich (Old Kingdom)	
AR	*Archaeological Reports* (Council of the Society for the Promotion of Hellenic Studies)	ArchRep
Ar	Arabic	
Arak.	*Arakin*	
Aram	Aramaic	
ArAnthr	*Archiv für Anthropologie*	AfA
ArAnz	*Archäologischer Anzeiger*	AA; ArchAnz
ArbT	*Arbeiten zur Theologie*	
ArBull	*Arab Bulletin: Bulletin of the Arab Bureau in Cairo*	
ARCE	American Research Center in Egypt	
ARCE Newsletter	*Newsletter of the American Research Center in Egypt*	NARCE
Arch	*Archaeology* (AIA)	
ArchAel	*Archaeologia Aeliana: Proceedings of the Society of Antiquaries of Newcastle upon Tyne*	
ArchAnz	*Archäologischer Anzeiger*	AA; ArAnz
ArchArm	*Archéologie armoricaine*	
ArchAusgr	*Archäologische Ausgrabungen*	
ArchAustr	*Archaeologia austriaca*	

Abbreviation	Citation	Abbreviation alternatives
ArchBibliogr	*Archäologische Bibliographie* [Supplement to ArchAnz, and JDAI]	
ArchCambr	*Archaeologia Cambrensis: Journal of the Cambrian Archaeological Association*	
ArchClass	*Archeologia classica: rivista della Scuola nazionale di archeologia*	
ArchDelt	*Archaiologicon Deltion*	
Archeion	*Archeion: archivo di storia della scienza* [Continues ASS]	
ArchEleph	Porten, Bezalel, *Archives from Elephantine*	
Archeologia (P)	*Archeologia: Trésor des âges* (Paris)	
Archeologia (R)	*Archeologia: Rivista bimestrale* (Rome)	
Archeologia (V)	*Archeologia* (Warsaw)	
Archéologie (S)	*Archéologie* (Sofia)	
Archéologie (W)	*Archéologie: Annales de la Société archéologie polonaise* (Wroclaw)	
ArchEph	*Archaiologike Ephemeris*	
ArchErt	*Archaelogiai Ertesítö*	
ArchForsch	*Archäologische Forschungen*	
ArchGeo	*Archaeologia geographica*	
ArchInf	*Archäologische Informationen: Mitteilungen für Ur- und Frühgeschichte*	
Archipel	*Archipel égéen* (Tours)	
ArchIsl	*Archéologie islamique*	
Architecture	A. Badawy, *History of Egyptian Architecture*	
ArchIug	*Archaeologia Iugoslavica*	
ArchivOr	*Archiv Orientální*	ArOr
ArchJourn	*Archaeological Journal* (Archaeological Institute of Great Britain and Ireland)	
ArchNews	*Archaeological News* (Department of Classics, University of Florida)	
ArchPal	W.F. Albright, *The Archaeology of Palestine*	
ArchPol	*Archaeologia polona*	
ArchRep	*Archaeological Reports* (Council of the Society for the Promotion of Hellenic Studies)	AR
ArchSchweiz	*Archäologie der Schweiz: Mitteilungsblatt der Schweizerischen Gesellschaft für Ur- und Frühgeschichte*	
Arch. Survey of Nubia	Archaeological Survey of Nubia	ASN
ArchTri	*Archeografo triestino*	
ArchVen	*Archaeologia veneta*	
ArchVer	*Archäologische Veröffentlichungen*	AV
ArchZeit	*Archäologische Zeitung*	
ARCM	*Annual Report of the Collegium Mediterranistorum* (Tokyo)	
ARCypr	*Annual Report of the Director of the Department of Antiquities* (Cyprus)	
ARE	J.H. Breasted, *Ancient Records of Egypt*	BAR; BARE
AREEF	*Archaeological Reports of the Egypt Exploration Society* [Continued by JEA]	
ArÉr	*Archaeologiai Értesitö*	
ARET	*Archivi reali di Ebla, Testi*	
ArF	*Archivio di filosofia* (Istituto di Studi Filosofici)	
ARG	*Archiv für Reformationsgeschichte*	
ArGiur	*Archivio giuridico*	
ArhEtn	*Arhaeologija un etnografija*	
ArhMold	*Arhaeologia moldovei*	
ArhPregl	*Arheoloshki pregled*	
ArhVest	*Arheoloski vestnik*	
ARI	W.F. Albright, *Archaeology and the Religion of Israel*	
ARID	*Analecta romana Instituti danici*	
Aris.Ex.	*Aristeas the Exegete*	
Aristob.	*Aristobulus*	
ArKorr	*Arabische Korrespondenz*	
ArLing	*Archivum linguisticum: Review of Comparative Philology and General Linguistics*	
ARM	*Archives royales de Mari*	
ArMar	*Archives marocaines*	
ARMT	*Archives royales de Mari: transcriptions et traductions*	
ARNA	F.V. Winnett and W.L. Reed, eds., *Ancient Records from North Arabia*	
ArOr	*Archiv Orientální*	ArchivOr
ArOtt	*Archivum ottomanicum*	
ARP	*Archiv für Religionspsychologie*	
ARp	*Archaeological Report Comprising the Recent Work of the Egypt Exploration Fund and the Progress of Egyptology*	
ArPh (P)	*Archives de philosophie* (Paris)	
ArPh (S)	*Archiv für Philosophie* (Stuttgart)	
ArPhil	*Archivum philologicum*	
ArqPort	*O arqueólogo português*	
ArRom	*Archivum romanicum*	
ArsIsl	*Ars Islamica* [Continued by ArsOr]	
ArsOr	*Ars Orientalis* [Continues ArsIsl]	
ArsPraehist	*Ars Praehistorica* (Barcelona)	
ArSten	*Archiv für Stenographie*	

Abbreviation	Citation	Abbreviation alternatives
ArStra	*Arabskie Strany*	
ArStud	*Arabian Studies*	
Art.	*Artapanus*	
ArtArch	*Art and Archaeology* (Washington, DC)	
ArtArh	*Art si arheologie*	
ArtAs	*Artibus Asiae* (Bern)	ArtAsBern
ArtBull	*Art Bulletin: Quarterly Published by the College Art Association of America*	
ArtFig	*Arti figurative: Rivista d'arte antica e moderne*	
Arti	*Le Arti* (Florence)	
Artibus Aegypti	H. de Meulenaere and L. Limme, eds., *Artibus Aegypti: Studia in honorem Bernardi V. Bothmer*	Fs Bothmer
ArtInd	*Art Index*	
ArtIsl	*Art islamique*	
ArtJourn	*Art Journal*	
ArtsIW	*Arts: The Islamic World*	
ArtsVirg	*Arts in Virginia*	
ARW	*Archiv für Religionswissenschaft*	AfR
ARWAW	*Abhandlungen der Rheinisch-Westfälischen Akademie der Wissenschaften*	
ArWorld	*Arab World*	
ARWP	*Archiv für Rechts und Wirtschaftsphilosophie*	
AS	*Assyriological Studies*	AssyrStud
ÄS	O. Firchow, ed., *Festschrift für Hermann Grapow zum 70. Geburtstag: Ägyptologische Studien*	Fs Grapow
ASA	*Annals of the American School of Athens*	AASA
ASAA	*Annuario della Scuola archeologica di Atene a delle Missioni italiane in Oriente*	
ASAB	*Annales de la Société archéologique de Bruxelles*	
ASAC	*Annales de la Société archéologique de la province de Constantine* (Société archéologique, historique et géographique de la wilaya de Constantine)	
ASAE	*Annales du Service des Antiquités de l'Égypte* [See also CASAE]	AnnServ
ASAE-Suppl.	*Supplément aux ASAE, Cahier*	CASAE; SASAE
ASAI	*Annales du Service archéologique de l'Iran*	
ASAK	*Anzeiger für schweizerische Altertumskunde*	
ASAN	*Annales de la Société archéologique de Namur*	
ASAW	*Abhandlungen der Sächsischen Akademie der Wissenschaften zu Leipzig* [To 1919: ASGW]	ASAW
Ascen.Is.	*Ascension of Isaiah*	
Asc.Jas.	*Ascents of James*	
ASCL	*Archivio storico per la Calabria e la Lucania*	
Asclepius	*Asclepius 21-29* (NHC VI,8)	
ASE	*Archaeological Survey of Egypt*	ASEg
ASE	*Memoir of the Archaeological Survey of Egypt*	ASE
ASEg	*Archaeological Survey of Egypt*	ASE
ASFI	*Archivio di storia della filosofia italiana*	
ASGP	*Annali del seminario giuridico* (Università di Palermo)	
ASGW	*Abhandlungen der Königlich Sächsischen Gesellschaft der Wissenschaften zu Leipzig* [1919 AAWL, from 1920 ASAW]	
ASHAL	*Annuaire de la Société d'histoire et d'archéologie de la Lorraine*	
ASHLL	*Acta Regiae Societatis Humaniorum Litterarum Lundensis*	
ASI	*Archivio storico italiano*	
ASM	*Archivio storico messinese*	
ASN	*Archaeological Survey of Nubia*	Arch.Survey of Nubia
ASNP	*Annali della Scuola normale superior di Pisa*	
ASNSL	*Archiv Studium Neueren Sprachen Literatur*	
ASNU	*Acta seminarii neotestamentici upsaliensis*	
ASOR	*The American Schools of Oriental Research*	
ASORDS	*American Schools of Oriental Research Dissertation Series*	
ASORMS	*American Schools of Oriental Research Monograph Series*	
ASP	*American Studies in Papyrology*	
ASPh	*Archiv für systematische Philosophie*	
ASPN	*Archivio storico per le provincie napoletane*	
ASPugl	*Archivio storico pugliese* [Continues Iapigia]	
ASQ	*Arab Studies Quarterly*	
ASR	*Archives de sociologie des religions* [Continued by ASSR]	
ASRS	*Archivio della Società romana di storia patria* [Continued by ADRS]	
ASS	*Acta sanctae sedis*	
ASS	*Archivio di storia della scienza* [Continued by Archeion]	
ASSard	*Archivio storico Sardo*	
AsSeign	*Assemblées du Seigneur*	
ASSic	*Archivio storico siciliano*	
Assiout	É. Chassinat and C. Palanque, *Une campagne de fouilles dans la nécropole d'Assiout* (MIFAO 24)	

Abbreviation	Citation	Abbreviation alternatives
Assiriologija i Egiptologija	*Assiriologiia i Egiptologiia: Sbornik statei V.V. Struve*	Fs Struve 1964
ASSO	*Archivio storico per la Sicilia orientale*	
ASSP	*Annuaire de la Société suisse de philosophie: Studia philosophica*	
ASSR	*Archives des sciences sociales des religions* [Continues ASR]	
Assum.Mos.	*Assumption of Moses*	
Assum.Vir.	*Assumption of the Virgin*	
Assyrian Dictionary	M. Civil et al., eds., *Assyrian Dictionary of the Oriental Institute of the University of Chicago*	ADOI; CAD
AssyrStud	*Assyriological Studies*	AS
AST	*Analecta sacra tarraconensia*	
ASTENE	Association for the Study of Travel in Egypt and the Near East	
ASTI	*Annual of the Swedish Theological Institute*	
ASU	*Der altsprachliche Unterricht: Arbeitshefte zur seiner wissenschaftlichen Begründung und praktischen Gestalt*	
ASV	American Standard Version	
AT, at	Altes Testament, alttestamentlich (Old Testament)	
ATAbh	*Alttestamentliche Abhandlungen*	
ATANT	*Abhandlungen zur Theologie des Alten und Neuen Testaments*	
ATAT	*Arbeiten zu Text und Sprache im Alten Testament*	
ATAug	*L'Année théologique augustinienne* [Continues AnTh, Continued by RÉAug]	
ATD	Altes Testament, Deutsch	
ATDan	*Acta theologica danica*	
ATG	*Archivo Teológico Granadino*	
Athribis	W.M.F. Petrie, *Athribis* (BSAE 14)	
Athribis	P. Vernus, *Athribis* (BdE 74)	
ATJ	*Ashland Theological Journal*	
ATM	*Archeion thessalonikon meleton*	
ATR	*Anglican Theological Review*	
AtRom	*Atene e Roma: Rassegna trimestrale dell'associazione italiana di cultura classica*	
ATS	*Arabic Translation Series of the Journal of Arabic Literature*	
Atti Arcad.	*Atti e memorie dell'Arcadia*	
Atti Bol.	*Atti e memorie della Regia deputazione di storia patria per le provincie di Romagna* (Bologna)	
Atti CNSR	*Atti del Congresso nazionale di studi romani*	
Atti CRDAC	*Atti del Centro ricerche e documentazione sull'Antichità classica*	
Atti CSDIR	*Atti del Centro studi e documentazione sull'Italia romana*	
Atti Istr.	*Atti e memorie della Società istriana di archeologia e storia patria*	
Atti Lig.	*Atti dell'Accademia ligure di scienze e lettere*	
Atti Mant.	*Atti e memorie dell'Accademia virgiliana di Mantova*	
Atti Med.	*Atti della Accademia Mediterranea delle scienze*	
Atti Mess.	*Atti della Accademia peloritana dei pericolanti* (Messina)	
Atti Mil.	*Atti del Sodalizio glottologico milanese*	
Atti Mod.	*Atti e memorie della Deputazione di storia patria per le antiche provincie modenesi*	
Atti Nap.	*Atti della Accademia di scienze morali e politiche della Società nazionale di scienze, lettere ed arti di Napoli*	
Atti Pad.	*Atti e memorie dell'Accademia di Padova*	
Atti Pal.	*Atti dell'Accademia di scienze, lettere e arti di Palermo*	
Atti Pat.	*Atti e memorie dell'Accademia patavina di scienze, lettere ed arti*	
Atti Pontan.	*Atti dell'Accademia pontaniana*	
Atti Pontif.	*Atti della pontificia Accademia romana di archeologia*	
Atti Rov.	*Atti della Accademia roveretana degli agiati*	
Atti SIP	*Atti della Società italiana per il progresso delle scienze*	
Atti SLSL	*Atti della Società linguistica di scienze e lettere di Genova*	
Atti SMG	*Atti e memorie della Società Magna Grecia*	
Atti SPA	*Atti della Società piemontese di archeologia e belle arti*	
Atti Tib.	*Atti e memorie della Società tiburtina di storia e d'arte*	
Atti Tor.	*Atti della Accademia delle scienze di Torino*	
Atti Tosc	*Atti e memorie dell'Accademia toscana di scienze e lettere "La Colombaria"*	
Atti Ven.	*Atti dell' Istituto veneto di scienze, lettere ed arti*	
Atti Ver.	*Atti e memorie delle Accademie di agricoltura, scienze e lettere di Verona*	
ÄUAT	*Ägypten und Altes Testament*	ÄAT
AUB	*Annales Universitatis budapestinensis de R. Eötvös nominatae*	
AUC	American University in Cairo	
AUC	*Anuarul Universitatii Cluj*	
AUF	*Archiv für Urkundenforschung*	

Abbreviation	Citation	Abbreviation alternatives
AUFer	*Annali del Università di Ferrara*	
AUG	*Annales de l'Université de Grenoble*	
Aug	*Augustinianum* (Institutum patristicum "Augustinianum"), Rome	
AugAge	Augustan Age	
AugStud	*Augustinian Studies*	
AulaOr	*Aula Orientalis*	AulOr
AUMurc	*Anales de la Universidad de Murcia*	
AUPar	*Annales de l'Université de Paris*	
AuS	G. Dalman, *Arbeit und Sitte in Palästina*	
AUSar	*Annales Universitatis saraviensis*	
AusBR	*Australian Biblical Review*	ABR
Ausf.Verz.	*Ausführliches Verzeichnis der ägyptischen Altertümer und Gipsabgüsse* (Berlin)	Berlin, Ausf.Verz.
AusgrFunde	*Ausgrabungen und Funde: Nachrichtenblatt für Vor- und Frühgeschichte*	
AUSof	*Annuaire de l'Université de Sofia*	
AUSS	*Andrews University Seminary Studies*	
Auth.Teach.	*Authoritative Teaching* (NHC VI,3)	
AUU	*Acta Universitatis Upsaliensis*	
AV	*Archäologische Veröffentlichungen*	
AV	Authorized Version	
ÄVA	*Aegyptische und Vorderasiatische Alterthümer aus den königlichen Museen zu Berlin*	
AVNA	*Annalen des Vereins für nassauische Altertumskunde*	
AW	*Antike Welt: Zeitschrift für Archäologie und Kulturgeschichte*	AntWelt
AW	*The Ancient World*	AncWorld
AWEAT	*Archiv für wissenschaftliche Erforschung des Alten Testaments*	
AWL	*Akademie der Wissenschaften und der Literatur in Mainz*	
AWM	*Aramco World Magazine*	
ÄZ	*Zeitschrift für Ägyptische Sprache und Altertumskunde*	ZÄS
AZP	*Allgemeine Zeitschrift für Philosophie*	
b.(Talm.)	*Babylonian (Talmud) = "Babli"*	
BA	*Biblical Archaeologist* [After 1998 NEA]	BiblArch
BAA	*British Archaeology Abstracts*	
BAAA	*Bibliographie analytique de l'Afrique antique*	
BAAC	*Bulletin de l'Association des Amis de l'Art Copte* [Continues BAAÉ]	
BAAÉ	*Bulletin de l'Association des Amis des églises et de l'art coptes* [Continued by BAAÉ]	
BAAfr	*Bulletin trimestriel des antiquités africaines*	
BAAlg	*Bulletin d'archéologie algérienne*	
BAAM	*Bulletin de l'art ancien et moderne* [Supplement to RAAM]	
BAAR	*Bollettino dell'Associazione archeologica romana*	
BAAS	*British Association for the Advancement of Science*	
BAB	*Bulletin antieke Beschaving: Annual Papers on Classical Archaeology* [Continues BVBKAB]	BABESCH
BÄBA	*Beiträge zur ägyptischen Bauforschung und Altertumskunde*	BeiträgeBf
BABESCH	*Bulletin antieke Beschaving: Annual Papers on Classical Archaeology* [Continues BVBKAB]	BAB
BABLB	*Boletín de la Academia de buenas letras de Barcelona*	
BAC	*Biblioteca de autores cristianos*	
BAC	*Bollettino di archeologia cristiana*	
BACA	*Butlleti de l'Associacion catalana d'antropologia*	
BACE	*Bulletin of the Australian Centre for Egyptology*	
BACl	*Bulletin semestriel de l'Association des classiques*	
BACPS	*Bulletin of the Center of Papyrological Studies* (Aïn Shams University) [Continued by BACPSI]	CPS
BACPSI	*Bulletin of (Ain-Shams University) Center of Papyrological Studies and Inscriptions* [Continues BACPS]	
BACT	*Bulletin archéologique du Comité des travaux historiques et scientifiques*	
BAe	*Bibliotheca Aegyptiaca*	BiAeg; Bibl.Aeg.
BAÉB	*Bulletin d'information et de coordination de l'Association internationale des études byzantines*	
Baedeker	K. Baedeker, *Ägypten und der Sudan: Handbuch für Reisende* (various editions)	
BAEO	*Boletín de la Asociación española de orientalistas*	
BAÉP	*Bulletin d'information et de liaison de l'Association internationale des études patristiques*	
BAF	*Bibliothèque des arabisants français*	
BAFG	*Bulletin de l'Association française de gemmologie*	

Abbreviation	Citation	Abbreviation alternatives
BAfO	*Beiheft des Archivs für Orientforschung*	BAOF
BAGB	*Bulletin de l'Association G. Budé*	
BAGB (Mex)	*Boletín de la Sección mexicana de la Association G. Budé*	
BAGB (SC)	*Bulletin de l'Association G. Budé, supplément critique*	
BAGD	W. Bauer et al., *Greek-English Lexicon of the New Testament*, 2d ed.	
BaghdMitt	*Baghdader Mitteilungen*	
BAH	*Bibliothèque archéologique et historique* (Paris)	
BAH (M)	*Boletín de la Academia de la historia* (Madrid)	
BAHD	*Bulletin d'archéologie et d'histoire dalmate*	
BAHipp	*Bulletin de l'Académie d'Hippone*	
BAHSL	*Bibliothèque archéologique et historique du Haut-Commissariat de la République française en Syrie et au Liban*	
BAIAS	*Bulletin of the Anglo-Israel Archaeological Society*	
BAL	*Bulletin des antiquités luxembourgeoises*	
BALAC	*Bulletin d'ancienne littérature et d'archéologie chrétienne* [Supplement to RevBén]	BLC
BalkStud	*Balkan Studies*	
BALRA	*Bulletin de l'Association lyonnaise de recherches archéologiques*	
Baltimore, W.A.G.	*Walters Art Gallery*	
BAM	*Bulletin d'archéologie marocaine*	
BAMA	*Bulletin d'information de l'Association internationale pour l'étude de la mosaïque antique*	
BANE	G.E. Wright, ed., *Bible in the Ancient Near East*	
BAO	*Bericht über die Ausgrabungen in Olympia*	
BAOF	*Beiheft des Archivs für Orientforschung*	BAfO
BAOM	*Bulletin of the Ancient Orient Museum* (Tokyo)	
BAPal	*Bollettino della Accademia di scienze, lettere e belle arti di Palermo*	
BAPI	*Bollettino dell'Archivio paleografico italiano*	
BAProv	*Bulletin archéologique de Provence*	
BAPSL	*Bulletin de l'Académie polonaise des sciences et des lettres*	
BAR	*Biblical Archaeologist Reader*	
BAR	*Biblical Archaeology Review*	BARev
BAR	J.H. Breasted, *Ancient Records of Egypt*	ARE; BARE
Bar	*Baruch*	
Bar.	*Baraita*	
BARB	*Bulletin de l'Académie royale de Belgique*	
BAR-BS	*British Archaeological Reports, British Series* [See also BAR-IS]	
BARE	J.H. Breasted, *Ancient Records of Egypt*	ARE; BAR
BARev	*Biblical Archaeology Review*	BAR
BARH	*Bulletin de l'Académie russe pour l'histoire de la culture matérielle*	
BARIS, BAR-IS	*British Archaeological Reports, International Series*	
Barn.	*Epistle of Barnabas*	Ep.Barn.
BARSH	*Bulletin de l'Académie roumaine, section historique*	
BASM	*Bollettino dell'Associazione internazionale degli studi mediterranei*	
BASOR	*Bulletin of the American Schools of Oriental Research*	
BASORSup; BASOR-Suppl.	*Bulletin of the American Schools of Oriental Research Supplement*	
BASP	*Bulletin of the American Society of Papyrologists*	
BASPR	*Bulletin of the American School of Prehistoric Research*	
BASPSup; BASP-Suppl.	*Bulletin of the American Society of Papyrologists, Supplements*	
BASR	*Bulletin de l'Académie des sciences de Russie* [Continued by BASU]	
BAss	*Beiträge zur Assyriologie und semitischen Sprachwissenschaft*	
BASTENE	*Bulletin of the Association for the Study of Travel in Egypt and the Near East*	
BASU	*Bulletin de l'Académie des sciences de l'URSS* [Continues BASR]	
BAT	*Bulletin d'archéologie des travaux historiques et scientifiques*	
BAT	*Die Botschaft des Alten Testaments*	
BATSH	*Berichte der Ausgrabung Tall Šeh Hamad*	
BAUB	*Beiträge zur Anthropologie und Urgeschichte Bayerns*	
Bauer	F. Vogelsang, *Kommentar zu den Klagen des Bauern* (UGAÄ 6)	
BAV	*Bibliotheca apostolica vaticana*	
BAVA	*Beiträge zur allgemeinen und vergleichenden Archäologie*	
BBA	*Berliner byzantinistische Arbeiten*	
B.Bat.	*Baba Batra*	

Abbreviation	Citation	Abbreviation alternatives
BBB	*Bonner biblische Beiträge*	
BBC	*Broadman Bible Commentary*	
BBET	*Beiträge zur biblischen Exegese und Theologie*	
BBF	*Bulletin des Bibliothèques de France*	
BBG	*Blätter für das Bayerische Gymnasialschulwesen*	
BBI	*Bulletin of the Byzantine Institute*	
BBLA; BBLAK	*Beiträge zur biblischen Landes- und Altertumskunde*	
BBMB	*Bulletin bibliographique du Musée belge*	
BBSAJ	*Bulletin of the British School of Archaeology in Jerusalem* [Continued by PEQ]	
BBV	*Berliner Beiträge zur Vor- und Frühgeschichte*	
BC	C.F. Keil and E. Delitzsch, eds., *Biblical Commentary*	
BCACR	*Bollettino della Commissione archeologica comunale di Roma* [See also BMCR, and BMIR]	
BCAF	*Bulletin du Comité de l'Afrique française*	
BCAGR	*Bollettino della Commissione archeologica del Governatorato di Roma*	
BCAI	*Bulletin critique des annales islamologiques* [Supplement to AnIsl]	
BCAK	*Blätter für christliche Archäologie und Kunst*	
BCAN	*Bulletin de la Commission archéologique de Narbonne*	
BCBL	*Bulletin du Cercle belge de linguistique*	
BCÉ	*Bulletin de liaison du Groupe international d'étude de la céramique égyptienne*	Bull.céram.
BCÉDA	*Bulletin du Centre d'études et de documentation archéologique de la conservation de Carthage*	
BCÉSS	*Bibliothèque des Centres d'études supérieures spécialisés*	CÉSS
BCH	*Bulletin de correspondance hellénique*	
BCH-Suppl.	*Bulletin de correspondance hellénique-Supplement*	
BCL	*Bibliotheca classica latina*	
BCLC	*Bulletin du Cercle linguistique de Copenhague*	
BCLF	*Bulletin critique du Livre français*	
BCMA	*Bulletin of the Cleveland Museum of Art*	
BCMI	*Buletinul Comisiunii monumentelor istorice*	
BCNHÉ	*Bibliothèque copte de Nag Hammadi Section Études*	
BCNHT	*Bibliothèque copte de Nag Hammadi Section Textes*	
BCO	*Bibliotheca classica orientalis: Dokumentation der altertumswissenschaftlichen Literatur sozialistischer Länder*	
BCPE	*Bollettino del Centro internazionale per lo studi dei papiri ercolanesi* [See also CronErc]	
BCPÉ	*Bulletin de Centre Protestant d'Études*	
BCPS	*Bulletin of the Center of Papyrological Studies* (Aïn Shams University) [Continued by BACPSI]	BACPS
BCSSA	*Bollettino del Centro di studi per la storia dell'architettura*	BCSSA
BCV	*Bibliothèque de la Casa Velázquez*	BCV
BD	Book of the Dead	BD
BD	T.G. Allen, *The Egyptian Book of the Dead* (OIP 82)	Tb (Allen)
BDB	F. Brown, S.R. Driver and C.A. Briggs, *A Hebrew and English Lexicon of the Old Testament*	
BdÉ	*Bibliothèque d'Étude* (IFAO)	BÉ; BiÉtud
BdÉC	*Bibliothèque d'études coptes* (IFAO)	BÉC
BDF	E. Blass, A. Debrunner and R.W. Funk, *Greek Grammar of the New Testament and Other Early Christian Literature*	
BDP	*Blätter für deutsche Philosophie*	
BDR	E. Blass et al., *Grammatik des neutestamentlichen Griechisch*	
BDR	*Bulletin de dialectologie romane*	
BÉ	*Bibliothèque d'Étude* (IFAO)	BdÉ; BiÉtud
BÉ	*Bibliothèque égyptologique* (Cairo)	BiÉg
BÉ	*Bulletin épigraphique: supplement du Revue des études grecques* [Supplement to RÉG]	
BÉ	G. Maspero, *Bibliothèque égyptologique* (Paris)	BiblÉg
BÉA	*Bulletin des études arabes: Intermédiaire des arabisants*	
BÉC	*Bibliothèque d'études coptes* (IFAO)	BdÉC
BÉCh	*Bibliothèque de l'École des chartes*	
BECl	*Boletim de estudios clássicos*	
BÉFAR	*Bibliothèque des Écoles françaises d'Athènes et de Rome*	
BÉHÉ	*Bibliothèque de l'École pratique des hautes études*	BÉPHÉ
BeiträgeBf	*Beiträge zur ägyptischen Bauforschung und Altertumskunde*	BÄBA
Bek.	*Bekorot*	
Bel	*Bel and the Dragon*	

Abbreviation	Citation	Abbreviation alternatives
Bened	*Benedictina*	
BeO	*Bibbia e Oriente: Rivista trimestrale per la conoscenza della Bibbia*	BibbOr
BÉO	*Bulletin d'études orientales*	BÉO
BÉPHÉ	*Bibliothèque de l'École pratique des hautes études*	BÉHÉ
Ber.	*Berakot*	Ber.
BerBerlin	*Amtliche Berichte aus den Königlichen Kunstsammlungen* (Berlin)	ABK
Berl.Inschr.	*Ägyptische Inschriften aus den Königlichen Museen zu Berlin*	ÄgInschr; ÄIB
Berlin, Ausf.Verz.	*Ausführliches Verzeichnis der ägyptischen Altertümer und Gipsabgüsse* (Berlin)	Ausf.Verz.
BerlMus	*Berliner Museen: Berichte aus den preussischen Kunstsammlungen*	
BES	*British Egyptology Societies*	
BES	*Brown Egyptological Studies*	
BES	*Bulletin of the Egyptological Seminar of New York*	
Besa	*Besa (= Yom Tob)*	
Bet El-Wali	G. Roeder, *Der Felsentempel von Bet El-Wali*	
BETL	*Bibliotheca ephemeridum theologicarum lovaniensium*	
BEvT	*Beiträge zur evangelischen Theologie*	
BFA: BFAC	*Bulletin of the Faculty of Arts of the Egyptian University* (Cairo)	
BFAM	*Bulletin of the Fogg Art Museum*	
BFC	*Bollettino di filologia classica*	
BFCT	*Beiträge zur Förderung christlicher Theologie*	
BFL (C)	*Bulletin de la Faculté des lettres* (Cairo University)	
BFL (L)	*Bulletin de la Faculté des lettres* (Université de Lille)	
BFL (M)	*Bulletin de la Faculté des lettres de Mulhouse*	
BFL (S)	*Bulletin de la Faculté des lettres* (Université de Strasbourg)	
BGA	*Bibliotheca geographorum arabicorum*	
BGASM	*Bulletin du Groupement archéologique de Seine et Marne*	
BGBE	*Beiträge zur Geschichte der biblischen Exegese*	
BGU	*Berlin Griechische Urkunden* (Staatlichen (Königliche) Museen zu Berlin)	
BHG	*Bibliotheca hagiographica graeca*	
BHH	B. Reicke, and L. Rost, eds., *Biblisch-Historisches Handwörterbuch*	
BHI	J. Bright, *A History of Israel*	
BHK	*Blätter für Heimatkunde*	
BHK	R. Kittel, ed., *Biblia hebraica*	
BHM	*Bulletin of the History of Medicine*	
BHNTC	*Black's/Harper's New Testament Commentaries*	
BHR	*Bibliothèque d'humanisme et Renaissance*	
BHS	*Biblia hebraica stuttgartensia*	
BHT	*Beiträge zur historischen Theologie*	
BIA	*Bulletin d'information archéologique* (IFAO)	
BIA(L)	*Bulletin of the Institute of Archaeology* (London)	
BIAB	*Bulletin de l'Institut archéologique bulgare*	
BiAeg	*Bibliotheca Aegyptiaca*	BAe; Bibl.Aeg.
BIAL	*Bulletin de l'Institut archéologique liégeois*	
BIARC	*Bulletin de l'Institut archéologique russe à Constantinople*	
BiArHisp	*Bibliotheca arabico-hispana*	
BIASA	*Bollettino del Istituto di archeologia e storia dell'arte*	
BIATC	*Bulletin d'information de l'Académie de Théologie Catholique*	
BIAUL	*Bulletin of the Institute of Anthropology* (University of London)	
BIAY	*Bulletin international de l'Académie Yugoslav*	
Bib	*Biblica: Commentarii editi a Pontificio Instituto Biblico*	
BibAT	*Biblical Archaeology Today: Proceedings of the International Congress on Biblical Archaeology* (Jerusalem, April 1984)	
BibB	*Biblische Beiträge*	
BibBh	*Biblebhashyam*	
BibbOr	*Bibbia e Oriente: Rivista trimestrale per la conoscenza della Bibbia*	BeO
BibKir	*Bibel und Kirche: Organ des Katholischen Bibelwerks Stuttgart, des Schweizerischen Katholischen Bibelwerks und des Österreichischen Katholischen Bibelwerks*	BK
Bibl.Aeg.	*Bibliotheca Aegyptiaca*	BAe; BiAeg
BiblArch	*Biblical Archaeologist* [After 1998 NEA]	BA
BibLeb	*Bibel und Leben*	
BiblÉg	G. Maspero, ed., *Bibliothèque égyptologique* (Paris)	BÉ
BibliogrPh	*Bibliographie de la philosophie*	
BibLit	*Bibel und Liturgie*	BLit
Bibl.nat.	*Bibliothèque Nationale*	
BiblNot	*Biblische Notizen*	BN
BiblRes	*Biblical Research*	BR

Abbreviation	Citation	Abbreviation alternatives
BiblTransl	*Bible Translator* (United Bible Societies)	BTrans
BiblZeits	*Biblische Zeitschrift*	BZ
BibOr	*Biblica et orientalia*	
BibS(F)	*Biblische Studien* (Freiburg, Germany)	
BibS(N)	*Biblische Studien* (Neukirchen)	
BICA	*Bollettino dell'Istituto di corrispondenza archeologica*	
BICH	*Bulletin of the International Commission of Historical Sciences*	
BICR	*Bollettino dell'Istituto centrale del Restauro*	
BICS	*Bulletin of the Institute of Classical Studies*	
BIDÉ	*Bulletin de l'Institut du desert d'Égypte*	
BIdÉ	*Bulletin de l'Institut d'Égypte*	BIÉ; Bull.Inst.Ég.
BIDR	*Bollettino dell'Istituto di diritto romano*	
BIÉ	*Bulletin de l'Institut d'Égypte*	BIdÉ; Bull.Inst.Ég.
BIÉ	*Bulletin de l'Institut égyptien*	
BiÉg	*Bibliothèque égyptologique* (Cairo)	BÉ
BIEH	*Boletín del Instituto de estudios helénicos*	
BIES	*Bulletin of the Israel Exploration Society* [Continues BJPES, Continued by Yediot]	
BIÉSO	*Bulletin de l'Institut pour l'étude de l'Europe sud-orientale*	
BiÉtud	*Bibliothèque d'Étude* (IFAO)	BiÉtud
BIFAI (1)	*Bibliothèque archéologique et historique de l'Institut français d'archéologie d'Istanbul* [Continued by BIFAI (2)]	
BIFAI (2)	*Bibliothèque de l'Institut français d'études anatoliennes d'Istanbul* [Continues BIFAI (1)]	
BIFAN	*Bulletin de l'Institut Fondamental d'Afrique Noire*	
BIFAO	*Bulletin de l'Institut français d'archéologie orientale*	Bull
BIFG	*Bollettino dell'Istituto di filologia greca*	
BIFP	*Bulletin et mémoires de l'Institut des fouilles de Provence et des Préalpes*	
Bigeh	A.M. Blackman, *The Temple of Bîgeh* (TemplImm.)	
BiGén	*Bibliothèque générale* (IFAO)	
BIHBR	*Bulletin de l'Institut historique belge de Rome*	
BII	*Bulletin of the Iranian Institute*	
Bij	*Bijdragen: Tijdschrift voor Filosofie en Theologie*	
Bik.	*Bikkurim*	
BIL	*Bollettino internazionale di informazioni sul latino*	
BIM	*Bulletin d'information méroïtique* [See also MeroitNewsl]	
BiMes	*Bibliotheca mesopotamica*	
BiMus	*Bibliothèque du Muséon*	
BIN	*Babylonian Inscriptions in the Collection of James B. Nies*	
BIN	*Bollettino italiano di numismatica*	
BiOr	*Bibliotheca Orientalis*	
BIOSCS	*Bulletin of the International Organization for Septuagint and Cognate Studies*	
BIRHT	*Bulletin d'information de l'Institut de recherche et d'histoire des textes* [Continued by RHT]	
BiWiss	*Bibliothek und Wissenschaft*	
BJ	*Bonner Jahrbücher des rheinischen Landesmuseums in Bonn und des Vereins von Altertumsfreunden im Rheinlande* [See also JVA]	BonnJb
BJPES	*Bulletin of the Jewish Palestine Exploration Society*	
BJRL	*Bulletin of the John Rylands University Library of Manchester*	BRL
BJS	*Brown Judaic Studies*	
BJV	*Berliner Jahrbuch für Vor- und Frühgeschichte*	
BK	*Bibel und Kirche: Organ des Katholischen Bibelwerks Stuttgart, des Schweizerischen Katholischen Bibelwerks und des Österreichischen Katholischen Bibelwerks*	BibKir
BK	E. Bresciani and M. Kamil, *Lettere aramaiche di Hermopoli*	
BKAT	*Biblischer Kommentar: Altes Testament*	
Bk.Barn.	*Book of the Resurrection of Christ by Barnabas the Apostle*	
Bk.Elch.	*Book of Elchasai*	
BKIS	*Beiträge zur Kunde der indogermanischen Sprachen*	
Bk.Noah	*Book of Noah*	
BKO	*Beiträge zur Kenntnis des Orients*	
BKT	*Berliner Klassikertexte*	
BKU	*Berliner koptische Urkunden*	
Blackman, MES	A.M. Blackman, *Middle Egyptian Stories I* (BAe 2)	
BLC	*Bulletin d'ancienne littérature et d'archéologie chrétienne* [Supplement to RevBén]	BALAC
BLE	*Bulletin de littérature ecclésiastique*	

Abbreviation	Citation	Abbreviation alternatives
BLe	H. Bauer and P. Leander, *Historische Grammatik der hebräischen Sprache*	
BLFLB	*Bulletin linguistique de la Faculté des lettres de Bucarest*	
BLit	*Bibel und Liturgie*	BibLit
BLR	*Bodleian Library Record*	
BLReinach	*Bulletin de liaison de la Société des amis de la Bibliothèque S. Reinach*	
BM	*British Museum*	
BM Guide 1924	E.A.W. Budge, *Guide to the 1st, 2nd and 3rd Egyptian Rooms*	
BM Stelae	*Hieroglyphic Texts from Egyptian Stelae, etc., in the British Museum*	Hiero.Texts; HTBM
BMA	*Brooklyn Museum Annual*	BrookMusA
BMA	*Brooklyn Museum of Art*	
BMAA	*Bulletin, Museum of Arts and Archaeology* (University of Michigan)	
BMAP	E.G. Kraeling, *The Brooklyn Museum Aramaic Papyri*	
BMB	*Berliner Münzblätter*	
BMB	*Bulletin du musée de Beyrouth*	BMBeyr
BMB	*The Brooklyn Museum Bulletin*	BMB
BMBeyr	*Bulletin du musée de Beyrouth*	BMB
BMBrux	*Bulletin des Musées royaux d'art et d'histoire = Bulletin van de Koninklijke Musea voor Kunst en Geschiedenis* Brussels	BMRAH; Bull. des Mus. roy.; Bull.Mus.Roy.
BMCR	*Bollettino del Museo della Civiltà romana* [Supplement to BCACR, Continues BMIR]	
BME	*British Museum Expeditions to Middle Egypt*	
B.Mes.	*Baba Mesi'a*	
BMF	*Bulletin des musées de France* [Continued by RevArts]	
BMFA	*Bulletin of the Museum of Fine Arts* Boston	
BMFEA	*Bulletin of the Museum of Far Eastern Antiquities*	
BMFr	*Blätter für Münzfreunde*	
BMGS	*Byzantine and Modern Greek Studies*	
BMH	*Bulletin du Musée hongrois des beaux-arts = Billetin a Szépművészeti Múzeum közleményei*	BMHBA
BMHA	*Bulletin pour la conservation des monuments historiques d'Alsace*	
BMHBA	*Bulletin du Musée hongrois des beaux-arts = Billetin a Szépművészeti Múzeum közleményei*	BMH
BMI	*Bulletin du musée Ingres*	
BMIR	*Bollettino del Museo dell'Impero Romano* [Supplement to BCACR, Continued by BMCR]	
BMKöln	*Museen in Köln, Bulletin*	
BMMA	*Bulletin of the Metropolitan Museum of Art*	MMA Bull.
BMMGP	*Bollettino: monumenti, musei e gallerie pontificie*	
BMMNEA	*Bulletin of the Museum of Mediterranean and Near Eastern Antiquities* Stockholm	
BMOP	*British Museum Occasional Papers*	
BMQ	*British Museum Quarterly*	
BMRA	*Bulletin des Musées Royaux des arts décoratifs et industriels à Bruxelles*	
BMRAH	*Bulletin des Musées royaux d'art et d'histoire = Bulletin van de Koninklijke Musea voor Kunst en Geschiedenis* Brussels	BMBrux; Bull. des Mus. roy.; Bull.Mus.Roy.
BMS	*Benediktinische Monatsschrift*	
BMS	J.P. Hyatt, ed., *Bible in Modern Scholarship*	
BMY	*British Museum Yearbook*	
BMZ	*Boletín Museo de Zaragoza*	
BN	*Biblische Notizen*	BiblNot
BNES	*Bulletin of the Near East Society* [Continued by Hebraica]	
BNF	*Beiträge zur Namenforschung*	
BNJ	*Byzantinisch-neugriechische Jahrbücher*	ByzJb
BNZ	*Berliner numismatische Zeitschrift*	
Bo	*Unpublished Bogazköy tablets (with catalog number)*	
BOIA	*Bulletin de l'Office international des Instituts d'archéologie et d'histoire de l'art* [Continued by Recherche]	
BolArq	*Boletín arqueológico* [Other name of ButArq]	
BolFil	*Boletim de filologia*	
Boll	*Bollettino*	
BollArte	*Bollettino d'arte* [See also CBA]	
BollCap	*Bollettino della capitale* [Continues Capitolium]	
BollClass	*Bollettino dei Classici*	
BollInf	*Bollettino d'informazioni* Cairo	
BollNum	*Bollettino di numismatica*	
BollSer	*Bollingen Series*	BS
Bonner geogr.Abh.	*Bonner geographische Abhandlungen*	
BonnJb	*Bonner Jahrbücher des rheinischen Landesmuseums in Bonn und des Vereins von Altertumsfreunden im Rheinlande* [See also JVA]	BJ
Bono homini donum	*Bono homini donum* (CILT 16)	
Booklist	*Booklist: The Society for Old Testament Study*	BSOTS

Abbreviation	Citation	Abbreviation alternatives
BOR	*The Babylonian and Oriental record*	
Boreas	*Boreas: Münstersche Beiträge zur Archäologie*	
Boreas	*Boreas: Uppsala Studies in Ancient Mediterranean and Near Eastern Civilizations*	
BOS	*Bonner orientalistische Studien*	
BOSA	*Bulletin on Sumerian Agriculture*	
BPAW	*Bericht über die zur Bekanntmachung geeigneten Verhandlungen der Königlich-Preußischen Akademie der Wissenschaften*	
BPC	*Bibliotheca philologica classica* [Supplement to JFAW]	
BPH	*Bibliotheca Praehistorica Hispana*	
BphW	*Berliner philologische Wochenschrift*	BPW
BPI	*Bollettino de paletnologia italiana*	
BPW	*Berliner philologische Wochenschrift*	BphW
B.Qam.	*Baba Qamma*	
BQR	*Bodleian Quarterly Record*	
BQR	*The British quarterly review*	
BR	*Biblical Research*	BiblRes
BRAH	*Boletin de la Real Academia de la historia de España*	
BRev	*Bible Review*	
BRevuo	*Biblia Revuo*	
BRGK	*Bericht der römisch-germanischen Kommission des deutschen archäologischen Instituts*	
Britannia	*Britannia: a journal of Romano-British and Kindred studies*	
BRL	*Bulletin of the John Rylands University Library of Manchester*	BJRL
BRL	K. Galling *Biblisches Reallexikon*	
BRM	A.T. Clay, ed., *Babylonian Records in the Library of J. Pierpont Morgan*	
BROB	*Berichten van de Rijksdienst voor het oudheidkundig Bodemonderzoek* [See also ROB]	
BrookMusA	*Brooklyn Museum Annual*	BMA
BrookMusQ	*Brooklyn Museum Quarterly*	
Brugsch, DG	H. Brugsch, *Dictionnaire géographique de l'ancienne Egypte*	
Brugsch, Rec.	H. Brugsch, *Recueil de monuments égyptiens*	Rec.dM; RecdM
Brugsch, Thes.	H. Brugsch, *Thesaurus Inscriptionum Aegyptiacarum*	
BS	*Bollingen Series*	BollSer
BSA (L)	*Bulletin de la Société d'anthropologie de Lyon*	
BSA (P)	*Bulletin de la Société d'anthropologie de Paris*	BSAP
BSAA	*Bulletin de la Société archéologique d'Alexandrie*	BullSocArch Alex
BSAAM	*Bulletin de la Société académique des antiquaires de la Morinie*	
BSAB	*Bulletin de la Société d'anthropologie de Bruxelles*	
BSABord	*Bulletin et mémoires de la Société archéologique de Bordeaux*	
BSABulg	*Bulletin de la Société archéologique bulgare*	
BSAC	*Bulletin de la Société d'archéologie copte*	
BSac	*Bibliotheca Sacra*	
BSAE	*British School of Archaeology in Egypt*	
BSAF	*Bulletin de la Société nationale des antiquaires de France*	
BSAFin	*Bulletin de la Société archéologique du Finistère*	
BSAL	*Bulletin de la Société archéologique du Limousin*	
BSAL	*Bulletin de la Société Linnéenne l'Anthropologie* Lyon	
BSAM	*Bulletin de la Société archéologique du Midi*	
BSAN	*Bulletin de la Société des antiquaires de Normandie*	
BSAO	*Bulletin de la Société des antiquaires de l'Ouest*	
BSAP	*Bulletin de la Société d'anthropologie de Paris*	BSA (P)
BSAP	*Bulletin trimestriel de la Société des antiquaires de Picardie*	
BSAR	*British School of Archaeology at Rome*	
BSAS	*Bulletin de la Société archéologique de Sens*	
BSAT	*Bulletin de la Société archéologique de Touraine*	
BSAW	*Berichte über die Verhandlungen der Sächsischen Akademie der Wissenschaften zu Leipzig*	
BSBR	*Bollettino sistematico di bibliografia romana*	
BSBS	*Bollettino storico-bibliografico subalpino*	
BSC	*Bible Study Commentary*	
BSC	*Bollettino storico catanese*	
BSE	*Bol'shaia sovetskaia entsiklopediia = Great Soviet Encyclopedia*	
BSEA	*British School of Egyptian Archaeology*	
BSEAA	*Boletín del Seminario de estudios de arte y arqueología*	

Abbreviation	Citation	Abbreviation alternatives
BSÉG	*Bulletin de la Société d'égyptologie de Genève*	
BSÉL	*Bulletin de la Société des études de lettres* [Continued by ÉtudLett]	
BSER	*Bulletin de la Société Ernest Renan*	
BSÉS	*Bulletin de la Société d'études historiques et géographiques de l'Isthme de Suez*	
BSF	*Beiträge zur Sudanforschung*	
BSFÉ	*Bulletin de la Société française d'égyptologie*	
BSFFA	*Bulletin de la Société française des fouilles archéologiques*	
BSFFT	*Bulletin de la Société des fouilles françaises de Tanis*	
BSFHM	*Bulletin de la Société française d'histoire de la médecine*	
BSFN	*Bulletin de la Société française de numismatique*	
BSFP	*Bulletin de la Société française de philosophie*	
BSGAO	*Bulletin trimestriel de la Société de géographique et archéologique d'Oran*	
BSGÉ	*Bulletin de la Société de géographie de l'Égypte*	
BSGF	*Bulletin de la Société géologique de France*	
BSGI	*Bollettino della Società geografica italiana*	
BSHG	*Bulletin de la Société d'histoire et de géographie de la région de Sétif*	
BSL	*Bollettino di studi latini: Periodico quadrimestrale d'informazione bibliografica*	
BSLL	*Bulletin de la Société royale des lettres* Lund	
BSLP	*Bulletin de la Société de linguistique de Paris*	
BSNTS	*Bulletin of the Studiorum Novi Testamenti Societatis* [Continued by NTS]	
BSOAS: BSOS	*Bulletin of the School of Oriental and African Studies*	BSOS
BSOTS	*Booklist: The Society for Old Testament Study*	Booklist
BSPA	*Bollettino della Società piemontese di archeologia*	
BSPF	*Bulletin de la Société préhistorique française*	
BSPFÉ	*Bulletin des sommaires des périodiques français et étrangers*	
BSPL	*Bulletin de la Société polonaise de linguistique*	
BSPM	*Bulletin de la Société internationale pour l'étude de la philosophie médiévale*	
BSRGÉ	*Bulletin de la Société Royale géographique d'Égypte*	
BSSAT	*Bollettino di studi storici ed archeologici di Tivoli e regione*	
BSSHY	*Bulletin de la Société des sciences historiques de l'Yonne*	
BSSI	*Bollettino storico della Svizzera italiana*	
BSSS	*Bulletin mensuel de la Société des sciences de Semur*	
BSTÉC	*Bulletin de la Société toulousaine d'études classiques*	
BSU	*Bollettino della Regia Deputazione di storia patria per l'Umbria*	
BTAM	*Bulletin de théologie ancienne et médiévale* [Supplement to RTAM]	
BTAVO	*Beihefte zum Tübinger Atlas des Vorderen Orients*	
BTB	*Biblical Theology Bulletin: Journal of Bible and Theology*	
BTF	*Bangalore Theological Forum*	
BTHA	*Bibliographie des travaux historiques et archéologiques*	
BTNT	R. Bultmann, *Theology of the New Testament*	
BToday	*The Bible Today*	TBT
BTrans	*Bible Translator* (United Bible Societies)	BiblTransl
BTS	*Bible et Terre Sainte* [Continued by MondBibl]	
BTZ	*Berliner Theologische Zeitschrift*	
BU	*Biblische Untersuchungen*	
BuA	B. Meissner, *Babylonien und Assyrien*	
Bucheum	R. Mond and O.H. Myers, *The Bucheum* (EES 41)	
BuckRev	*Bucknell Review*	
Budge, BD	E.A.W. Budge, *Book of the Dead: The Chapters of Coming Forth by Day*	Tb (Budge)
BudRég	*Budapest régiségei*	
Bull	*Bulletin de l'Institut français d'archéologie orientale*	BIFAO
Bull.céram.	*Bulletin de liaison du Groupe international d'étude de la céramique égyptienne*	BCÉ
BullCrit	*Bulletin critique* Paris	
Bull. des Mus. roy.	*Bulletin des Musées royaux d'art et d'histoire = Bulletin van de Koninklijke Musea voor Kunst en Geschiedenis* Brussels	BMBrux; BMRAH; Bull.Mus.Roy.
BullDian	*Bulletin de la Diana*	
Bulletin du centenaire	*Bulletin du centenaire* (Supplement to BIFAO 81)	

Abbreviation	Citation	Abbreviation alternatives
Bulletin Épigraphique	*Bulletin épigraphique: supplement du Revue des études grecques* [Supplement to RÉG]	BÉ
Bulletin Férussac	*Bulletin universel des sciences et de l'industrie: section 7, bulletin des sciences historiques, antiquités, philologie*	
BullHisp	*Bulletin hispanique*	
Bull.Inst.Ég.	*Bulletin de l'Institut d'Égypte*	BIdÉ; BIÉ
BullMon	*Bulletin Monumental*	
Bull.Mus.Roy.	*Bulletin des Musées royaux d'art et d'histoire = Bulletin van de Koninklijke Musea voor Kunst en Geschiedenis* Brussels	BMBrux; BMRAH; Bull.des Mus.roy.
BullNum	*Bulletin de numismatique*	
Bull.SFFT	*Bulletin périodique de la Société française des fouilles de Tanis*	
BullSocArch Alex	*Bulletin de la Société archéologique d'Alexandrie*	BSAA
BUP	*Bulletin of the University of Pittsburgh*	
BURG	*Bibliothèque universelle et Revue de Genève*	
Burg; Burgense	*Burgense* (Facultad de Teología del Norte de España), Burgos (Spain)	
BurH	*Buried History* Melbourne	
BUS	*Bulletin de l'université de Strasbourg*	
Bustan	*Bustan: Österreichische Zeitschrift für Kultur, Politik und Wirtschaft der islamischen Länder*	
ButArq	*Butlleti arqueològic* [Other name of BolArq]	
BVAB; BVBKAB	*Bulletin van de Vereeniging tot Bevordering der Kennis van de Antieke Beschaving* [Continued by BAB]	
BVC	*Bericht des Vereins Carnuntum*	
BVC; BVChr	*Bible et vie chrétienne: Revue de doctrine de spiritualité et de pastorale bibliques*	
BVMG	*Bibliothèque du Vulgarisation du Musée Guimet*	
BVSG	*Berichte über die Verhandlungen der Königlichen Sächsischen Gesellschaft der Wissenschaften zu Leipzig*	LpBer
BWANT	*Beiträge zur Wissenschaft vom Alten und Neuen Testament*	
BWG	*Berichte zur Wissenschaftsgeschichte*	
BWL	W.G. Lambert, *Babylonian Wisdom Literature*	
ByF	*Biblia y Fe*	
Byzantiaka	*Byzantiaka: Epistemonikon Organon Hellenikes Historike Etaireias*	
Byzantina	*Byzantina: Epistemonikon Organon Kentrou Byzantinon Ereunon Philosophikes Scholes Aristoteleiou Panepistemiou*	
Byzantion	*Byzantion: revue internationale des études byzantines*	
Byzantis	*Byzantis: Epitheoresis ton byzantinon spoudon*	
ByzAr	*Byzantinisches Archiv*	
ByzChron	*Byzantina chronica*	
ByzForsch	*Byzantinische Forschungen: Internationale Zeitschrift für Byzantinistik*	
ByzJb	*Byzantinisch-neugriechische Jahrbücher*	BNJ
ByzMet	*Byzantina-Metabyzantina: a journal of Byzantine and modern Greek studies*	
ByzSlav	*Byzantin-slavica*	
ByzZeit	*Byzantinische Zeitschrift*	
BZ	*Biblische Zeitschrift*	BiblZeits
BZAW	*Beiheft zur Zeitschrift für die alttestamentliche Wissenschaft*	
BZES	*Beihefte zur Zeitschrift für eingeborenen Sprachen*	
BZGA	*Baseler Zeitschrift für Geschichte und Altertumskunde*	
BZNW	*Beihefte zur Zeitschrift für die neutestamentliche Wissenschaft*	
BZRGG	*Beihefte zur Zeitschrift für Religions- und Geistesgeschichte*	
BZVO	*Berliner Beiträge zum Vorderen Orient*	
C	*Codex Ephraemi*	
C&AH	*Catastrophism and Ancient History*	
CAA	*Corpus Antiquitatum Aegyptiacarum: Lose-Blatt Katalog ägyptischer Altertümer*	
CAAAH	*Cahiers alsaciens d'archéologie, d'art et d'histoire* [Continues CAHA]	
CaByr	*Cahiers de Byrsa*	CahByrsa
CAD	M. Civil et al., eds., *Assyrian Dictionary of the Oriental Institute of the University of Chicago*	ADOI; Assyrian Dictionary
CaÉ	*Cahiers Évangile* [Continues Évangile]	CahÉv
Caesaraugusta	*Caesaraugusta: Publicaciones del Seminario de Arqueología y Numismática Aragonesas*	
Caesarodunum	*Caesarodunum* Tours	
CaesMarit	*Joint Expedition to Caesarea Maritima: Excavation Reports*	
CAF	*Citius altius fortius: Estudios deportivos*	
CAFr	*Congrès archéologique de France*	

Abbreviation	Citation	Abbreviation alternatives
CAG	*Commentaria in Aristotelem Graeca*	
CAH	*Cambridge Ancient History*	
CAHA	*Cahiers d'archéologie et de l'histoire d'Alsace* [Continued by CAAAH]	
CahArch	*Cahiers archéologiques: fin de l'antiquité et Moyen âge*	
CahArt	*Cahiers d'art*	
CahByrsa	*Cahiers de Byrsa*	CaByr
CahByrsa-SM	*Cahiers de Byrsa: Serie monographies*	
CAHC	*Cuadernos de arqueología e historia de la Ciudad*	
CahCoptes	*Cahiers coptes*	
CahÉv	*Cahiers Évangile* [Continues Évangile]	CaÉ
CahHist	*Cahiers d'histoire*	
Cahiers de la Soc.As.	*Cahiers de la Société asiatique*	CSA
Cahiers du CÉPOA	*Cahiers du Centre d'étude du Proche-Orient ancien*	CCÉPOA
CahKarn	*Cahiers de Karnak* [Continues Kêmi]	Karnak
CahNum	*Cahiers numismatiques: Bulletin de la Société d'études numismatiques et archéologiques*	CaNum
CahRB	*Cahiers de la Revue biblique*	
CahSion	*Cahiers sioniens*	
CahThéol	*Cahiers Théologiques*	
CahTun	*Cahiers de Tunisie*	
CAI	*Cahiers des annales islamologiques*	
Cairo CG	*Catalogue général du musée du Caire*	Cat.Caire; CG; CGC
Cairo Temp.	*Cairo Temporary Number*	
CAJ	*College Art Journal* (College Art Association of America) [Continues Parnassus]	
Caminos, LEM	R.A. Caminos, *Late-Egyptian Miscellanies*	
Cant	*Canticles of Canticles (= Song of Songs)*	
CaNum	*Cahiers numismatiques: Bulletin de la Société d'études numismatiques et archéologiques*	CahNum
CAP	A.E. Cowley, *Aramaic Papyri of the Fifth Century B.C.*	
CapAng	*Caput anguli: Revista del Instituto de Cultura Clásica Leopoldo Lugones*	
Capitolium	*Capitolium: Rassegna mensile del governatorato* [Continued by BollCap]	
CARS	*Cahiers de l'actualité religieuse et sociale*	
CAS	*Cahiers d'archéologie subaquatique*	

Abbreviation	Citation	Abbreviation alternatives
CASA	*Cronache di archeologia e di storia dell'arte*	
CASAÉ	*Supplément aux ASAE, Cahier*	ASAÉ-Suppl.; SASAÉ
CAT	*Commentaire de l'Ancien Testament*	
Cat.Caire	*Catalogue général du musée du Caire*	Cairo CG; CG; CGC
Cath	*Catholica*	
Cav.Tr.	*Cave of Treasures*	
CB	*Cultura biblica*	CultBibl
CBA	*Cronaca delle belle arti* [Supplement to BollArte]	
CBC	*Cambridge Bible Commentary on the New English Bible*	
CBFV	*Cahiers bibliques Foi et Vie* [Supplement to Foi et Vie]	
CBI	*Cuadernos de la biblioteca islámica "Félix María Pareja"*	
CBOTS	*Coniectanea biblica. Old Testament series*	
CBQ	*The Catholic Biblical Quarterly*	
CBQ-Monogr.; CBQMS	*Catholic Biblical Quarterly Monograph Series*	
CBSC	*Cambridge Bible for Schools and Colleges*	
CC	*Cross Currents*	
CCA	*Collection du Centenaire de l'Algérie*	
CCAB	*Corsi di cultura sull'arte ravennate e bizantina*	
CCath	*Corpus Catholicorum*	
CCC	*Civiltà classica e cristiana*	
CCÉ	*Cahiers de la céramique égyptienne*	
CCÉC	*Cahiers du Centre d'études chypriotes*	
CCÉPOA	*Cahiers du Centre d'étude du Proche-Orient ancien*	Cahiers du CÉPOA
CCER	*Cahiers du Cercle Ernest Renan*	
CCER	*Centre for Computer-aided Egyptological Research*	
CCF	*Cesky casopis filologicky*	
CCGR	*Cahiers du Centre George-Radet*	
CChr	*Corpus Christianorum*	
CCM	*Cahiers de civilisation médiévale*	
CCMAA	*Comité de conservation des monuments de l'art arabe*	
CCV	*Collection de la Casa Velázquez*	
CD	*Cairo (Genizah),Damascus Document*	
CD	R.O. Faulkner, *A Concise Dictionary of Middle Egyptian*	Faulkner, CD; FCD
CDAFI	*Cahiers de la Délégation archéologique française en Iran*	

Abbreviation	Citation	Abbreviation alternatives
CdÉ	*Chronique d'Égypte*	Chron.d'Ég.; ChronÉg
CÉA	*Cahiers des études anciennes*	
CEAfr	*Cuadernos de estudios africos*	
CÉDAÉ	*Centre d'étude et de documentation sur l'ancienne Égypte* [Other name of Centre de Documentation et d'Études sur l'Ancienne Égypte]	
CÉDAÉ	*Collection scientifique* (CÉDAÉ)	Collsc; CS
CÉFR	*Collection de l'École française de Rome*	
Centaurus	*Centaurus: International Magazine of the History of Science and Medicine*	
Cerný, oDeM	Cerný, Jaroslav, *Catalogue des ostraca hiératiques non littéraires de Deir el Médineh, Nos. 1-456* (DFIFAO 3-7)	
CÉSS	*Bibliothèque des Centres d'études supérieures spécialisés*	BCÉSS
CFC	*Cuadernos de filología clásica*	
CFCR	*Cuadernos de filología Colegio Universitario de Ciudad Real* [See also RCUCR, and Stylus]	
CFÉÉTK	*Centre franco-égyptien d'étude des temples de Karnak*	
CFS	*Cahiers Ferdinand de Saussure*	
CG; CGC	*Catalogue général du musée du Caire*	Cairo CG; Cat.CaireCGC
CGITA	*Cahiers du Groupe interdisciplinaire du théâtre antique*	
CGRAR	*Cahiers du Groupe de recherches sur l'armée romaine et les provinces*	
CGT	A. Fabretti et al., *Regio Museo di Torino: antichità egizie (Catalogo generale dei Musei di Antiquità e degli oggetti d'arte raccolti nelle gallerie e biblioteche del Regno ser 1, 1-2)*	Turin Cat.; Turin CG
CGTC	*Cambridge Greek Testament Commentary*	
CGTSC	*Cambridge Greek Testament for Schools and Colleges*	
CH	*Church History*	ChHist
CH	*Code of Hammurabi (Babylonian Laws)*	
CHA	*Cahiers d'histoire et d'archéologie* Nimes	
CHAL	*Cambridge History of Arabic Literature*	
CHAL	Holladay, W.L., ed., *A Concise Hebrew and Aramaic Lexicon of the Old Testament*	
Champ.Mon.	J.F. Champollion, *Monuments de l'Égypte et de la Nubie*	
Champ.Not. descr.	J.F.Champollion, *Monuments de l'Égypte et de la Nubie, Notices descriptives*	
CHB	P.R. Ackroyd et al., eds., *The Cambridge History of the Bible*	
CHD	*Chicago Hittite Dictionary*	
CHÉ	*Cahiers d'histoire égyptienne*	
Cher	Philo, *De cherubim*	
ChHist	*Church History*	CH
CHI	*Cambridge History of Iran*	
CHI	*Cuadernos de historia del Islam*	
Chic.O.I.C.	*Oriental Institute Communications*	OIC
Chiron	*Chiron: Mitteilungen der Kommission für alte Geschichte und Epigraphie des DAI*	
CHJ	*Cambridge Historical Journal*	
CHJ; CHJud	W.D. Davies and Louis Finkelstein, eds., *The Cambridge History of Judaism*	
CHM	*Cahiers d'histoire mondiale* [Continued by Cultures]	
CHR	*Catholic Historical Review*	
Chron.d'Ég.; ChronÉg	*Chronique d'Égypte*	CdÉ
ChrWiss	*Christentum und Wissenschaft*	
CHSP	*Center for Hermeneutical Studies Protocol Series*	
Chymia	*Chymia: Annual Studies in the History of Chemistry* [Continued by HSPS]	
CIA	*Corpus inscriptionum atticarum*	
Cicero	*Cicero: commentarii auspice Collegio Studiis Ciceronianis Provehendis editi*	
Ciceroniana	*Ciceroniana: Rivista di studi ciceroniani*	
CIE	*Corpus inscriptionum etruscarum*	
CiencTom	*Ciencia tomista*	
CIF	*Cuadernos de investigación filológica*	
CIFAO	*Conferences de l'Institut français d'archéologie orientale*	
CIG	*Corpus Inscriptionum Graecarum*	
CII	*Corpus inscriptionum indicarum*	
CII	*Corpus inscriptionum iranicarum*	
CIJ	Frey, J.B., ed., *Corpus inscriptionum iudaicarum*	
CIL	*Corpus Inscriptionum Latinarum*	
CILT	*Amsterdam Studies in the Theory and History of Linguistic Science, Series IV: Current Issues in Linguistic Theory*	
CIMA	*Cahiers de l'Institut du moyen âge grec et latin*	
CIS	*Corpus inscriptionum semiticarum*	

Abbreviation	Citation	Abbreviation alternatives
CISA	*Contributi dell'Istituto di storia antica*	
CiuD	*Ciudad de Dios*	
CivCatt	*Civiltà cattolica*	
CivMod	*Civiltà moderna*	
CJ	*Concordia Journal*	
CJAS	*Canadian Journal of African Studies*	
CJP	*Classical Journal of Philosophy*	
CJT	*Canadian Journal of Theology*	
CL	*Communautés et Liturgies*	
CL	R.R. Steele, *Code of Lipit-Ishtar* (AJA 52)	
CLA	*Canon Law Abstracts*	
Class	*Classical, Classique, Classica*	
ClassAnt	*Classical Antiquity*	
ClassBull	*Classical Bulletin*	
ClassFol	*Classical folia: Studies in the Christian Perpetuation of the Classics* [Continues Folia]	
ClassJourn	*Classical Journal* (University of Georgia)	
ClassJourn (M)	*Classical Journal* (Virgil Society. Royal Malta University Branch)	
ClassMed	*Classica et Mediaevalia: Revue danoise de philologie et d'histoire*	
ClassNeolat	*Classici e neolatini*	
ClassOut	*Classical Outlook: Journal of the American Classical League*	
ClassPhil	*Classical Philology*	CP
ClassQuart	*Classical Quarterly*	
ClassRev	*The Classical Review*	CR
ClassStud	*Classical Studies* (Department of Classics, University of Kyoto)	
ClassWeek	*Classical Weekly*	
ClassWorld	*Classical World* (Duquesne University)	
Cles	*Cles: Spécial Égypte. -- v. 7, no. 1* (1975)	
Clio; Clio (P)	*Clio: Introduction aux études historiques* Paris	
Clio (R)	*Clio: Rivista trimestrale di studi storici* Rome	
ClioMed	*Clio medica: Acta Academiae Internationalis Historiae Medicinae*	
Cl.Mal.	*Cleodemus Malchus*	
ClRh	*Clara Rhodos*	
CLS	*Comparative Literature Studies* (University of Illinois)	
CMC	*Cahiers du musée Champollion Histoire et archéologie*	
CME	*Collection de monographies ethnographiques*	
CMF	*Ceske Museum filologické*	
CMH	*Cambridge Mediaeval History*	
CMHE	F.M. Cross, *Canaanite Myth and Hebrew Epic*	
CMI Bull.; CMIB	*Canadian Mediterranean Institute Bulletin*	
CML	*Classical and Modern Literature*	
CMO	*Collection de la Maison de l'Orient*	
CMS	*Corpus der minoischen und mykenischen Siegel*	
CNFI	*Christian News from Israel*	
CNIP	*The Carsten Niebuhr Institute of Ancient Near East Studies, Publications*	
CNRS	*Centre national de la recherche scientifique*	
CNS	*Cristianesimo nella Storia*	CristSt
CNT	*Commentaire du Nouveau Testament*	
CO	*Commentationes orientales*	
COA	*Cahiers d'onomastique arabe*	
CoA	*The City of Akhenaten* (EEF 38, 40, 44)	
COC	*Cahiers de l'Orient contemporain*	
CodCosm	*Codrul cosminului: buletinul "Institutului de istorie si Limba"*	
CodMan	*Codices manuscripti: Zeitschrift für Handschriftenkunde*	
Col	*Colossians*	
CollHell	*Collectanea Hellenistica*	
CollLatomus	*Collection Latomus*	
CollLing	*Collection linguistique*	
Coll.Ny Carlsberg	*From the Collections of the Ny Carlsberg Glyptothek*	
Colloquium	*Colloquium* Auckland and Sydney	
Collsc	*Collection scientifique* (CÉDAÉ)	CÉDAÉ; CS
ColT	*Collectanea Theologica*	
Comm	*Commentationes*	
CommAen	*Commentationes aenipontannae*	
CommMon	*Communication Monographs* [Continues SpeechMon]	
Communio	*Communio: revue catholique internationale*	
CommViat	*Communio Viatorum: A Theological Quarterly*	
CommVind	*Commentationes vindobonenses*	
CompHum	*Computers and the Humanities*	
CompLit	*Comparative Literature* (University of Oregon)	
Comptes rendus	*Comptes rendus (des séances) de l'Académie des inscriptions et belles-lettres*	CRAI; CRAIBL; CRAL
ComViat	*Communio Viatorum: A Theological Quarterly*	CommViat
ConBNT	*Coniectanea biblica, New Testament*	

Abbreviation	Citation	Abbreviation alternatives
ConBOT	*Coniectanea biblica, Old Testament*	
Concilium	*Concilium: revue internationale de théologie*	
Conf	Philo, *De confusione linguarum*	
Congr	Philo, *De congressu eruditionis gratia*	
Conimbriga	*Conimbriga: Revista do Instituto de Arqueologia da Faculdade de Letras da Universidade de Coimbra*	
ConnHell	*Connaissance hellénique*	
Connoisseur	*The Connoisseur*	
ConNT	*Coniectanea neotestamentica*	
ContiRossini	K. Conti Rossini, *Chrestomathia Arabica meridionalis ephigraphica*	
ContrPrim.	*Contributions to Primatology*	
Convivium (Barc)	*Convivium: filosofia, psicologia, humanidades* Barcelona	
Convivium (Bol)	*Convivium* Bologna	
ConvLit	*Convorbiri literare*	
Copenhagen NCG	*Ny Carlsberg Glyptothek*	Kopenhagen, NCG
Copenhague, NCG, AEIN	*Glyptothek Ny Carlsberg, Inventory no. of the Egyptian collection*	
Corinth	*Corinth: Results of Excavations Conducted by the American School of Classical Studies at Athens*	
CorLond	*Corolla Londiniensis*	
Correspondant	*Le Correspondant*	
CorrOr	*Correspondance d'Orient*	
CorsHist	*Corse historique* [Continued by RÉCors]	
COut	*Commentaar op het Oude Testament*	
CP	*Classical Philology*	ClassPhil
CPAC	*Cuadernos de Prehistoria y Arqueologia Castellonenses*	
CPCA	*California Publications in Classical Archaeology*	
CPCP	*California Publications in Classical Philology*	
CPF	*Cahiers des Portes de Fer*	
CPI	*Commentationes philologae ienenses*	
CPJ	A. Tcherikover, ed., *Corpus papyrorum Judicarum*	
CPPJ	*Cahiers de philosophie politique et juridique*	
CPR	*Corpus papyrorum Raineri*	
CQ	*Church Quarterly*	
CQR	*Church Quarterly Review*	
CR	*Clergy Review*	
CR	*The Classical Review*	ClassRev
CR(C)IG	*Comptes rendus du Congrès international de géographie* Cairo	CRCG
CRA	*Cahiers de la recherche architecturale*	
CRAI; CRAIBL; CRAL	*Comptes rendus (des séances) de l'Académie des inscriptions et belles-lettres*	Comptes rendus
CRAL	*Compte rendu de l'Académie lyonnaise de recherche archéologique*	
CRAS	*Comptes rendus hebdomadaires des séances de l'Académie des Sciences*	
CRASBA	*Comptes rendus de l'Académie des sciences et des beaux-arts*	
CRASMP	*Comptes rendus de l'Académie des sciences morales et politiques*	
CRASOM	*Comptes rendus de l'Académie des Sciences d'Outre-Mer*	
CRASR	*Comptes rendus de l'Académie des sciences de Russie*	
Cratyle	*Cratyle: Cahiers de recherche en linguistique appliquée à l'enseignement du grec*	
CRBR	*Critical Review of Books in Religion*	
CRCG	*Comptes rendus du Congrès international de géographie* Cairo	CR(C)IG
CRCIA	*Compte rendu de la Commission impériale archéologique*	
CRHPR	*Cahiers de la Revue d'histoire et de philosophie religieuses*	
CRINT	*Compendia rerum iudaicarum ad novum testamentum*	
CRIPÉL	*Cahier de recherches de l'Institut de papyrologie et égyptologie de Lille*	
CristSt	*Cristianesimo nella Storia*	CNS
CritArte	*Critica d'arte: rivista bimestrale di arti figurative per il mondo antico*	
Critica	*Critica: rivista di letteratura, storia e filosofia* Bari [Continued by QuadCrit]	
CritSt (F)	*Critica storica* Florence	
CritSt (M)	*Critica storica* Messina	
CronErc	*Cronache ercolanensi* [Other name of BCPÉ]	
CronPomp	*Cronache pompeiane*	
CRRA	*Compte Rendu de Recontre Assyriologique Internationale*	
CRTL	*Cahiers de la Revue théologique de Louvain* [See also RTL]	
CRTP	*Cahiers de la Revue de théologie et de philosophie* [See also RTP]	
Crum, CD	W.E. Crum, *A Coptic Dictionary*	
Crux	*Crux* Vancouver (BC)	

Abbreviation	Citation	Abbreviation alternatives
CS	*Chicago Studies* Mundelein (IL)	
CS	*Collection scientifique* (CÉDAÉ)	CÉDAÉ; Collsc
CSA	*Cahiers de la Société asiatique*	Cahiers de la Soc.As.
CSCA	*California Studies in Classical Antiquity*	
CSCO	*Corpus scriptorum christianorum orientalium*	
CSCP	*Cornell Studies in Classical Philology*	
CSÉG	*Cahiers de la Société d'égyptologie* Geneva	
CSEL	*Corpus scriptorum ecclesiasticorum latinorum*	
CSHB	*Corpus scriptorum historiae byzantinae*	
CSJ	*Cairo Scientific Journal*	
CSR	*Christian Scholars Review*	
CSSH	*Comparative Studies in Society and History*	
CT	A. de Buck, *The Egyptian Coffin Texts*	
CT	*Cuneiform Texts from Babylonian Tablets in the British Museum*	
CTA	*Cahiers techniques de l'art*	
CTA	A. Herdner, *Corpus des tablettes en cunéiformes alphabétiques découvertes à Ras Shamra-Ugarit de 1929 à 1939* (MRS 10)	
CTAED	S. Ahituv, *Canaanite Toponyms in Ancient Egyptian Documents*	
CTEER	*Italica: cuadernos de trabajos de la Escuela Española de Historia y Arqueología en Roma* Madrid	Italica (E)
CTH	E. Laroche, *Catalogue des textes hittites*	
CThM	*Calwer Theologische Monographien*	
CTJ	*Calvin Theological Journal*	
CTM	*Concordia Theological Monthly*	
CToday	*Christianity Today*	
CTQ	*Concordia Theological Quarterly*	
CTSAP	*Catholic Theological Society of America Proceedings*	
CTSSR	*College Theology Society Studies in Religion*	
CU	*Code of Ur-Nammu*	
CUA	*Catholic University of America* Washington (DC)	
CuadF	*Cuadernos de filosofía*	
CuadLit	*Cuadernos de literatura*	
CULR	*Catholic University Law Review*	
CultBibl	*Cultura biblica*	CB
CultScuola	*Cultura e scuola*	
Cultura (M)	*La Cultura* Milan and Rome	
Cultura (R)	*La Cultura: Rivista trimestrale* Rome	
Culture	*Culture: Revue mensuelle de l'université de Neuilly*	
Cultures	*Cultures* (UNESCO) [Continues CHM]	
CUOS	*Columbia University Oriental Studies*	
CUQ	*Columbia University Quarterly*	
CurTM	*Currents in Theology and Mission*	
CVA	*Corpus vasorum antiquorum*	
CVC	*Cahiers du Vieux Conflans*	
CW	*The Classical World* New York	
D	E. Chassinat and F. Daumas, *Le Temple de Dendara*	Dend.; Dendara
D	*Deuteronomic source; or Codex Bezae*	
DA	*Dialoghi di Archeologia*	DialArch
Dacia	*Dacia: Revue d'Archéologie et d'Histoire Ancienne*	
DACL	F. Cabrol and H. Leclercq, *Dictionnaire d'archéologie chrétienne et de liturgie*	
Dacoromania (B)	*Dacoromania: Buletinul Muzeului Limbei Române* Bucarest	
Dacoromania (F)	*Dacoromania: Jahrbuch für östliche Latinität* Freiburg (Germany)	
DAGR	C. Daremberg and E. Saglio, eds., *Dictionnaire des antiquités grecques et romaines d'après les textes et les monuments*	
Dahchour	J. de Morgan, *Fouilles à Dahchour*	
DAI	*Deutsches Archäologisches Institut*	
DAIK	*Deutsches Archäologisches Institut, Abteilung Kairo*	
DAIT	*Deutsches Archäologisches Institut, Abteilung Teheran*	
Dakke	G. Roeder and W. Ruppel, *Der Tempel von Dakke (TemplImm.)*	
DAM	*Documents d'archéologie méridionale*	
DamMitt	*Damaszener Mitteilungen*	
Dan	*Daniel*	
Das Altertum	*Das Altertum* Berlin	Altertum
Dawson (and Gray), Cat. BM I	W.R. Dawson and P.H.K. Gray, *Catalogue of Egyptian Antiquities in the British Museum 1: Mummies and Human Remains*	
DAWW	*Denkschrift der Kaiserlichen Akademie der Wissenschaften in Wien* [From 1950: DÖAW]	
DB	E. Vigouroux, ed., *Dictionnaire de la Bible*	

Abbreviation	Citation	Abbreviation alternatives
DBAT	*Dielheimer Blätter zum Alten Testament und seiner Rezeption in der Alten Kirche*	
DBG	*Deutsche Buchgesellschaft*	
DBM	*Deltion Biblikon Meleton*	
DBSup	L. Pirot et al., eds., *Dictionnaire de la Bible, Supplément* [Supplement to DB]	
DBTh	X. Léon-Dufour, ed., *Dictionary of Biblical Theology*	
DD	*Dor le Dor*	
DDSR	*Duke Divinity School Review*	
DE	*Discussions in Egyptology*	DiscEg
Debod bis Kalabsche	G. Roeder and F. Zucker, *Debod bis Kalabsche (TemplImm.)*	
Dec	Philo, *De decalogo*	
Dédalo (M)	*Dédalo* Milan	
Dédalo (SP)	*Dédalo: revista de arte e arqueologia* São Paulo (Brazil)	
Deir el Médineh	B. Bruyère, *Rapport sur les fouilles de Deir el Médineh 1922-51* (FIFAO 1, pt. 1; 2, pt. 2; 3, pt. 3; 4, pt. 3; 5, pt. 2; 6, pt. 2; 7, pt. 2; 8, pt. 3; 10, pt. 1; 14-16; 20-21; 26)	
Deir el-Bahari	E. Naville, *The Temple of Deir el-Bahari and The XIth Dynasty Temple at Deir el-Bahari* (EEF 12-14, 16, 19, 27, 28-30, 32)	Naville, Deir el-Bahari (XIth Dyn.Temple)
Deir el-Gebrawi	N. de G. Davies*The Rock Tombs of Deir el-Gebrawi* (ASE 11-12)	
Délos	*Délos: Exploration archéologique de Délos*	
Delta	*Delta: Rivista di critica e di cultura*	
Dem.	*Demai*	
Dem.	*Demetrius (the Chronographer)*	
Demareteion	*Demareteion: numismatique-glyptique-archéologie, haute curiosité*	
De Morgan, Cat.des Mon.	J. de Morgan et al., *Catalogue des monuments et inscriptions de l'Egypte antique*	
Dem.Stud.; DemStud	*Demotische Studien*	
Dend.; Dendera	E. Chassinat and F. Daumas, *Le Temple de Dendara*	D
Dend., Mam.	F. Daumas, *Les mammisis de Dendara*	
Dend Mar	A. Mariette, *Dendérah: Description générale du grand temple de cette ville*	Mariette, Dend.
Dendûr	A.M. Blackman, *The Temple of Dendûr (TemplImm.)*	
Denkm.memphit.Theologie	H. Junker, *Die Götterlehre von Memphis* (APAW 1939, Nr. 23)	
Denkschr.ÖAW; DenkschrWien	*Denkschrift der Österreichischen Akademie der Wissenschaften* [To 1950: DAWW]	DÖAW

Abbreviation	Citation	Abbreviation alternatives
Deo	Philo, *De Deo*	
Der.Er.Rab.	*Derek Eres Rabba*	
Der.Er.Zut.	*Derek Eres Zuta*	
Derr	A.M. Blackman, *The Temple of Derr (TemplImm.)*	
Descr.de l'Égypte; Description	*Description de l'Égypte ou recueil des observations et des recherches qui ont été faites en Égypte pendant l'expédition de l'armée française*	
Descr.somm.	*Cairo Museum: Description sommaire des principaux monuments*	
Deshasheh	W.M.F. Petrie, *Deshasheh 1897* (EEF 15)	
Deut	*Deuteronomy*	
DeutschRev	*Deutsche Revue*	
DeutschRunds	*Deutsche Rundschau*	
DFIFAO	*Documents de fouilles de l'Institut français d'archéologie orientale du Caire*	
DGA	*Deutsche Gesellschaft für Anthropologie, Ethnologie und Urgeschichte*	
DGT	*Drevnejsije Gosudartsva na territorii SSSR*	
DH	*Deuteronomistic History/ Historian*	
DHA	*Dialogues d'histoire ancienne*	
DHRP	*Dissertationes ad historiam religionum pertinentes*	
DialArch	*Dialoghi di Archeologia*	DA
Dialectica	*Dialectica: international review of philosophy of knowledge*	
Dialogue	*Dialogue: Revue canadienne de philosophie*	
Dial.Sav.	*Dialogue of the Savior* (NHC III,5)	
Dial.Trypho	Justin, *Dialogue with Trypho*	
Did	*Didaskalia*	
Did.	*Didache*	
Didaskalos	*Didaskalos: Journal of the Joint Association of Classical Teachers* [See also Hesperiam, and JACT]	
Diogène	*Diogène* (Conseil international de la philosophie et des sciences humaines)	
Diogn.	*Epistle to Diognetes*	
Dioniso	*Dioniso: rivista di studi sul teatro a antico*	
Dionysius	*Dionysius* (Department of Classics, Dalhousie University)	
Diotima	*Diotima: Review of philosophical research*	
Direction	*Direction* Fresno (CA)	
Disc.8-9	*Discourse on the Eighth and Ninth* (NHC VI,6)	

Abbreviation	Citation	Abbreviation alternatives
DiscEg	*Discussions in Egyptology*	DE
Discorsi	*Discorsi: Ricerche di storia della filosofia*	
DISO	Jean, C.-F. and J. Hoftijzer, *Dictionnaire des inscriptions sémitiques de l'ouest*	
DissAb	*Dissertation Abstracts International*	
DissPan	*Dissertationes pannonicae*	
Div	*Divinitas* Vatican City	
DivT; DivThom	*Divus Thomas: commentarium de philosophia et theologia*	
DJD	*Discoveries in the Judean Desert*	
Djedefhor	H. Brunner, "Ein weiteres Djedefhor-Zitat," MDAIK 19 (1963)	
Djedefhor	H. Brunner, "Eine neue Entlehnung aus der Lehre des Djedefhor," *MDAIK 14 (1956)*	
Djedefhor	W. Helck, *Lehre eines Mannes an seinen Sohn, Djedefhor* (KÄT)	
Djedefhor	G. Posener, "Le début de l'enseignnement de Hardjedef," RdE 9 (1952)	
DJN	*Deutsches Jahrbuch für Numismatik*	
DL	*Doctrine and Life*	
DLZ	*Deutsche Literaturzeitung für Kritik der internationalen Wissenschaft*	
DMA	*Documenta Mundi: Aegyptiaca*	
DMOA	*Documenta et Monumenta Orientis Antiqui*	
DN	*divine name*	
DÖAW	*Denkschrift der Österreichischen Akademie der Wissenschaften* [To 1950: DAWW]	Denkschr.ÖAW; DenkschrWien
DocArch	*Documents Archeologia* [Continued by DossArch]	
Dodone	*Dodone: Epistemonike epeteris tes Philosophikes Scholes tou Panepistemiou Ioanninon*	
DOG	*Deutsche Orientgesellschaft*	
Dolgozatok	*Dolgozatok: Travaux de la section numismatique et archéologique du musée de Transylvanie*	
DOP	*Dumbarton Oaks Papers*	
DOS	*Dumbarton Oaks Studies*	
DOSA	J. Biella, *Dictionary of Old South Arabic: Sabaean Dialect (HSS 25)*	
DossArch	*Dossiers d'archéologie, Documents* [Continues DocArch, Continued by HistArch]	
DOT	*Deutscher Orientalistentag*	
DOTT	D.W. Thomas, ed., *Documents from Old Testament Times*	
DownRev	*Downside Review*	DRev
Doxa	*Doxa: rassegna critica di antichita classica*	
DPA	*Dissertationes philologae argentoratenses*	
DPAA	*Dissertazioni della Pontificia Accademia romana di archeologia*	
DPARA	*Atti della Pontificia Accademia Romana di Archeologia: ser. 1-2, dissertazioni*	
DPH	*Dissertationes philologicae Halenses*	
DPUC	*The Decennial Publications of the University of Chicago*	
DPV	*Dissertationes philologae Vindobonenses*	
DRev	*Downside Review*	DownRev
Drevnii Egipet	*Drevnii Egipet i Drevnii Afrika: Sbornik statei*	
Drevnii Mir	*Drevnii mir, Sbornik statei V.V. Struve*	Fs Struve 1962
Drevnii Nubija	*Drevnii Nubija: Rezul'taty nabot archeologiceskoi Ekspedicii A.N. SSSR v Obedinennoi Arabskoi Respublike 1961-1962*	
Drevnii Vostok	*Drevnii Vostok i anticnyi mir: Sbornik statei*	
DS	Denzinger-Schönmetzer, *Enchiridion symbolorum*	
DTC	*Dictionnaire de théologie catholique*	
DTT	*Dansk Teologisk Tidsskrift*	
DUJ	*Durham University Journal*	DUJ
Düm Geogr Inschr (DGI); Dümichen, GI	J. Dümichen, *Geographische Inschriften altägyptischer Denkmäler*	
DunRev	*Dunwoodie Review*	
Durius	*Durius: Boletín castellano de estudios clasicos*	
DVSM	*Kongelike Danske Videnskabernes Selskabs Meddelelser*	
DVSS	*Kongelike Danske Videnskabernes Selskabs Skrifter*	
Dynamis	*Dynamis* (Departamento de Historia de la Medicina, Universidad de Granada)	
DZGM	*Deutsche Zeitschrift für Geschichtswissenschaft, Monatsblätter*	
DZGV	*Deutsche Zeitschrift für Geschichtswissenschaft, Vierteljahrsschrift*	
E	*Elohist source*	
E	de Rochemonteix and É. Chassinat, *Le Temple d'Edfou* Cairo	Edfou
E&L	*Egypt and the Levant*	
EA	J.A. Knudtzon, *Die El-Amarna-Tafeln*	

Abbreviation	Citation	Abbreviation alternatives
EAA	*Enciclopedia dell'arte antica, classica e orientale*	
ÉAC	*Études d'archéologie classique*	
EAE	*Excavaciones arqueológicas en España*	
EAEHL	M. Avi-Yonah, ed., *Encyclopedia of Archaeological Excavations in the Holy Land*	
EAJ	*East African Journal of Literature and Society*	
EAJET	*East Africa Journal of Evangelical Theology*	
EAJT	*East Asia Journal of Theology*	
EAPI	*Epitheoresis archaias philologias kai historias*	
EastWest	*East and West* Rome	EW
EAZ	*Ethnographisch-Archäologische Zeitschrift*	
EB	*Early Bronze (Age)*	
EB	*Echter Bibel*	
EB	*Encyclopaedia Britannica*	EncBrit
Ebert, RL	M. Ebert, *Reallexikon der Vorgeschichte*	RVG
Ébib	*Études bibliques*	
Ebr	Philo, *De ebrietate*	
Ec	*The Ecumenist*	
ÉC	*Études classique* Namur	ÉtudClass (N)
Eccl or Qoh	*Ecclesiastes or Qoheleth*	
ÉchOr	*Échos d'Orient*	
ECQ	*Eastern Church Quarterly*	
EcR	*The Ecumenical Review*	
ÉcrTemps	*L'Écrit du temps*	
Ecu	*Ecumenismo*	
ED	*Early Dynastic period*	
Ed.	*Eduyyot*	
EDB	L.E. Hartman, ed., *Encyclopedic Dictionary of the Bible*	
Edda	*Edda: Nordisk tidsskrift for literaturforskning*	
Edebiyât	*Edebiyât: Journal of Middle Eastern Literature*	
Edfou	de Rochemonteix and É. Chassinat, *Le Temple d'Edfou* Cairo	E
Edfou Mam.	E. Chassinat, *Le mammisi d'Edfou* (MIFAO 16)	
EdRev	*Educational Review*	
EEA	*Epistemonike Epeteris tes philosophikes Scholes tou Panepistemiou Athenon*	
EEF	*Egypt Exploration Fund*	
EEF	*Egypt Exploration Fund Memoirs*	MEEF
EEF	*Egyptologist's Electronic Forum*	
EEMM	*Metropolitan Museum of Art, Egyptian Expedition* [Supplement to BMMA]	MMA Eg.Exp.; MMAEE
EES	*Egypt Exploration Society*	
EES; EESm	*Egypt Exploration Society Memoirs*	EM; ExcMem; MEES
EET	*Epistemonike Epeteris tes philosophikes Scholes tou Aristoteleiou Panepistemiou Thessalonikes*	
EFG	*Estudios de filología griega*	
EgArch	*Egyptian Archaeology*	
ÉgCont	*Egypte contemporaine: revue de la société khédiviale d'économie politique, de statistique et de législation*	
Egitto e Vicino Oriente	*Egitto e Vicino Oriente: Rivista della sezione orientalistica dell'Istituto di Storia Antica, Università degli Studi di Pisa*	EVO
ÉglTh	*Église et Théologie: Bulletin de la Faculté de théologie protestante de Paris*	
ÉgMA	*Égypte et monde arabe*	
EgRel	*Egyptian Religion* New York	Egyptian Religion; ER
ÉgT	*Église et Théologie* Ottawa	
EgToday	*Egyptology Today*	
Egypt and the Hellenistic World	E. van't Dack et al., eds., *Egypt and the Hellenistic World: Proceedings of the International Colloquium Leuven, 24 - 26 May 1982 (Stud. Hellen. 27)*	
Egyptes	*Egyptes: Histoires et cultures*	
Egyptian Religion	*Egyptian Religion* New York	EgRel; ER
Egyptological Miscellanies	J.K. Hoffmeier and E.S. Meltzer, eds., *Egyptological Miscellanies: A Tribute to Professor Ronald J. Williams* (The Ancient World 6, 1983)	Fs Williams
Egyptological Studies	*Egyptological Studies* Jerusalem	
Egypt Trav.Mag.	*Egypt Travel Magazine*	
EHAT	*Exegetisches Handbuch zum Alten Testament*	
EHBS	*Epeteris Hetaireias byzantinon spoudon*	
EHEM	*Epeteris tes Hetaireias eleiakon meleton*	
EHHD	*Epeteris tou Kentrou ereunes tes historias tou hellenikou dikaiou*	
EHI	R. de Vaux, *The Early History of Israel*	
ÉHPR	*Études d'histoire et de philosophie religieuses*	
EHR	*English Historical Review*	
EHS	*Einleitung in die Heilige Schrift*	
EI	*Encyclopédie de l'Islam*	EncIsl
EI	*Eretz Israel: Archaeological and Geographical Studies*	ErIsr

Abbreviation	Citation	Abbreviation alternatives
Eidos	*Eidos: Journal of Painting, Sculpture and Design*	
ÉIE	*Études indo-européennes*	
EIM	*Epigraphia indo-moslemica*	
Eirene	*Eirene: Studia Graeca et Latina*	
EJ	J. Klutzkin and I. Elbogen, eds., *Encyclopedia Judaica*	
EKKNT	*Evangelisch-katholischer Kommentar zum Neuen Testament*	
EKL	*Evangelisches Kirchenlexikon*	
El Amrah and Abydos	D. Randall-Maciver and A.C. Mace, *El Amrah and Abydos 1899-1901* (EEF 23)	
ÉLAN	*Études lorraines d'archéologie nationale*	
El Arábah	J. Garstang, *El Arábah* (ERA 6)	
El Bersheh	*El Bersheh* (ASE 3, 4)	
Elenchos	*Elenchos: rivista di studi sul pensiero antico*	
ELF	*Ensaios de literatura e filologia*	
El Kab	J.E. Quibell, *El Kab* (ERA 3)	
Ellinisticeskii Bliznii Vostok	*Ellinisticeskii Bliznii Vostok* Moscow	
El.Mod.	*Eldad and Modad*	
EM	*Egypt Exploration Society Memoirs*	EES; EESm; ExcMem; MEES
EM	*Ephemerides Mexicanae*	
ÉMC	*Échos du monde classique: Classical Views*	
Emerita	*Emerita: revista de linguistica y filología clásica*	
Emm	*Emmanuel*	
Empúries	*Empúries* [Continues Ampurias]	
En	*Enchoria: Zeitschrift für Demotistik und Koptologie*	Enchoria
EncBib	T.K. Cheyne, ed., *Encyclopaedia Biblica* London	
EncBibBarc	A. Diez Macho and S. Bartina, eds., *Enciclopedia de la Biblia* Barcelona	
EncBrit	*Encyclopaedia Britannica*	EB
EnchBib	*Enchiridion biblicum*	
Enchoria	*Enchoria: Zeitschrift für Demotistik und Koptologie*	En
EncIr	*Encyclopaedia iranica*	
EncIsl	*Encyclopédie de l'Islam*	EI
EncJud	*Encyclopaedia Judaica*	
EncMiqr	*Entsiqlopedia Miqra'it = Encyclopaedia Biblica* Jerusalem	
EncRel	M. Eliade, M., *Encyclopedia of Religion*	
Encycl.phot. Caire	*Encyclopédie photographique de l'art: Le Musée du Caire*	
EnsChr	*L'Enseignement chrétien*	
EnsPub	*Enseignement public: Revue pédogogique*	

Abbreviation	Citation	Abbreviation alternatives
Entr	*Encounter* Indianapolis (IN)	
EnvDes	*Environmental Design: Journal of the Islamic Environmental Design Research Center*	
Eos	*Eos: Commentari Societatis philologae polonorum* [Merged with KwarKlas]	
Ep.Alex.	*Epistle to the Alexandrians*	
EpAnat	*Epigraphica anatolica: Zeitschrift für Epigraphik und historische Geographie Anatoliens*	
Ep.Apos.	*Epistle to the Apostles*	
Ep.Barn.	*Epistle of Barnabas*	Barn.
Ep.Chr.Abg.	*Epistle of Christ and Abgar*	
Ep.Chr.Heav.	*Epistle of Christ from Heaven*	
Eph	*Ephemeris*	
Eph	*Ephesians*	
Eph.	*Ignatius, Letter to the Ephesians*	Ign.Eph.
EphC	*Ephemerides Carmelitica*	
EphDac	*Ephemeris Dacoromana: Annuario della Scuola romena di Roma*	
ÉPHÉ	*Annuaire d'École pratique des hautes études, Ve section: Sciences religieuses*	AÉHÉ V
ÉPHÉ	*École pratique des hautes études* Paris	
Ephem	Lidzbarski, M., *Ephemeris für semitische Epigraphik*	
EphEp	*Ephemeris epigraphica*	
Ephesos	*Ephesos: Forschungen in Ephesos* (ÖAW)	
EphLit	*Ephemerides Liturgicae*	
EphMar	*Ephemerides Mariologicae*	
Epigraphica	*Epigraphica: Rivista italiana di epigrafia*	
Episteme	*Episteme: Rivista critica di storia delle scienze mediche e biologiche*	
Ep Jer	*Epistle of Jeremiah*	
EPK	*Egyetemes Philologiai Közlöny*	
Ep.Lao.	*Epistle to the Laodiceans*	
Ep.Lent.	*Epistle of Lentulus*	
EPM	*Egyptian prehistory monographs*	
Ep.Paul Sen.	*Epistles of Paul and Seneca*	
Ep.Pet.Phil.	*Letter of Peter to Philip (NHC VIII,2)*	
Ep.Pol.	*Epistles of Polycarp*	
ÉPRO	*Études préliminaires aux religions orientales dans l'Empire romain* [Continued by RGRW]	
Ep.Tit.(Apoc.)	*Apocryphal Epistle of Titus*	
ER	*Egyptian Religion* New York	EgRel; Egyptian Religion
ER	*Epworth Review*	
ERA	*Egyptian Research Account*	

Abbreviation	Citation	Abbreviation alternatives
Eranos	*Eranos: Acta philologica suecana*	
Eranos-Jb	*Eranos Jahrbuch*	ErJb
Erasmus	*Erasmus: Speculum scientiarum: International bulletin of contemporary scholarship*	
ÉRAUL	*Études et recherches archéologiques de l'université de Liège*	
ErbAuf	*Erbe und Auftrag*	
ERE	*Encyclopaedia of Religions and Ethics*	
ErFor	*Erträge der Forschung*	
ErfThSt	*Erfurter Theologische Studien*	
Erg.-H.	*Ergänzungsheft (supplementary volume)*	
ErIsr	*Eretz Israel: Archaeological and Geographical Studies*	EI
ErJb	*Eranos Jahrbuch*	
Erman, ÄG	A. Erman, *Ägyptische Grammatik*	
Erman, Lit.	A. Erman, *Die Literatur der Ägypter*	
Erman, NG	A. Erman, *Neuägyptische Grammatik*	
ERT	*Evangelical Review of Theology*	
ERT; ERTR	*Egyptian Religious Texts and Representations*	
Erub.	*Erubin*	
ÉSA	*Études sud-arabiques*	
ESAnt	*Eurasia septentrionalis antiqua*	
Escr Vedat	*Escritos del Vedat*	
ÉSHG	*Études suisses d'histoire générale*	
ESI	*Excavations and Surveys in Israel*	
Eskolot	*Eskolot* [Other name of Scholia]	
ESLP	B.V. Bothmer, *Egyptian Sculpture of the Late Period*	
Esna	S. Sauneron, *Esna* (PIFAO)	
ESNY	*Egyptological Seminar of New York*	
EspVie	*Esprit et Vie*	
EstBib	*Estudios Bíblicos*	EstudBibl
EstEcl	*Estudios eclesiásticos: Revista teológica de investigación e información*	EstudEcl
EstFranc	*Estudios Franciscanos*	
Esth	*Esther*	
EstTeo	*Estudios Teológicos*	
Estud	*Estudios*	
EstudBibl	*Estudios Bíblicos*	EstBib
EstudClás	*Estudios clásicos*	
EstudEcl	*Estudios eclesiásticos: Revista teológica de investigación e información*	EstEcl
EstudHum	*Estudios humanísticos*	
EstudOr	*Estudios orientales*	

Abbreviation	Citation	Abbreviation alternatives
ET	*English translation*	
ÉT	*Études et Travaux: Travaux du centre d'archéologie méditerranéenne de l'Academie polonaise de sciences*	ÉtudTrav
ETF	*Espacio, tiempo y forma*	
Eth	*Ethiopic*	
EthnAnz	*Ethnologischer Anzeiger*	
EthnMous	*Ethnikon Mouseion*	
Ethnographie	*Ethnographie* Paris	
ETL	*Ephemerides theologicae lovanienses*	
ETOT	W. Eichrodt, *Theology of the Old Testament*	
ÉtPap	*Études de papyrologie* (Société Royale égyptienne de Papyrologie), Cairo	ÉtudPap
ÉTR	*Études théologiques et religieuses*	
ÉtudArch	*Études archéologiques*	
ÉtudByz	*Études byzantines* [Continued by RÉB]	
ÉtudCelt	*Études celtiques*	
ÉtudChypr	*Études chypriotes*	
ÉtudClass (G)	*Études classiques (Publications universitaires de lettres et sciences humaines d'Aix-en-Provence)*	
ÉtudClass (N)	*Études classique* Namur	ÉC
ÉtudCors	*Études corses*	
Études	*Études: Revue catholique d'intérêt général*	
Études nubiennes	*Études nubiennes: Colloque de Chantilly (2-6 Juillet 1975)*	
ÉtudLett	*Études de lettres* (Université de Lausanne) [Continues BSÉL]	
ÉtudMéd	*Études méditerranéennes*	
ÉtudNum	*Études numismatiques*	
ÉtudPap	*Études de papyrologie* (Société Royale égyptienne de Papyrologie), Cairo	ÉtPap
ÉtudPh	*Études philosophiques*	
ÉtudRhod	*Études rhodaniennes* [See also RGL]	
ÉtudThas	*Études thasiennes*	
ÉtudTrav	*Études et Travaux: Travaux du centre d'archéologie méditerranéenne de l'Academie polonaise de sciences*	ÉT
ÉtudUrb	*Études urbaines*	
EU	*Egyptologische uitgaven*	
EUC	*Estudis universitaris catalans* [Supplement to ListFil]	
Eudemus	*Eudemus: An International Journal Devoted to the History of Mathematics and Astronomy*	

Abbreviation	Citation	Abbreviation alternatives
Eugnostos	*Eugnostos the Blessed (NHC III,3; V,1)*	
Eunomia	*Eunomia* [Supplement to List-Fil, See also RevArch (Pr)]	
EuntDoc	*Euntes Docete*	
Eup.	*Eupolemus*	
Euphrosyne	*Euphrosyne: Revista de filologia clássica*	
EUQ	*Emory University Quarterly*	
Euresis	*Euresis: Notizie e scritti di varia indole del Liceo class. M. Tullio Cicerone di Sala Consilina*	
EV(V)	*English version(s)*	
Évangile	*Évangile* Paris [Continued by CahÉv]	
EvJ	*Evangelical Journal*	
EvK	*Evangelische Kommentare*	
EVO	*Egitto e Vicino Oriente: Rivista della sezione orientalistica dell'Istituto di Storia Antica, Università degli Studi di Pisa*	Egitto e Vicino Oriente
EvQ	*Evangelical Quarterly*	
EvT; EvTh	*Evangelische Theologie*	
EW	*East and West* Rome	EastWest
EWNT	H. Balz, and G. Schneider, eds., *Exegetisches Wörterbuch zum Neuen Testament*	
Ex	*Explor* Evanston (IL)	
Ex Orbe Religionum	*Ex Orbe Religionum: Studio Geo Widengren*	
Ex Oriente Lux	*Jaarbericht van het Vooraziatisch-Egyptisch Genootschap (Gezelschap) "Ex Oriente Lux"*	JEOL; JVEG
ExB	*Expositor's Bible*	
Excavations	*Excavations and Studies* Tel Aviv	
Excav.Saqq.	*Excavations at Saqqara* (SAE)	
ExcMem	*Egypt Exploration Society Memoirs*	EES; EESm; EMMEES
Exeg.Soul	*Exegesis on the Soul (NHC II,6)*	
Exod	*Exodus*	
Expedition	*Expedition: The Bulletin of the University Museum of the University of Pennsylvania*	
Expl.	*Exemplar*	
ExpT: ExpTim(es)	*The Expository Times*	
Ezek	*Ezekiel*	
Ezek.Trag.	*Ezekiel the Tragedian*	
Fabrica	*Fabrica: Quaderni di Retorica e di Euristica Letteraria*	
Fabula	*Fabula: Zeitschrift für Erzählforschung*	
FAS	*Freiburger Altorientalische Studien*	
FastArch	*Fasti Archaeologici: Annual Bulletin of Classical Archaeology*	

Abbreviation	Citation	Abbreviation alternatives
Faulkner, CD	R.O. Faulkner, *A Concise Dictionary of Middle Egyptian*	CD; FCD
Faulkner, Pyr.	R.O. Faulkner, *The Ancient Egyptian Pyramid Texts and Supplement of Hieroglyphic Texts*	
FB	*Forschung zur Bibel*	
FB	*Frühbronzezeit (Early Bronze Age)*	
FBBS	*Facet Books: Biblical Series*	
FBW	*Fundberichte aus Baden-Württemberg*	
FC	*Fathers of the Church*	
FCD	R.O. Faulkner, *A Concise Dictionary of Middle Egyptian*	CD; Faulkner, CD
FelRav	*Felix Ravenna*	
Fenix	*Fenix: revista de la Biblioteca Nacional* Lima	
FÉRÉ	*Fondation égyptologique Reine Élisabeth (Bruxelles)*	
Festgabe Will	*Festgabe für Dr. Walter Will: Ehrensenator der Universität München, zum 70. Geburtstag am 12. November 1966*	Festgabe Will
Festschrift Ägyptisches Museum Berlin	*Festschrift zum 150jährigen Bestehen des Berliner Ägyptischen Museums*	Fs Mus.Berlin
Festschrift Papyrus Erzherzog Rainer	*Papyrus Erzherzog Rainer (P. Rainer Cent.): Festschrift zum 100-jährigen Bestehen der Papyrussammlung der österreichischen Nationalbibliothek*	
FFC; FFCommunications	*Folklore Fellows Communications*	
FFF	*Från filologiska föreningen*	
FFNT	*Foundations and Facets: New Testament*	
FFP	*Fouilles franco-polonaises*	
FFS	*Fouilles franco-suisses*	
FGH	F. Jacoby, *Die Fragmente der griechischen Historiker*	FGrH
FGLP	*Forschungen zur Geschichte und Lehre des Protestantismus*	
FGrH	F. Jacoby, *Die Fragmente der griechischen Historiker*	FGH
FH	*Fides et Historia*	
FHG	K. Müller, *Fragmenta historicorum graecorum*	
FichEp	*Ficheiro epigràfico: Suplemento de Conimbriga*	
FIFAO	*Fouilles de l'Institut français d'archéologie orientale*	
Figlina	*Figlina* (Société française d'étude de la céramique antique en Gaule), Lyon	
FilOb	*Filologicheskoe obozrenie*	
Filosofia	*Filosofia: Rivista trimestrale* Turin	

Abbreviation	Citation	Abbreviation alternatives
Fischer WG	*Fischer Weltgeschichte*	
FKT	*Forum Katholische Theologie*	
Flacc	Philo, *In Flaccum*	
Florilegium	*Florilegium: Carleton University Annual Papers on Classical Antiquity and the Middle Ages*	
FM	*Field Museum* Chicago	
FMA	*Forma maris antiqui*	
FMAfr	*La France méditerranéenne et africaine*	
FmäS	W. Schenkel, *Frühmittelägyptische Studien*	
FMS	*Frühmittelalterliche Studien: Jahrbuch des Instituts für Frühmittelalterforschung der Universität Münster*	
FMZ	*Frankfurter Münzzeitung*	
FO	*Folia Orientalia*	FolOr
Foi et Vie; FoiVie	*Foi et vie* Paris [See also CBFV]	
FolArch	*Folia archaeologica*	
Folia	*Folia: Studies in the Christian Perpetuation of the Classics* [Continued by ClassFol]	
FolLing	*Folia linguistica: acta societatis linguisticae Europaeae*	
FolOr	*Folia Orientalia*	FO
Fond	*Fondamenti* Brescia	
Fontes atque Pontes	M. Görg, ed., *Fontes atque Pontes: Eine Festgabe für Hellmut Brunner*	Fs Brunner
Fonti	S. Donadoni, ed., *Fonti Indirette della Storia Egiziana = Les Sources Indirectes de l'histoire égyptienne*	
ForIul	*Forum Iulii: Annuario del Museo archeologico nazionale di Cividale del Friuli*	
ForLett	*Forum der Letteren* [Continues Museum (L)]	
ForschBer	*Forschungen und Berichte*	FuB
ForschFortsch	*Forschungen und Fortschritte*	FuF
Forum	*Forum* Bonner (MT)	
FOTL	*Forms of Old Testament Literature*	
Fouilles	*Fouilles en Nubie (1959-1961)*	
FouillesDelph	*Fouilles de Delphes*	
Fouilles Saqq.; FouillesSaqq	*Fouilles à Saqqarah* (SAE)	
FPA	*France-Pays arabes*	
FR	*Freiburger Rundbrief*	
FR	A. Furtwängler, K. Reichhold, *Griechische Vasenmalerei*	
FRA	*Freiburger rechtsgeschichtliche Abhandlungen*	
Fragen an die altägyp. Literatur	J. Assmann, et al., eds. *Fragen an die altägyptische Literatur: Gedenkschrift an Eberhard Otto*	Fs Otto; Gs Otto
Fran	*Franciscanum* Bogota	
Francia	*Francia: Forschungen zur Westeuropäischen Geschichte*	
Frg.Tg.	*Fragmentary Targum*	
Frgs.Hist.Wrks.	*Fragments of Historical Works*	
Frgs.Poet.Wrks.	*Fragments of Poetic Works*	
FRLANT	*Forschungen zur Religion und Literatur des Alten und Neuen Testaments*	
Frm.	*Fragments* (NHC XII,3)	
FrZt	*Frühzeit (early period)*	
FS	*Numbering of Mastabas in Saqqara according to Firth*	
Fs	*Festschrift (celebratory essays)*	
FSAC	W. F. Albright, *From the Stone Age to Christianity*	
Fs Adriani	*Alessandria e il mondo ellenistico-romano: Studi in onore di Achille Adriani*	
Fs Albright	A. Malamat, ed., *W. F. Albright Volume*	
Fs Aldred	*Chief of seers: Egyptian studies in memory of Cyril Aldred* (Studies in Egyptology)	
Fs Arangio-Ruiz	*Studi in onore di Vincenzo Arangio-Ruiz nel 45 anno del suo insegnamento*	
Fs Barocas	*Egyptological Studies for Claudio Barocas*	
Fs Barta	*Gedenkschrift für Winfried Barta* (MÄU 4)	Gs Barta
Fs Bertholet	W. Baumgartner, O. Eißfeld, eds., *Festschrift für Alfred Bertholet zum 80. Geburtstag gewidme*	
Fs Bleeker	*Liber Amicorum: Studies in Honour of Professor Dr. C. J. Bleeker*	Liber Amicorum
Fs Bothmer	H. de Meulenaere, and L. Limme, eds., *Artibus Aegypti: Studia in honorem Bernardi V. Bothmer*	Artibus Aegypti
Fs Botti	*Studi in onore di Giuseppe Botti*	
Fs Brunner	M. Görg, ed., *Fontes atque Pontes: Eine Festgabe für Hellmut Brunner*	Fontes atque Pontes
Fs Carsten Niebuhr Instituttet	*Mellem Nilen og Tigris: Festskrift for Carsten Niebuhr Instituttet*	
Fs Champollion (1922)	*Recueil d'études égyptologiques dédiées à la mémoire de Jean-François Champollion* (BEHE 234)	
Fs Champollion (1972)	*Textes et langages de l'Egypte pharaonique: Hommage à Jean-François Champollion* (BdE 64)	

Abbreviation	Citation	Abbreviation alternatives
Fs Crum	*Coptic Studies in Honour of Walter Ewing Crum*	
Fs Dunand	*Mélanges offerts à M. Maurice Dunand*	Mélanges Dunand
Fs Dunham	*Studies in ancient Egypt, the Aegean, and the Sudan: essays in honor of Dows Dunham on the occasion of his 90th birthday, June 1, 1980*	
Fs Dussaud	*Mélanges syriens offerts à M. René Dussaud par ses amis et élèves*	Mél.Dussaud
Fs Ebers	*Aegyptiaca: Festschrift für Georg Ebers*	
Fs Edel	M. Görg, and E. Pusch, eds., *Festschrift Elmar Edel (12. März 1979)* (ÄUAT 1)	
Fs Edwards	*Pyramid studies and other essays presented to I.E.S. Edwards* (EES)	
Fs Eißfeld	J. Fück, ed., *Festschrift Otto Eißfeld zum 60. Geburtstag 1. September 1947*	
Fs Emerton	*Wisdom in ancient Israel: Essays in honour of J.A. Emerton*	
Fs Fairman	J. Ruffle et al., eds., *Glimpses of Ancient Egypt*	Glimpses of Ancient Egypt
Fs Freedman	*Fortunate the Eyes that See: Essays in Honor of David Noel Freedman in Celebration of His Seventieth Birthday*	
Fs Freedman	C.L. Meyers, and M. O'Connor, eds., *The Word of the Lord Shall Go Forth: Essays in Honor of David Noel Freedman*	WLSGF
Fs Galling	*Archäologie und Altes Testament: Festschrift für Kurt Galling zum 8. Jan. 1970*	
Fs Glueck	*Near Eastern Archaeology in the Twentieth Century: Essays in Honor of Nelson Glueck*	
Fs Golenischeff	*Drevnii Egipet*	
Fs Gordon	*Orient and Occident: Essays presented to Cyrus H. Gordon* (AOAT 22)	
Fs Grapow	O. Firchow, ed., *Festschrift für Hermann Grapow zum 70. Geburtstag: Ägyptologische Studien*	ÄS
Fs Grégoire	*PAGKARPEIA: Mélanges Henri Grégoire*	PAGKARPEIA
Fs Griffith	*Studies Presented to Francis Llewellyn Griffith*	
Fs Grossmann	*Themelia: Spätantike und koptologische Studien: Peter Grossmann zum 65. Geburstag*	
Fs Gundlach	*Wege öffnen: Festschrift für Rolf Gundlach zum 65. Geburtstag* (ÄAT 35)	
Fs Gutbub	*Mélanges Adolphe Gutbub*	Mélanges Gutbub
Fs Hintze	*Ägypten und Kusch*	
Fs Hughes	*Studies in Honor of George R. Hughes* (SAOC 39)	Studies Hughes
Fs Junker	*Festschrift zum 80. Geburtstag von Hermann Junker*	
Fs Kees	*Festschrift zum 70. Geburtstag von Hermann Kees*	
Fs Leclant	*Hommages à Jean Leclant* (BdE 106)	
Fs Lüddeckens	H. Thissen, and K. Zauzich, eds., *Grammata Demotica: Festschrift für Erich Lüddeckens zum 15. Juni 1983*	
Fs Mansel	*Mélanges Mansel - Mansel'e armagan. Türk Tarih Kurumu yayinlari, dizi 6, 60a-c*	Mélanges Mansel
Fs Mariette	*Mélanges Mariette* (BdE 32)	Mél.Mar.; Mélanges Mariette
Fs Maspero	*Mélanges Maspero* (MIFAO 66 and 67)	Mél.Masp.; Mélanges Maspero
Fs Michalowski	*Mélanges offerts à Kazimierz Michalowski*	Mélanges Michalowski
Fs Mokhtar	*Mélanges Gamal Eddin Mokhtar* (BdE 97)	
Fs Moortgart	*Festschrift für Anton Moortgart zum 65. Geburtstag*	
Fs Mus.Berlin	*Festschrift zum 150jährigen Bestehen des Berliner Ägyptischen Museums*	Festschrift Ägyptisches Museum Berlin
Fs Naster	*Studia Paulo Naster Oblata II: Orientalia Antiqua*	Studia Naster II
Fs Orsolina Montevecchi	E. Bresciani, ed., *Scritti in onore di Orsolina Montevecchi*	Scritti O.Montevecchi
Fs Otten	E. Neu and C. Rüster, eds., *Festschrift für Heinrich Otten*	
Fs Otto	J. Assmann et al., eds., *Fragen an die altägyptische Literatur: Gedenkschrift an Eberhard Otto*	Fragen an die altägyp.Literatur; Gs Otto
Fs Papyrussammlung Wien	*Festschrift zum 100jährigen Bestehen der Papyrussammlung der Österreichischen Nationalbibliothek. Papyrus Erzherzog Rainer (pRainer cent.)*	
Fs Parker	L.H. Lesko, ed., *Egyptological Studies in Honor of Richard A. Parker*	
Fs Pedersen	*Studia Orientalia Ioanni Pedersen septuagenario*	
Fs Pirenne	*Dédié à la Mémoire de Jacques Pirenne* (AIP 20)	Mélanges Pirenne
Fs Polotsky (1964)	*Studies in Egyptology and Linguistics in Honour of Hans Jacob Polotsky* (1964)	Studies Polotsky (1964)
Fs Polotsky (1981)	*Studies presented to Hans Jakob Polotsky* (1981)	Studies Polotsky (1981)

Abbreviation	Citation	Abbreviation alternatives
Fs Quaegebeur	*Egyptian religion: the last thousand years: studies dedicated to the memory of Jan Quaegebeur* (OLA 84-85)	
Fs Ricke	*Aufsätze zum 70. Geburtstag von Herbert Ricke*	
Fs Robert	*Mélanges bibliques rédigés en honneur de André Robert*	
Fs Rosellini, Scritti	*Scritti dedicati alla memoria di Ippolito Rosellini*	Scritti Rosellini
Fs Rosellini, Studi	*Studi in memoria di Ippolito Rosellini nel primo centenario della morte*	Studi Rosellini
Fs Sauneron (1)	*Volume dédié à la mémoire de Serge Sauneron* (BIFAO 77)	Hommage Sauneron
Fs Sauneron (2)	*Hommages à la Serge Sauneron* (BdE 81-82)	Hommages Sauneron
Fs Säve-Söderbergh	*Sundries in Honour of Torgny Säve-Söderbergh* (Boreas 13)	Säve-Söderbergh; Sundries Säve-Söderbergh
Fs Schenkel	*Per aspera ad astra: Wolfgang Schenkel zum neunundfünfzigsten Geburtstag*	
Fs Schott	*Festschrift für Siegfried Schott zu seinem 70. Geburtstag*	
Fs Schubart	*Aus Antike und Orient: Festschrift für Wilhelm Schubart zum 75. Geburtstag*	
Fs Schulman	*Dedicated to Alan R. Schulman* (BES 10) (ESNY)	
Fs Simpson	*Studies in honor of William Kelly Simpson*	
Fs Spuler	H. R. Roemer and A. Noth, eds., *Studien zur Geschichte und Kultur des Vorderen Orients: Festschrift für Bertold Spuler zum 70. Geburtstag*	
Fs Stadelmann	*Stationen: Beiträge zur Kulturgeschichte Ägyptens: Rainer Stadelmann gewidmet*	
Fs Struve 1962	*Drevnii mir, Sbornik statei V.V. Struve*	Drevnii Mir
Fs Struve 1964	*Assiriologiia i Egiptologiia: Sbornik statei V.V. Struve*	Assiriologija i Egiptologija
Fs van der Leeuw	*Pro Regno Pro Sanctuario: Een bundel studies en bijdragen van vrienden en vereerders bij de zestigste verjaardag van Gerardus van der Leeuw*	
Fs Vergote	*Miscellanea in honorem Josephi Vergote* (OLP 6-7)	Miscellanea Vergote
Fs Vermaseren	*Hommages à Maarten J. Vermaseren*	Hommages Vermaseren
Fs Ward	*Ancient Egyptian and Mediterranean studies: in memory of William A. Ward*	
Fs Wessetzky	*Studia iuvenum in honorem Vilmos Wessetzky*	
Fs Westendorf	*Studien zu Sprache und Religion Ägyptens: Zu Ehren von Wolfhart Westendorf überreicht von seinen Freunden und Schülern*	Studien Westendorf
Fs Will	*Festgabe für Dr. Walter Will: Ehrensenator der Universität München, zum 70. Geburtstag am 12. November 1966*	Fs Will
Fs Williams	J.K. Hoffmeier and E.S. Meltzer, eds., *Egyptological Miscellanies: A Tribute to Professor Ronald J. Williams* (The Ancient World 6, 1983)	Egyptological Miscellanies
Fs Williams	*Studies in Philology in Honour of Ronald James Williams*	Studies Williams
Fs Wilson	*Studies in Honour of John A. Wilson* (SAOC 35)	Studies Wilson
Fs Winter	*Aspekte spätägyptischer Kultur: Festschrift für Erich Winter zum 65. Geburtstag (AegTrev 7)*	
Fs Zandee	*Studies in Egyptian Religion Dedicated to Professor Jan Zandee*	
Fs Zucker	W. Müller, ed., *Festschrift für Friedrich Zucker zum 70. Geburtstag*	
FTS	*Freiburger Theologische Studien*	
FUB	*Furman University Bulletin*	
FuB	*Forschungen und Berichte*	ForschBer
FuF	*Forschungen und Fortschritte*	ForschFortsch
Fuga	Philo, *De fuga et inventione*	
Fund	*Fundamentum: Zeitschrift der Freien Evangelisch-Theologischen Akademie Basel.*	
FundSchw	*Fundberichte aus Schwaben*	
Furrow	*Furrow* Maynooth (Ireland)	
FWSDFML	*Funk and Wagnall's Standard Dictionary of Folklore, Mythology and Legend*	
FZPT	*Freiburger Zeitschrift für Philosophie und Theologie*	
G + no.	*Grab Gisa (Giza Tomb)*	
GAAL	*Goettinger Arbeitshefte zur Altorientalischen Literatur*	
GacNum	*Gaceta numismática*	
GAG	W. von Soden, *Grundriss der akkadischen Grammatik* (AnOr 33/47)	
Gaium	Philo, *Legatio ad Gaium*	
Gal	*Galatians*	
Gallia	*Gallia: fouilles et monuments archéologiques en France métropolitaine*	
GalliaPréhist	*Gallia préhistoire*	
Gallia-Suppl.	*Gallia, Supplément* Paris	
Gardiner, AEO	A.H. Gardiner, *Ancient Egyptian Onomastica*	AEO

Abbreviation	Citation	Abbreviation alternatives
Gardiner, EG	A.H. Gardiner, *Egyptian Grammar*	
Gardiner, LEM	A.H. Gardiner, *Late-Egyptian Miscellanies* (BAe 7)	LEM
Gardiner, LES	A.H. Gardiner, *Late-Egyptian Stories* (BAe 1)	LES
Gardiner, RCT	A.H. Gardiner, *The Royal Canon of Turin*	RCT
GARI	A.K. Grayson, *Assyrian Royal Inscriptions*	
Gauthier, D(N)G	H. Gauthier, *Dictionnaire des noms géographiques*	
GazArch	*Gazette archéologique: recueil de monuments pour servià la connaissance et à l'histoire de l'art dans l'antiquité et le moyen-âge*	
GB	D. Baly, *Geography of the Bible*	
GBA	*Gazette des beaux-arts*	
GBS	*Guides to Biblical Scholarship*	
GCFI	*Giornale critico della filosofia italiana*	
GCS	*Die griechischen christlichen Schrifsteller der ersten drei Jahrhunderte*	
Gebel es-Silsilah I	R.A. Caminos and T.G.H. James, *Gebel es-Silsilah I* (ASE 31)	
GECJ; GEC Journal	*General Electric Company Journal*	
GeistArb	*Geistige Arbeit: Zeitung aus der wissenschaftlichen Welt*	
Gem.	*Gemara*	
Gen	*Genesis*	
GenAfr	*Genève-Afrique = Geneva-Africa*	
Genava	*Genava: bulletin du musee d'art et d'histoire*	
GenHum	*Le Genre humain*	
GeoAnz	*Geographischer Anzeiger*	
Geo-archeologia	*Geo-archeologia: Periodico semestrale dell'Associazione geo-archeologica italiana*	
Géographie	*La Géographie*	
GeoJb	*Geographisches Jahrbuch*	
GeoJourn	*Geographical Journal*	GJ
GeoMag	*Geographical Magazine*	
GeoRev	*Geographical Review*	
GeoRunds	*Geographische Rundschau*	
GeoTids	*Geografisk Tidsskrift*	
GeoZeits	*Geographische Zeitschrift*	
Germania	*Germania: Anzeiger der Römisch-germanischen Kommission des deutschen archäologischen Instituts*	
Germanien	*Germanien: Monatshefte für Germanenkunde zur Erkenntnis deutschen Wesens*	
GermStud	*German Studies: a review of German-language research contributions on literature, music, and fine arts with bibliographies*	
Gerzeh and Mazghuneh	W.M.F. Petrie, *The Labyrinth, Gerzeh and Mazghuneh* (BSAE 21)	
GesB	W. Gesenius and F. Buhl, eds., *Hebräisches und aramäisches Handwörterbuch*	
Geschichtsfreund	*Der Geschichtsfreund: Mitteilungen des historischen Vereins der fünf Orte Luzern, Uri, Schwyz, Unterwalden ob und nid dem Wald und Zug*	
Gesnerus	*Gesnerus: Swiss journal of the history of medicine and sciences*	
GettyMusJ	*J. Paul Getty Museum Journal*	
GFF	*Giornale filologico ferrarese*	
GGA	*Göttingische Gelehrte Anzeigen*	
GGM	*Geographi Graeci Minores*	
GGR	M.P. Nilsson, *Geschichte der griechische Religion*	
GHÅ	*Göteborgs Högskolas Årsskrift*	
GHBW	R.R. Wilson, *Genealogy and History in the Biblical World*	
GIF	*Giornale italiano di filologia: Revista trimestrale di cultura*	
Gig	Philo, *De gigantibus*	
Giornale	G. Botti and T.E. Peet, *Il giornale della necropoli di Tebe*	
GiornMet	*Giornale di Metafisica*	
GIP	*Grundriss der iranischen Philologie*	
Git.	*Gittin*	
Gizeh and Rifeh	W.M.F. Petrie, *Gizeh and Rifeh* (BSAE 13)	
GJ	*Geographical Journal*	GeoJourn
GJV	E. Schürer, *Geschichte des jüdisches Volkes im Zeitalter Jesu Christi*	
GK	E. Kautzsch, ed., *Gesenius' Hebräische Grammatik, 28th ed.*	
Gk.Apoc.Ezra	*Greek Apocalypse of Ezra*	
Gladius	*Gladius: Études sur les armes anciennes, l'art militaire et la vie culturelle en orient et occident*	
GLÉCS	*Comptes rendus du Groupe linguistique d'études chamito-sémitiques*	
Glimpses of Ancient Egypt	J. Ruffle et al., eds., *Glimpses of Ancient Egypt*	Fs Fairman
GLO	*Graecolatina et orientalia*	GrOr
Glossa	*Glossa: An international journal of linguistics*	

Abbreviation	Citation	Abbreviation alternatives
Glotta	*Glotta: Zeitschrift für griechische und lateinische Sprache*	
GLP	*Graecolatina Pragensia: Acta Universitatis Carolinae, Philologia*	
GM	*Göttinger Miszellen*	GöttMisc
GMS	*Gibb Memorial Series*	
GMT	W. Westendorf, *Grammatik der medizinischen Texte* (Grundriß der Medizin 8)	Westendorf, Med. Gramm./GMT; Med.Gramm.
GN	Gercke and Norden, *Einleitung in die Altertumswissenschaft*	
GNB	*Good News Bible*	
GNC	*Good News Commentary*	
Gnomon	*Gnomon: Kritische Zeitschrift für die gesamte klassische Altertumswissenschaft*	
Gnosticisme et monde hellénistique	*Gnosticisme et monde hellénistique: Actes du Colloque de Louvain-la-Neuve (11-14 mars 1980)*	
GNS	*Gazette numismatique suisse*	
GNS	*Good News Studies*	
GNT	*Grundrisse zum Neuen Testament*	
GO	*Göttinger Orientforschungen*	GOF
Godisnjak	*Godisnjak* Sarajevo	
GOF	*Göttinger Orientforschungen*	GO
Gos.Barn.	*Gospel of Barnabas*	
Gos.Bart.	*Gospel of Bartholomew*	
Gos.Bas.	*Gospel of Basilides*	
Gos.Bir.Mary	*Gospel of the Birth of Mary*	
Gos.Eb.	*Gospel of the Ebionites*	
Gos.Eg.	*Gospel of the Egyptians* (NHC III,2; IV,2)	
Gos.Eve	*Gospel of Eve*	
Gos.Gam.	*Gospel of Gamaliel*	
Gos.Heb.	*Gospel of the Hebrews*	
Gos.Inf.	*Infancy Gospels*	
Gos.Inf.(Arab)	*Gospel of the Infancy (Arabic)*	
Gos.Inf.(Arm)	*Gospel of the Infancy (Armenian)*	
Gos.John (Apocr.)	*Gospel of John (Apocryphal)*	
Gos.Marcion	*Gospel of Marcion*	
Gos.Mary	*Gospel of Mary*	
Gos.Naass.	*Gospel of the Naassenes*	
Gos.Naz.	*Gospel of the Nazarenes*	
Gos.Nic.	*Gospel of Nicodemus*	
Gos.Pet.	*Gospel of Peter*	
Gos.Phil.	*Gospel of Philip* (NHC II,3)	
Gos.Thom.	*Gospel According to Thomas* (NHC II,2)	
Gos.Trad.Mth.	*Gospel and Traditions of Matthias*	

Abbreviation	Citation	Abbreviation alternatives
Gos.Truth	*Gospel of Truth* (NHC I,3; XII,2)	
GOTR	*Greek Orthodox Theological Review*	
Göttinger Vorträge	S. Schott, ed., *Göttinger Vorträge vom Ägyptologischen Kolloquium der Akademie am 25. und 26. August 1964*	
GöttMisc	*Göttinger Miszellen*	GM
GP	F.M. Abel, *Géographie de la Palestine*	
Gr.	*Gramm (gram)*	
GrazBeitr	*Grazer Beiträge: Zeitschrift für die klassische Altertumswissenschaft*	
GRBM	*Greek, Roman and Byzantine Monographs*	
GRBS	*Greek, Roman and Byzantine Studies*	
GRBSA	*Greek, Roman and Byzantine Scholarly Aids*	
Great Pow.	*The Concept of Our Great Power* (NHC VI,4)	
Greg; Gregorianum	*Gregorianum: Commentarii de re theologica et philosophica editi a professoribus Pontificiae Universitatis Gregorianae*	
GRM	*Germanisch-romanische Monatsschrift*	
GrOr	*Graecolatina et orientalia*	GrOr
GrRom	*Greece and Rome*	
GrSuf	*Grai si Suflet*	
Grundriß der Medizin	H. Grapow et al., *Grundriß der Medizin der alten Ägypter*	
Gs	*Gedenkschrift (commemorative essays)*	
GSAI	*Giornale della Società Asiatica Italiana*	
GSAT	*Gesammelte Studien zum Alten Testament*	
Gs Barta	*Gedenkschrift für Winfried Barta* (MÄU 4)	Fs Barta
GSKA	*Glas Srpske Kraljevske Akademije* Belgrade	
Gs Otto	J. Assmann et al., eds., *Fragen an die altägyptische Literatur: Gedenkschrift an Eberhard Otto*	Fragen an die altägyp.Literatur; Fs Otto
GTA	*Göttinger theologische Arbeiten*	
GTJ	*Grace Theological Journal*	
GTT	*Gereformeerd Theologisch Tijdschrift*	
GTTOT	J.J. Simons, *The Geographical and Topographical Texts of the Old Testament*	
GuL	*Geist und Leben*	
Gurob	G. Brunton and R. Engelbach, *Gurob* (BSAE 41)	
GVÉP	*Groupe vendéen d'études préhistoriques*	

Abbreviation	Citation	Abbreviation alternatives
GVG	C. Brockelmann, *Grundriss der vergleichenden Grammatik der semitischen Sprachen*	
GWU	*Geschichte in Wissenschaft und Unterricht*	
Gymnasium	*Gymnasium: Zeitschrift für Kultur der Antike und humanistische Bildung* [Continues HumGym]	
HAB	*Harper's Atlas of the Bible*	
Hab	*Habakkuk*	
HÄB	*Hildesheimer Ägyptologische Beiträge*	
Habis	*Habis: Arqueologia, Filologia clasica*	
HAD	G. Fohrer, ed., *Hebrew and Aramaic Dictionary of the OT*	
HadArkh	*Hadashot Arkheologiyot: Archeological Newsletter of the Israel Department of Antiquities and Museums* [See also ESI]	
Hag	*Haggai*	
Hag.	*Hagiga*	
HallWPr	*Hallisches Winckelmannsprogramm*	
HAIJ	J.M. Miller and J.H. Hayes, *A History of Ancient Israel and Judah*	
Hal.	*Halla*	
HALAT	W. Baumgartner, ed., *Hebräisches und aramäisches Lexikon zum Alten Testament*	
HamHeh	*Hamizrah Hehadash: The Near East*	HH; HM
Hamito-Semitica	*Hamito-Semitica : proceedings of a colloquium held by the Historical Section of the Linguistics Association, Great Britain at the School of Oriental and African Studies, University of London, on the 18th, 19th and 20th of March 1970*	
Handlist	H. Murray and Mary Nuttal, *A Handlist to Howard Carter's Catalogue of Objects in Tutᶜankhamun's Tomb* (Tutᶜankhamun's Tomb Series 1)	
HANE.M	*History of the Ancient Near East / Monographs*	
HANE.S	*History of the Ancient Near East / Studies*	
HAR	*Hebrew Annual Review*	
Harageh	R. Engelbach and B. Gunn, *Harageh* (BSAE 28)	
HAS	*Harvard African Studies*	
HÄS	*Hamburger Ägyptologische Studien*	
HASB	*Hefte des archäologischen Seminars* Bern	
HAT	*Handbuch zum Alten Testament*	
Hatnub	R. Anthes, *Die Felseninschriften von Hatnub* (UGAÄ 9)	
HAW	*Handbuch der Altertumswissenschaften*	HdA
HBA	*Hamburger Beiträge zur Archäologie*	
HbArch	*Handbuch der Archäologie*	
HBC	*Harper's Bible Commentary*	
HBD	P.J. Achtemeier, ed., *Harper's Bible Dictionary*	
HBN	*Hamburger Beiträge zur Numismatik*	
HbOr	*Handbuch der Orientalistik*	HdO; HO
HBT	*Horizons in Biblical Theology*	
HBV	*Hessische Blätter für Volkskunde*	
HdA	*Handbuch der Altertumswissenschaften*	HAW
HDB	J. Hastings, ed., *Dictionary of the Bible*	
HdO	*Handbuch der Orientalistik*	HbOr; HO
HDR	*Harvard Dissertations in Religion*	
HDS	*Harvard Dissertation Series*	
Hdt.	*Herodotus*	
H.E.	*Haute Egypte (Upper Egypt)*	
Heb	*Hebrew Epistle to the Hebrews*	
Heb.Apoc.El.	*Hebrew Apocalypse of Elijah*	
Hebraica	*Hebraica: Quarterly Journal in the interest of Semitic Studies* [Continues BNES, Continued by AJSL]	
Hec.Ab	*Hecataeus of Abdera*	
HeilLand	*Das heilige Land (Holy Land)*	
Hekanakhte Papers	T.G.H. James, *The Hekanakhte Papers and other Early Middle-Kingdom Documents* (PMMA 19)	
HÉL	*Histoire, épistémologie, langage*	
Helck, Materialien Indexband	I. Hofmann, *Indices zu W. Helck, Materialien zur Wirtschaftsgeschichte des Neuen Reiches*	
Helikon	*Helikon: rivista di tradizione e cultura classica dell'Università di Messina*	
Helinium	*Helinium: Revue consacrée à l'archéologie des Pays-Bas, de la Belgique et du Grand Duché du Luxemburg*	
Heliopolis; Heliopolis, Kafr Ammar and Shurafa	W.M.F. Petrie and E. Mackay, *Heliopolis, Kafr Ammar and Shurafa* (BSAE 24)	
Helios	*Helios: Journal of the Classical Association of the Southwestern United States*	
Hell.	*Hellenistic, hellénistique, hellenistisch*	
HellasJb	*Hellas Jahrbuch*	
HellCont	*L'Hellénisme contemporain*	

Abbreviation	Citation	Abbreviation alternatives
Hellenika	*Hellenika: Philologikon istorikon kai laographikon periodikon syngramma*	
HellHor	*Hellenikon Horizontes*	
Helmantica	*Helmantica: Revista de filologia clasica y hebrea*	
Hel.Syn.Pr.	*Hellenistic Synagogal Prayers*	
HelvArch	*Helvetia archaeologica* [Continues SuissPrim]	
Hen	*Henoch: Studi storicofilologici sull'ebraismo redatti presso la Biblioteca Paul Kahle dell'Istituto di orientalistica dell'Università di Torino*	Henoch
Henoch	*Henoch: Studi storicofilologici sull'ebraismo redatti presso la Biblioteca Paul Kahle dell'Istituto di orientalistica dell'Università di Torino*	Hen; Henoch
Hephaistos (B)	*Hephaistos: kritische Zeitschrift zur Theorie und Praxis der Archäologie und angrenzender Wissenschaften* Bremen	
Hephaistos (P)	*Hephaistos: A quarterly devoted to computer research in the humanities* Philadelphia	
Heres	Philo, *Quis rerum divinarum heres*	
Herm	*Hermathena*	
Hermeneia	*Hermeneia: A Critical and Historical Commentary on the Bible*	
Hermeneus	*Hermeneus: Tijdschrift voor de antieke cultuur*	
Hermes	*Hermes: Zeitschrift für klassische Philologie*	
Herm.Man.	*Hermas, Mandate*	
Herm.Sim.	*Hermas, Similitude*	
Herm.Vis.	*Hermas, Vision*	
Herodot	*Herodoti Historiae recognovit Carolus Hude*	
Hesperia	*Hesperia: Journal of the American School of Classical Studies at Athens*	
Hesperiam	*Hesperiam: Journal of the Joint Association of Classics Teachers* [See also Didaskalos, and JACT]	
Hespéris	*Hespéris: archives berbères et bulletin de l'Institut des hautes-études marocaines* [Continued by HespTam]	
HespTam	*Hespéris Tamuda* [Continues Hespéris]	Tamuda
Het Boek	*Het Boek* The Hague	
Hev	*Nahal Hever texts*	
HeyJ; HeythJourn	*The Heythrop Journal: a quarterly review of philosophy and theology*	
HG	J. Friedrich, *Die hethitischen Gesetze* (DMOA 7)	
HGB	Z. Kallai, *Historical Geography of the Bible*	
HH	*Hamizrah Hehadash: The Near East*	HamHeh; HM
HHI	S. Herrmann, *History of Israel in Old Testament Times*	
HibJ; HibJourn	*Hibbert journal: a quarterly review of religion, theology, and philosophy*	
Hierakonpolis	J.E. Quibell and F.W. Green, *Hierakonpolis* (BSAE 4-5)	
Hiero.Texts	*Hieroglyphic Texts from Egyptian Stelae, etc., in the British Museum*	BM Stelae; HTBM
HIOTP	H. Jagersma, *History of Israel in the Old Testament Period*	
Hippokrates	*Hippokrates: Annales Societatis Historiae Medicinae Fennicae*	
Hispania	*Hispania: Revista española de historia*	
HispAnt	*Hispania antiqua: Revista de historia antigua*	
HistArch	*Histoire et archéologie: Les Dossiers* [Continues DossArch]	
Hist.Eccl.	Eusebius, *Historia ecclesiastica = Church History*	
HistJb	*Historisches Jahrbuch*	
Hist.Jos.	*History of Joseph*	
Hist.Jos.Carp.	*History of Joseph the Carpenter*	
HistMath	*Historia mathematica: International Journal of History of Mathematics* New York and London	
Historia; Historia (W)	*Historia: Zeitschrift für alte Geschichte* Wiesbaden	
Historia (M)	*Historia: studi storici per l'antichità classica* Milan	
Historia Lausiaca	Butler, Cuthbert, *Lausiac History of Palladius*	
History	*History: Quarterly Journal of the Historical Association* London	
HistrArch	*Histria archaeologica*	
Hist.Rech.	*History of the Rechabites*	
HistRel	*History of Religions: An international journal for comparative historical studies*	HR
HistSc	*History of Science*	
HistTd	*History Today: Monthly Magazine*	
HistTechn	*History of Technology*	
HistTh	*History and Theory: Studies in the Philosophy of History*	
HistZeits	*Historische Zeitschrift*	HZ
Hit	*Hittite*	
HJP (1)	E. Schürer et al., *History of the Jewish People in the Time of Jesus Christ, 1886-1890*	

Abbreviation	Citation	Abbreviation alternatives
HJP (2)	G. Vermes, ed., *History of the Jewish People in the Age of Jesus Christ, 1973-1987*	
HKAT	*Handkommentar zum Alten Testament*	
HKL	Borger, R., *Handbuch der Keilschriftliteratur*	
HKNT	*Handkommentar zum Neuen Testament*	
HL	"Hittite Laws," in *Ancient Near Eastern Texts Relating to the Old Testament,* 3d ed	
HLB	*Harvard Library Bulletin*	
HM	*Hamizrah Hehadash: The Near East*	HamHeh; HH
HM	*Historia Mathematica* Toronto	
HNT	*Handbuch zum Neuen Testament*	
HNTC	*Harper's New Testament Commentaries*	
HO	*Handbuch der Orientalistik*	HbOr; HdO
Hokhma	*Hokhma: revue de réflexion théologique*	
Hommage Sauneron	*Volume dédié à la mémoire de Serge Sauneron* (BIFAO 77)	Fs Sauneron (1)
Hommages Sauneron	*Hommages à la Serge Sauneron* (BdE 81-82)	Fs Sauneron (2)
Hommages Vermaseren	*Hommages à Maarten J. Vermaseren*	Fs Vermaseren
Homme	*Homme: journal illustré des sciences anthropologiques*	
Homo	*Homo: internationale Zeitschrift für die vergleichende Forschung am Menschen*	
Homonoia	*Homonoia: Yearbook of the Chair of Greek Philology*	
Hor	*Horizons*	
Hor.	*Horayot*	
Horizon	*Horizon* New York	
Horos	*Horos: Hena archaiognostiko periodiko*	
Hos	*Hosea*	
HP	*Hoherpriester, High Priest*	
HPBM	*Hieratic Papyri in the British Museum*	
HPLS	*History and Philosophy of the Life Sciences*	
HPM	*High Priest of Memphis*	
HPQ	*History of Philosophy Quarterly*	
HPR	*Homiletic and Pastoral Review*	
HPS	*Hellenikos philologikos syllogos en Konstantinopolei*	
HPT	*History of Political Thought*	
HPT	M. Noth, *A History of Pentateuchal Traditions*	
HR	*History of Religions: An international journal for comparative historical studies*	HistRel
HS	*Hebrew Studies*	

Abbreviation	Citation	Abbreviation alternatives
HSAO	*Heidelberger Studien zum Alten Orient*	
HSAT	E. Kautzsch and A. Bertholet, eds., *Die Heilige Schrift des Alten Testaments*	
HSCL	*Harvard Studies in Comparative Literature*	
HSCP	*Harvard Studies in Classical Philology*	
HSF	*Historische Sprachforschung*	
HSM	*Harvard Semitic Monographs*	
HSM	*Histoire des sciences médicales*	
HSPS	*Historical Studies in the Physical Sciences* [Continues Chymia]	
HSS	*Harvard Semitic Studies*	
HTBM	*Hieroglyphic Texts from Egyptian Stelae, etc., in the British Museum*	BM Stelae; Hiero.Texts
HTKNT	*Herders theologischer Kommentar zum Neuen Testament*	
HTR	*Harvard Theological Review*	
HTS	*Harvard Theological Studies*	
HUCA	*Hebrew Union College Annual*	
Hul.	*Hullin*	
Humanidades (B)	*Humanidades* Buenos Aires	
Humanidades (S)	*Humanidades* (Universidad Pontificia de Comillas), Santander	
Humanisme	*Humanisme: Bulletin de l'Association humanisme* Brussels	
Humanitas (A)	*Humanitas: Nouvelle revue des humanités* Arlon (Belgium)	
Humanitas (C)	*Humanitas* Coimbra	
Humanitats	*Humanitats: Revue internationale de philologie classique et humanités*	
Humanités	*Humanités: Revue d'enseignement secondaire et d'éducation*	
HumGym	*Humanistisches Gymnasium* [Continued by Gymnasium]	
HumIsl	*Humaniora islamica: An annual publication of Islamic studies and humanities*	
HumLov	*Humanistica Lovaniensia*	
HumRen	*Humanisme et Renaissance*	
HVJ	*Historische Vierteljahrsschrift*	
Hymn Dance	*Hymn of the Dance*	
Hyp.Arch.	*Hypostasis of the Archons* (NHC II,4)	
Hypo	Philo, *Hypothetica*	
Hypoth.	*Hypothesis*	
Hypsiph.	*Hypsiphrone* (NHC XI,4)	
HZ	*Historische Zeitschrift*	HistZeits
HZM	*Handelingen der Zuidnederlandse Maatschapij voor Taal- & Letterkunde en Geschiedenis*	
IAB	*Institute of Archaeology Bulletin*	

Abbreviation	Citation	Abbreviation alternatives
IACS	*International Association of Coptic Studies*	
IACS Newsl(etter)	*International Association for Coptic Studies Newsletter*	
IAE	*International Archives of Ethnography, Internationales Archiv für Ethnographie*	
IAE	*International Association of Egyptologists*	
IÄF	P. Kaplony, *Die Inschriften der ägyptischen Frühzeit*	
IAMB	*Istanbul Arkeoloji Müzelerinde Bulunan Bogazköy Tabletleri*	IBoT
IAMN	*Istanbul Arkeologi Müizeleri Nesriyati* Istanbul	
IAMY	*Istanbul Arkeologi Müizeleri Yilligi*	
Iapigia	*Iapigia* [Continued by ASPugl]	
IazLit	*Iazyk i literatura*	
IB	*Interpreter's Bible*	
IBAES	*Internet-Beiträge zur Ägyptologie und Sudanarchäologie*	
IBC	*Interpretation: A Bible Commentary for Teaching and Preaching*	
IBHR	*International Bibliography of the History of Religions*	
IBHS	*International Bibliography of Historical Sciences*	
IBIS	J. Leclant and G. Clerc, *Inventaire bibliographique des isiaca* (EPRO 18)	
Ibis	*De Ibis*	
IBLA	*Institut des belles-lettres arabes* Tunis	
IBoT	*Istanbul Arkeoloji Müzelerinde Bulunan Bogazköy Tabletleri*	IAMB
IBS	*Irish Biblical Studies*	
ICC	*The International Critical Commentary on the Holy Scriptures of the Old and New Testaments*	
ICCROM	*International Centre for Conservation and Restauration of Cultural Property in Rome*	
ICE	*International Congress of Egyptology*	
IcRel	*Iconography of Religions*	
ICS	*Illinois Classical Studies*	
IDB	G.A. Buttrick, ed., *Interpreter's Dictionary of the Bible*	
IDBSup	K. Crim, ed., *Interpreter's Dictionary of the Bible Supplementary Volume*	
Idö és történelem	*Idö és történelem (Zeit und Geschichte, Vorträge)* Budapest	
IdVal	*Ideas y valores*	
IEJ	*Israel Exploration Journal*	
IF	*Indogermanische Forschungen*	IGF
IFAO	*Institut français d'archéologie orientale du Caire*	
IFD	*Institut français de Damas* [later IFÉAD]	
IFÉAD	*Institut français d'études arabes de Damas* [earlier IFD]	
IFJ	*Istoriko-filosofsky jezegodnik = History of Philosophy Yearbook* Moscow	
IG	*Inscriptiones Graecae* Chicago [See also InscrGr]	
IG	*Istorijski Glasnik* Belgrade	
IGCS	*International Guide to Classical Studies*	
IGF	*Indogermanische Forschungen*	IF
IGJ	*Indogermanisches Jahrbuch*	
IGLS	*Inscriptions grecques et latines de la Syrie*	
IGMS	*International Guide to Medieval Studies*	
Ign.Eph.	*Ignatius, Letter to the Ephesians*	Eph.
Ign.Magn.	*Ignatius, Letter to the Magnesians*	Magn.
Ign.Phld.	*Ignatius, Letter to the Philadelphians*	Phld.
Ign.Pol.	*Ignatius, Letter to Polycarp*	Pol.
Ign.Rom.	*Ignatius, Letter to the Romans*	Rom.
Ign.Smyrn.	*Ignatius, Letter to the Smyrnaeans*	Smyrn.
Ign.Trall.	*Ignatius, Letter to the Trallians*	Trall.
IGRR	*Inscriptiones graecae ad res romanas pertinentes*	
IGSK; IGSKA	*Inschriften griechischer Städte aus Kleinasien*	
IHA	*L'Information de l'histoire de l'art*	
IJAHS	*The International Journal of African Historical Studies*	
IJCS (L)	*International Journal of Comparative Sociology* Leiden	
IJCS (T)	*International Journal of Comparative Sociology* Toronto	
IJH	J.H. Hayes and M. Miller, eds., *Israelite and Judean History* (OTL)	
IJMES	*International Journal of Middle Eastern Studies*	
IJNA	*International Journal of Nautical Archaeology and Underwater Exploration*	
IJT	*Indian Journal of Theology*	
IKirZ; IKZ	*Internationale Kirchliche Zeitschrift*	
Illahun, Kahun, Gurob	W.M.F. Petrie, *Illahun, Kahun and Gurob*	
Illustration	*L'Illustration* Paris	
IllVat	*Illustrazione Vaticana*	
ILN	*The Illustrated London News*	
ILR	*International Library Review*	

Abbreviation	Citation	Abbreviation alternatives
ILS	H. Dessau, *Inscriptiones latinae selectae*	
IM	*Inventar Mirgissa*	
IMEO	*Istituto Italiano per il Medio ed Estremo Oriente*	
Imm; Immanuel	*Immanuel: Semi-annual Bulletin of Religious Thought and Research in Israel*	
IMS	*Internationale Monatsschrift*	
IMU	*Italia medioevale e umanistica*	
IncLing	*Incontri Linguistici*	
Index	*Index: Quaderni camerti di studi romanistici = International Survey of Roman Law*	
InfÉg	*Informatique et égyptologie*	
Inf.Gos.Thom.	*Infancy Gospel of Thomas*	
InfGram	*L'Information grammaticale*	
InfHist	*L'Information historique*	
InFil	*Inozemna filolohija*	
InfLitt	*L'Information littéraire*	
INJ	*Israel Numismatic Journal*	
Inscr.Hier.Char.	*Inscriptions in the Hieratic and Demotic Character from the Collections of the British Museum*	
InscrCret	*Inscriptiones creticae*	
InscrGr	*Inscriptiones graecae* Berlin [See also IG]	
InscrIt	*Inscriptiones Italiae*	
Inscr.Sinai	A.H. Gardiner, *Inscriptions of Sinai*	
Inst	*Institut, Institute*	
Int	*Interpretation: Journal of Bible and Theology* Richmond (VA) [Continues UTSR]	Interpretation (R)
Interp.Know.	*Interpretation of Knowledge* (NHC XI,1)	
Interpretation (NY)	*Interpretation: Journal of Political Philosophy* New York	
Interpretation (R)	*Interpretation: Journal of Bible and Theology* Richmond (VA) [Continues UTSR]	Int
InvLuc	*Invigilata lucernis* (Università di Bari)	
IOS	*Israel Oriental Studies*	
IOTS	B.S. Childs, *Introduction to the Old Testament as Scripture*	
I.P.	*Intermediate Period*	
IPN	M. Noth, *Die israelitischen Personennamen*	
IPQ	*International Philosophical Quarterly*	
Iran (Lond.)	*Iran: Journal of the British Institute of Persian Studies*	
Iran (St-Pet.)	*Iran* (Academy of Sciences of the USSR), St. Petersburg	
IrAnt	*Iranica antiqua*	
Iraq	*Iraq* (British School of Archaeology in Iraq)	
IrJur	*Irish Jurist*	
IrNam	*Iran Nameh: Persian Journal of Iranian Studies*	
IrStud	*Iranian Studies: Journal of the Society for Iranian Studies*	
IRT	*Issues in Religion and Theology*	
Isa	*Isaiah*	
ISBE	G.W. Bromiley, ed., *International Standard Bible Encyclopedia*	
ISEELA	*Instituto Superior de Estudios Eclesiasticos Libro Annual*	
Isis	*Isis: International Review devoted to the History of Science and its Cultural Influences* [See also Osiris]	
Islam	*Der Islam: Zeitschrift für Geschichte und Kultur des islamischen Orients*	
Islam Today	*Islam Today = L'Islam aujourd'hui*	
Islamica	*Islamica: Zeitschrift für die Erforschung der Sprachen und der Kulturen der islamischen Völker*	
Islamicochristiana	*Islamicochristiana: Revue annuelle*	
IslAns	*Islâm ansiklopedisi*	
IslArt	*Islamic Art: An Annual Dedicated to the Art and Culture of the Muslim World*	
IslCult	*Islamic Culture: An English Quarterly*	
IslQuart	*Islamic Quarterly: Review of Islamic Culture*	
IslRev	*Islamic Review*	
IslStud	*Islamic Studies*	
ISP	*International Studies in Philosophy* [Continues StudFil]	
ISPCS	*Israel Society for the Promotion of Classical Studies*	
IsrBull	*Israel Bulletin*	
ISS	*International Studies in Sociology and Social Anthropology*	
IstForsch	*Istanbuler Forschungen*	
Istina	*Istina* Paris	
IstMitt	*Istanbuler Mitteilungen*	
IstMitt-B	*Istanbuler Mitteilungen, Beihefte*	
Istros	*Istros: Revue roumaine d'archéologie et d'histoire ancienne*	
Isvestija	*Isvestija: Bulletin de la Commission impériale archéologique de Pétersbourg*	
Italica (AA)	*Italica: Review of the American Association of Teachers of Italian* Ann Arbor (MI)	
Italica (E)	*Italica: cuadernos de trabajos de la Escuela Española de Historia y Arqueología en Roma* Madrid	CTEER

Abbreviation	Citation	Abbreviation alternatives
ItAnt	*L'Italia antichissima*	
ITC	*International Theological Commentary*	
ItDial	*L'Italia dialettale* [See also SSL]	
ITQ	*Irish Theological Quarterly*	
ITS	*Indian Theological Studies*	
ItScr	*L'Italia che scrive: Rassegna per coloro che leggono*	
IulDert	*Iulia dertona* Tortona	
Iura	*Iura: rivista internazionale di diritto romano e antico*	
IvEph	H.Wankel, ed., *Die Inschriften von Ephesos*	
IZBG	*Internationale Zeitschriftenschau für Bibelwissenschaft und Grenzgebiete*	
j.(Talm.)	*Jerusalem (Talmud)*	j.(Talm.)
JA	*Journal asiatique*	JournAs
JAA	*Journal of Anthropological Archaeology*	
JAAL	*Journal of Afroasiatic Languages*	
JAAmst	*Jaarboek van de Akademie te Amsterdam*	
JAAR	*Journal of the American Academy of Religion*	
JAAS (NY)	*Journal of Asian and African Studies* New York	
JAAS (T)	*Journal of Asian and African Studies* Tokyo	
JAC	*Jahrbuch für Antike und Christentum*	
JAC; JACiv	*Journal of Ancient Civilization*	
JACF	*Journal of the Ancient Chronology Forum*	
JACT	*Journal of the Joint Association of Classical Teachers* [See also Didaskalos, and Hesperiam]	
JAH	*Journal of African History*	
Jahrb.RGZM	*Jahrbuch des Römisch-Germanischen Zentralmuseums*	JRGZ
JAI	*Journal of the Royal Anthropological Institute of Great Britain and Ireland*	JRAI
JAIA	*Journal of Archaeological Institute of America*	
JAK	*Jahresberichte aus Augst und Kaiseraugst*	
JAL	*Journal of Arabic Literature*	
JANES; JANES(CU)	*The Journal of the Ancient Near Eastern Society of Columbia University*	
Jan.Jam.	*Jannes and Jambres*	
Janssen, AEB	*Annual Egyptological Bibliography*	AEB
Janus	*Janus: Revue internationale de l'histoire des sciences, de la médecine, de la pharmacie et de la technique*	

Abbreviation	Citation	Abbreviation alternatives
JAOS	*Journal of the American Oriental Society*	
JAOSSup; JAOS-Suppl.	*Journal of the American Oriental Society Supplement*	
JARCE	*Journal of the American Research Center in Egypt*	
JAS	*Journal of Archaeological Science*	
JAS	*Journal of Asian Studies*	
Jas	*James*	
JASAH	*Journal of the American Society of Architectural Historians*	
JASGB	*Journal of the Asiatic Society of Great Britain and Ireland*	
JASO	*Journal of the Anthropological Society of Oxford*	
JASOR	*Journal of the American Society of Oriental Research*	
JAULLA	*Journal of the Australasian Universities Language and Literature Association*	
JAWG	*Jahrbuch der Akademie der Wissenschaften* Göttingen	
JAWLM	*Jahrbuch der Akademie der Wissenschaften und der Literatur* Mainz	
JAZU	*Jugoslavenske Akademije Znanosti i Umjetnosti*	
Jazyki Afriki	*Jazyki Afriki: Voprosy struktury istorii i tipologii*	
JB	*Jerusalem Bible*	
JBA	*Journal of Biblical Archaeology*	
JBAA	*Journal of the British Archaeological Association*	
JBAW	*Jahrbuch der Bayerische Akademie der Wissenschaften*	
JBC	R.E. Brown et al., eds., *The Jerome Biblical Commentary*	
JBHM	*Jahrbuch des Bernischen Historischen Museums*	
JbKSW	*Jahrbuch der Kunsthistorischen Sammlung des Allerhöchsten Kaiserhauses* Vienna	
JBL	*Journal of Biblical Literature*	
JBL-Monogr.	*Journal of Biblical Literature: Monograph Series*	
JBM	*Jahrbuch der Berliner Museen*	
JBR	*Journal of Bible and Religion*	
JCCAR	*Journal of the Central Conference of American Rabbis* [Continued by JRJ]	
JcoptS	*Journal of Coptic Studies*	
JCS	*Journal of Classical Studies: Journal of the Classsical Society of Japan*	
JCS; JCunStud	*Journal of Cuneiform Studies*	
JDAI	*Jahrbuch des Deutschen Archäologischen Instituts*	JdI

Abbreviation	Citation	Abbreviation alternatives
JDAI; JDAI-Erg.	*Jahrbuch des Deutschen Archäologischen Instituts: Ergänzungshefte*	JdI
JdE	*Journal d'Entrée du musée du Caire*	JE
JdI	*Jahrbuch des Deutschen Archäologischen Instituts*	JDAI
JdI	*Jahrbuch des Deutschen Archäologischen Instituts: Ergänzungshefte*	JDAI; JDAI-Erg.
JDS	*Judean Desert Studies*	
Jdt	*Judith*	
JE	*Journal d'Entrée du musée du Caire*	JdE
JEA	*Journal of Egyptian Archaeology*	Journ
JEAN	*Japan Egyptological Association News*	
JEcumenStud	*Journal of Ecumenical Studies*	JES
Jeev	*Jeevadhara*	
JEH	*Journal of Ecclesiastical History*	
JEnc	*Jewish Encyclopaedia*	JewEnc
JEOL	*Jaarbericht van het Vooraziatisch-Egyptisch Genootschap (Gezelschap) "Ex Oriente Lux"*	Ex Oriente Lux; JVEG
Jer	*Jeremiah*	
JES	*Journal of Ecumenical Studies*	JEcumenStud
JES	*Journal of Ethiopian Studies*	
JESHO	*Journal of the Economic and Social History of the Orient*	
JETS	*Journal of the Evangelical Theological Society*	
JeunAfr	*Jeune Afrique*	
JewArt	*Jewish Art: Journal of the Center for Jewish Art*	
JewEnc	*Jewish Encyclopaedia*	JEnc
JFA	*Journal of Field Archaeology.*	
JFA (C)	*Journal of the Faculty of Archaeology* (Cairo University)	
JFASI	*The Journal of the Faculty of Archaeology Special Issue* Cairo	Journal Faculty of Archaeology
JFAW	*Jahresbericht über die Fortschritte der Altertumswissenschaft*	
JFSR	*Journal of Feminist Studies in Religion*	
JGG	*Jahrbuch zur Geschichte und Gesellschaft des Vorderen und Mittleren Orients*	
JGS	*Journal of Glass Studies*	
JGW	*Jahrbuch für Geschichtswissenschaft*	
JHA	*Journal for the History of Astronomy*	
JHAS	*Journal for the History of Arabic Science*	
JHAW	*Jahrbuch der Heidelberger Akademie der Wissenschaften*	
JHB	*Journal of the History of Biology*	

Abbreviation	Citation	Abbreviation alternatives
JHI	*Journal of the History of Ideas*	
JHistStud	*Journal of Historic Studies*	
JHM	*Journal of the History of Medicine and Allied Sciences*	
JHNES	*Johns Hopkins Near Eastern Studies*	
JHP	*Journal of the History of Philosophy*	
JHS	*Journal of Hebrew Scriptures*	
JHS	*Journal of Hellenic Studies*	
JHSch	*Jahrbuch für das höhere Schulwesen*	
JIA	*Journal of Industrial Archaeology*	
JIAN	*Journal international d'archéologie numismatique*	
JIBS	*Journal of Indian and Buddhist Studies*	
JIES	*Journal of Indo-European Studies*	
JIPh	*Journal of Indian Philosophy*	
JIS	*Journal of Islamic Studies*	
JITC	*Journal of the Interdenominational Theological Center*	
JJP	*Journal of Juristic Papyrology*	
JJS	*Journal of Jewish Studies*	
JKAF	*Jahrbuch für kleinasiatische Forschung*	
JKAHS	*Journal of the Kerry Archaeological and Historical Society*	
JKP	*Jahrbuch für klassische Philologie*	
JKSW	*Jahrbuch der Kunsthistorischen Sammlungen in Wien*	
JLA	*The Jewish Law Annual*	
JLAEA	*Journal of the Language Association of Eastern Africa*	
JLA-Suppl.	*The Jewish Law Annual, Supplementary Studies*	
JLW	*Jahrbuch für Liturgiewissenschaft*	
JMA	*Journal of Mediterranean Archaeology*	
JMEOS	*Journal of the Manchester Egyptian and Oriental Society*	
JMES	*Journal of Middle Eastern Studies*	
JMES	*Journal of the Middle East Society*	
JMH	*Journal of Medieval History*	
JMIR	*Journal du Ministère de l'Instruction Publique en Russie*	
JMRS	*Journal of Medieval and Renaissance Studies*	
JMS	*Journal of Mithraic Studies*	
JNES	*Journal of Near Eastern Studies*	
JNG	*Jahrbuch für Numismatik und Geldgeschichte*	
JNS	*Journal of the Royal Numismatic Society*	
JNSL	*Journal of Northwest Semitic Languages*	

Abbreviation	Citation	Abbreviation alternatives
JÖAI	*Jahreshefte des Österreichischen Archäologischen Instituts in Wien*	ÖJh
JÖAI-B	*Jahreshefte des österreichischen archäologischen Instituts, Beiblatt*	
JÖB	*Jahrbuch der österreichischen Byzantinistik*	
JÖBG	*Jahrbuch der österreichischen byzantinischen Gesellschaft*	
JOI	*Journal of the Oriental Institute*	
JOS	Philo, *De Iosepho*	
Jos.	*Josephus*	Joseph.
Jos.Asen.	*Joseph and Asenath*	
Joseph.	*Josephus*	Jos.
josh	*Joshua*	
Journ	*Journal of Egyptian Archaeology*	JEA
JournAfr	*Journal des africanistes*	
Journal Faculty of Archaeology	*The Journal of the Faculty of Archaeology Special Issue* Cairo	JFASI
JournAs	*Journal asiatique*	JA
JournÉtud	*Journées d'études: Conferences de la Société d'études latines de Bruxelles*	
JournLing	*Journal of Linguistics*	
JournPh	*Journal of Philosophy*	
JournPhil	*Journal of Philology*	
JournRel	*Journal of Religion*	JR
JournSav	*Journal des savants* (Académie des inscriptions et belles-lettres), Paris	JS
JPA	*Journal of Palestinian Archaeology* (PIA)	
JPEK	*Jahrbuch für Prähistorische und Ethnographische Kunst*	
JPFG	*Jahrbuch der philosophischen Fakultät der Georg August-Universität zu Göttingen*	
JPK; JPKS	*Jahrbuch der Preußischen Kunstsammlungen*	
JPOS	*Journal of the Palestine Oriental Society*	
JPR	*Journal of Prehistoric Religion*	
JPS	*Journal of Palestine Studies*	
JPSV	*Jewish Publication Society Version*	
JPT	*Journal of Psychology and Theology*	
JPVB	*Jahresbericht des philologischen Vereins zu Berlin*	
JQR	*Jewish Quarterly Review*	
JQRMS	*Jewish Quarterly Review Monograph Series*	
JR	*Journal of Religion*	JournRel
JRA	*Journal of Roman Archaeology*	
JRAfrS	*Journal of the Royal African Society*	
JRAI	*Journal of the Royal Anthropological Institute of Great Britain and Ireland*	JAI
JRAS; JRAsS	*Journal of the Royal Asiatic Society of Great Britain and Ireland*	
JRE	*Journal of Religious Ethics*	
JRelS	*Journal of Religious Studies*	
JRGS	*Journal of the Royal Geographic Society*	
JRGZ	*Jahrbuch des Römisch-Germanischen Zentralmuseums*	Jahrb.RGZM
JRH	*Journal of Religious History*	
JRIBA	*Journal of the Royal Institute of British Architects*	
JRJ	*Journal of Reform Judaism*	
JRS	*Journal of Roman Studies*	
JRT	*Journal of Religious Thought*	
JS	*Journal des savants* (Académie des inscriptions et belles-lettres), Paris	JournSav
JSAH	*Journal of the Society of Architectural Historians*	
JSAI	*Jerusalem Studies in Arabic and Islam*	
JSAN	*Journal of the Society of Ancient Numismatics*	
JSAS	*Journal of the Society for Armenian Studies*	
JSBL	*Journal of the Society of Biblical Literature*	
JSFO	*Journal de la Société finno-ougrienne*	
JSGU	*Jahrbuch der schweizerischen Gesellschaft für Ur- und Frühgeschichte*	
JSHRZ	*Jüdische Schriften aus hellenistisch-römischer Zeit*	
JSJ	*Journal for the Study of Judaism*	
JSNT	*Journal for the Study of the New Testament*	
JSNTSup; JSNT-Suppl.	*Journal for the Study of the New Testament Supplement Series*	
JSOR	*Journal of the Society of Oriental Research*	
JSOT	*Journal for the Study of the Old Testament*	
JSOTSup; JSOT-Suppl.	*Journal for the Study of the Old Testament Supplement Series*	
JSP	*Journal for the Study of the Pseudepigrapha*	
JSPK	*Jahrbuch der Stiftung Preußischer Kulturbesitz*	
JSPSup	*Journal for the Study of the Pseudepigrapha Supplement*	
JSS	*Journal of Semitic Studies*	
JSSEA	*Journal of the Society for the Study of Egyptian Antiquities* Toronto	SSEA(J); SSEAJ

Abbreviation	Citation	Abbreviation alternatives
JSS-Monogr.	*Journal of Semitic Studies, Monographs*	
JSSR	*Journal of the Scientific Study of Religion*	
JTC	*Journal for Theology and the Church*	
JThSt; JTS	*Journal of Theological Studies*	
JTSoA	*Journal of Theology for Southern Africa*	
JTurkStud	*Journal of Turkish Studies*	
JUAG	*Jahrbuch der Ungarischen archäologischen Gesellschaft*	
Jub.	*Jubilees*	
JUD	*Jahrbuch der Universität Düsseldorf*	
Judaica	*Judaica: Beiträge zum Verständnis des judischen Schicksals in Vergangenheit und Gegenwart*	
Judaism	*Judaism* New York	
Judg	*Judges*	
JudRunds	*Judische Rundschau*	
jul.	*Julian Calendar, Julianischer Kalender*	
JVA	*Jahrbuch des Vereins von Altertumsfreunden im Rheinlande* [See also BonnJb]	
JVEG	*Jaarbericht van het Vooraziatisch-Egyptisch Genootschap (Gezelschap) "Ex Oriente Lux"*	Ex Oriente Lux; JEOL
JVSG	*Jahrbuch des Vereins Schweizerischer Gymnasiallehrer*	
JW	Josephus, *Bellum Judaicum = Jewish War*	
JWAG	*Journal of the Walters Art Gallery*	
JWG	*Jahrbuch für Wirtschaftsgeschichte*	
JWH	*Journal of World History*	
JWI	*Journal of the Warburg and Courtauld Institutes*	
K	*Kethib*	
K	*Tablets in the Kouyunjik collection of the British Museum [cited by number]*	
Kadmos	*Kadmos: Zeitschrift für vor- und frühgriechische Epigraphik*	
KAF	*Kleinasiatische Forschungen*	KlF
Kagemni	*The Instructions for Kagemni*	
Kahun, Gurob, Hawara	W.M.F. Petrie, *Kahun, Gurob and Hawara*	
KAI	H. Donner, and W. Röllig, eds., *Kanaanäische and aramäische Inschriften*	
Kairos	*Kairos: Zeitschrift fur Religionswissenschaft und Theologie*	
KAJ	E. Ebeling, ed., *Keilschrifttexte aus Assur juristischen Inhalts* (WVDOG 50)	
Kalabchah	H. Gauthier, *Le temple de Kalabchah (TemplImm.)*	
Kamosestele	L. Habachi, *The Second Stela of Kamose* (ADAIK, Ägyptologische Reihe 8)	
KantStud	*Kant-Studien: Philosophische Zeitschrift*	
KAR	E. Ebeling, ed., *Keilschrifttexte aus Assur religiösen Inhalts* (WVDOG 28/34)	
Karnak	*Cahiers de Karnak* [Continues Kêmi]	CahKarn
Karnak I	A. Varille, *Karnak I* (FIFAO 19)	
Karnak V	*Karnak V (1970-1972)* (Centre franco-égyptien d'étude des temples de Karnak)	
Karnak-Nord	C. Robichon et al., eds., *Karnak Nord III-IV* (FIFAO 23, 25)	
Karthago	*Karthago: revue d'archéologie africaine*	
Kasr el-Agoûz	D. Mallet, *Le Kasr el-Agoûz* (MIFAO 11)	
KAT	*Kommentar zum Alten Testament*	
KÄT	*Kleine Ägyptische Texte*	
KAV	O. Schroeder, ed., *Keilschrifttexte aus Assur verschiedenen Inhalts* (WVDOG 35)	
Kawa	M.F.L. Macadam, *The Temples of Kawa*	
KB	L. Koehler and W. Baumgartner, *Lexicon in Veteris Testamenti libros*	
KB	E. Schrader, ed., *Keilschriftliche Bibliothek*	
KBANT	*Kommentare und Beiträge zum Alten und Neuen Testament*	
KBGG	*Korrespondenzblatt des Gesamtvereins der deutschen Geschichts- und Altertumsvereine*	
KBKL	*Kritische Berichte zur kunstgeschichtlichen Literatur*	
KBo	*Keilschrifttexte aus Boghazköi* (WVDOG)	
KBSW	*Korrespondenzblatt für die höheren Schulen Württembergs*	
KBVS	*Korrespondenzblatt des Vereins für Siebenbürgische Landeskunde*	
KBWZ	*Korrespondenzblatt der westdeutschen Zeitung*	
KCT	*Katholiek Cultureel Tijdschrift*	
KD	*Kerygma und Dogma*	KerDog
KEHAT	O.F. Fridelin, ed., *Kurzgefasstes exegetisches Handbuch zum Alten Testament*	
KelSz	*Keleti Szemle: Revue orientale*	

Abbreviation	Citation	Abbreviation alternatives
Kêmi	*Kêmi: Revue de philologie et d'archéologie égyptiennes et coptes* [See also Karnak]	
Kenkhreai	*Kenkhreai: Eastern Port of Corinth, Results of Investigations*	
Kentron	*Kentron* Caen	
Ker.	*Keritot*	
Kerameikos	*Kerameikos: Ergebnisse der Ausgrabungen*	
KerDog	*Kerygma und Dogma*	KD
Kernos	*Kernos: revue internationale et pluridisciplinaire de religion grecque antique*	
Ketub.	*Ketubot*	
KG	Frankfort, Henri, *Kingship and the Gods*	
KGB	*Vereinigung für baugeschichtliche Forschung: Bericht über die Tagung für Ausgrabungswissenschaft und Bauforschung* (Koldewey-Gesellschaft)	
KHC	Marti, K., ed., *Kurzer Handcommentar zum Alten Testament*	
KI	*C-14 Berechnung nach dem Geologisch-Paläontologischen Kieler Institut*	
KIAM	*Kultura i iskusstvo anticnovo mira*	
Kil.	*Kil'ayim*	
KirchZeits	*Kirchliche Zeitschrift*	
KirSeph	*Kirjath Sepher: Bibliographical Quaterly of the Jewish National and University Library*	
KJV	*King James Version*	
KK	*Katorikku Kenkyu*	
Klearchos	*Klearchos: Bollettino dell'Associazione Amici del Museo Nazionale di Reggio Calabria*	
Kleio	*Kleio: Tijdschrift voor oude Talen en antieke Kultuur*	
KlF	*Kleinasiatische Forschungen*	KAF
Klio	*Klio: Beiträge zur alten Geschichte*	
Klosterman	E. Klosterman, *Eusebius: Das Onomastikon der Biblischen Ortsnamen*	
Kl.Pauly; KlPauly	*Der kleine Pauly*	
Kl.Schr.; KlSchr	*Kleine Schriften*	
KlT	*Kleine Texte*	
KMAS	*Kelsey Museum of Archaeology Studies*	
KMT	*KMT: A Modern Journal of Ancient Egypt*	
K.O.; KO	*Kom Ombo*	
Koinonia	*Koinonia* (Associazione di studi tardoantichi)	
Kokalos	*Kokalos* (Istituto di Storia Antica dell'Università di Palermo)	
KölnJb	*Kölner Jahrbuch für Vor- und Frühgeschichte*	
Kon.Nederl. AdW	*Koninglijke Nederlandse Akademie van Wetenschappen*	
Kopenhagen, NCG	*Ny Carlsberg Glyptothek*	Copenhagen NCG
KoptHWb	W. Westendorf, *Koptisches Handwörterbuch*	
Koptos	W.M.F. Petrie, *Koptos*	
Kopt.Stud.	*Koptologische Studien in der DDR*	
Koroth	*Koroth: Bulletin Devoted to the History of Medicine and Science*	
Korr.Zus.	*Korrektur-Zusatz*	
KPA	A. Kirchner, *Prosopographia attica*	
KPAB	*Kentucky Philological Association Bulletin*	
Kratkie soobtschenija	*Kratkie soobtschenija, Instituta narodov Azii*	
KratSoob (K)	*Kratkie Soobshcheniia Instituta Arkheologii* Kiev	
KratSoob (M)	*Kratkie Soobshcheniia Instituta Arkheologii* Moscow	
Kratylos	*Kratylos: Kritisches Berichts- und Rezensionsorgan für indogermanische und allgemeine Sprachwissenschaft*	
KRI	Y. Kaufmann, *Religion of Israel*	
KRI	K.A. Kitchen, *Ramesside Inscriptions*	RI
Kriterion	*Kriterion* Belo Horizonte (Brazil)	
KSIE	*Kratkie Soobscenija Instituta Ethnografiy*	
Ktèma	*Ktèma: civilisations de l'Orient, de la Grèce et de Rome antiques*	
KTR	*King's Theological Review*	
KTU	M. Dietrich et al., eds., *Keilalphabetischen Texte aus Ugarit I* (AOAT 24)	
KUB	*Keilschrifturkunden aus Boghazköi*	
KultSpr	*Kultur und Sprache*	
KunstÅrs	*Kunstmuseets Årsskrift*	
KunstKünst	*Kunst und Künstler*	
KunstOr	*Kunst des Orients*	
Kush	*Kush: Journal of the Sudan Antiquities Service*	
KV	*Kings' Valley = Valley of the Kings*	
KVJG	*Kritische Vierteljahressehriften für Gezetsgebung und Rechtswissenschaft*	
KwarKlas	*Kwartalnik Klasyczny*	
LÄ	*Lexikon der Ägyptologie*	LdÄ

Abbreviation	Citation	Abbreviation alternatives
LAAA	*Annals of Archaeology and Anthropology* Liverpool	AAA; AAALiv; Liv.Ann.
L.A.B.	*Liber Antiquitatum Biblicarum*	
Labeo	*Labeo: rassegna di diritto romano*	
Lacau, TR	P. Lacau, *Textes religieux* (RdT 26)	
Lad.Jac.	*Ladder of Jacob*	
L.A.E.	*Life of Adam and Eve*	
LAE	W.K. Simpson, ed., *The Literature of Ancient Egypt*	
Lahun I	G. Brunton, *Lahun I: The Treasure* (BSAE 27)	
Lahun II	W.M.F. Petrie et al., *Lahun II: The Pyramid* (BSAE 33)	
Lalies	*Lalies: Actes des sessiones de linguistique et de littérature*	
Lam	*Lamentations*	
Lampadion	*Lampadion* Amsterdam [Continued by Lampas]	
Lampas	*Lampas: Tijdschiift voor Nederlandse classici* [Continues Lampadion]	
Lane	Lane, E.W., *Arabic-English Lexicon*	
Langages	*Langages* Paris	
Language	*Language: Journal of the Linguistic Society of America*	
LAnn	*Liber Annuus* (Studium Biblicum Franciscanum)	LASBF; LibAnn; SBF
Laographia	*Laographia: Deltion tes Hellenikes laographikes Hetaireias*	
LAPO	*Littératures anciennes du Proche-Orient*	
LAR	D.D. Luckenbill, *Ancient Records of Assyria and Babylonia*	
LAS	D.D. Luckenbill, *Annals of Sennacerib* (OIP 2)	
LÄS	*Leipziger Ägyptologische Studien*	
LASBF	*Liber Annuus* (Studium Biblicum Franciscanum)	LAnn; LibAnn; SBF
Lat	*Lateranum* (Facultas Theologica Pontificii Athenaei Lateranensis), Vatican City	
LatGr	*Latina et graeca*	
Latinitas	*Latinitas: commentarii linguae latinae excolendae provehendae*	
Latomus	*Latomus: Revue d'études latines*	
Lauer, PD	J.-P. Lauer and P. Lacau, *Pyramide à degrés* (Fouilles Saqq.)	PD
Laur	*Laurentianum*	
LavTP	*Laval théologique et philosophique*	LTP
LB	*Late Bronze (Age)*	
LB	*Linguistica biblica: Interdisziplinäre Zeitschrift für Theologie und Linguistik*	LingBibl

Abbreviation	Citation	Abbreviation alternatives
LBAT	T.G. Pinches and A. Sachs, eds., *Late Babylonian Astronomical and Related Texts*	
LBHG	Y. Aharoni, *The Land of the Bible: a historical geography*	
LBS	*Library of Biblical Studies*	
LCC	*Library of Christian Classics*	
LCL	*Loeb Classical Library*	
LCM	*Liverpool Classical Monthly*	
LD	*Lectio divina*	
LD	K.R. Lepsius, *Denkmaeler aus Aegypten und Aethiopien*	
LdÄ	*Lexikon der Ägyptologie*	LÄ
LDAB	*Leuven Database of Ancient Books*	
LdM	*Livre des morts (Book of the Dead)*	L.Morts
L.E.	*Lower Egypt*	
LE	A. Goetze, *The Laws of Eshnunna* (AASOR 31)	
Le rêve d'égyptien	*Le rêve d'égyptien* (Silex 13, 1979)	
LEAU	*Latina ephemeris aegyptiaca universa*	
LEC	*Library of Early Christianity*	
Leemans, Mon.Ég.	C. Leemans, *Monumens égyptiens du Musée d'antiquités des Pays-Bas à Leide*	
Leg All I-III	Philo, *Legum allegoriae I-III*	
LehrpLehrg	*Lehrproben und Lehrgänge*	
LEM	A.H. Gardiner, *Late-Egyptian Miscellanies* (BAe 7)	Gardiner, LEM
Leonardo	*Leonardo: rassegna bibliografica*	
Les; Lesônênú	*Lesônênú: A journal for the study of the Hebrew language and cognate subjects*	
LES	A.H. Gardiner, *Late-Egyptian Stories* (BAe 1)	
Let.Aris.	*Letter of Aristeas*	
Lev	*Leviticus*	
Levant	*Levant: Journal of the British School of Archaeology in Jerusalem*	
Levante	*Levante* Rome	
Lexis (AT)	*Lexis: poetica, retorica e comunicazione nella tradizione classica* Abano Terme	
Lexis (L)	*Lexis: Studien zur Sprachphilosophie, Sprachgeschichte und Begriffsforschung* Lahr	
LexLingAeth	A. Dillmann, *Lexicon linguae aethiopicae*	
LexSyr	C. Brockelmann, *Lexicon Syriacum*	
LHA	F. Zorrell, *Lexicon Hebraicum et Aramaicum Veteris Testamenti*	
L'Homme	*L'Homme: revue française d'anthropologie*	

Abbreviation	Citation	Abbreviation alternatives
LHPC	*Leuven Homepage of Papyrus collections*	
LIAO	*Lettre d'information: Archéologie orientale*	
LibAnn	*Liber Annuus* (Studium Biblicum Franciscanum)	LAnn; LASBF; SBF
LibAnt	*Libya antiqua: Annual of the Department of Antiquity of Libya*	
Liber Amicorum	*Liber Amicorum: Studies in Honour of Professor Dr. C. J. Bleeker*	Fs Bleeker
LibNot	*Library Notes: Bulletin Issued for the Friends of Duke University Library*	
LibStud	*Libyan Studies*	
Libya	*Libya* Rome	
Libyca	*Libyca* Algiers	
Licht	J.E. Gautier and G. Jéquier, *Mémoire sur les fouilles de Licht* (MIFAO 6)	
Life	Josephus, *Vita = Life*	
LIMC	*Lexicon iconographicum mythologiae classicae*	
Limes	*Limes: Centro de Estudios Clásicos, Universidad Metropolitana de Ciencias de la Educación* Santiago	
Limesblatt	*Limesblatt* Trier	
LingAeg	*Lingua Aegyptia: Journal of Egyptian Studies*	
LingBibl	*Linguistica biblica: Interdisziplinäre Zeitschrift für Theologie und Linguistik*	LB
LingLit	*Lingua e literatura* São Paulo (Brazil)	
LingStile	*Lingua e stile*	
Lingua	*Lingua: International review of general linguistics*	
Linguistique	*La Linguistique* Paris	
Link	*Link: Review of Mediaeval and Modern Greek*	
List	*Listening: Journal of Religion and Culture*	
ListFil	*Listy filologické* [See also Eunomia]	
LitHand	*Literarischer Handweiser*	
Litteris	*Litteris: An International Critical Review of the Humanities*	
LiturgArts	*Liturgical Arts*	
LiturgJb	*Liturgisches Jahrbuch*	
LitWoch	*Literarische Wochenschrift*	
Liv.Ann.	*Annals of Archaeology and Anthropology* Liverpool	AAA; AAA-Liv; LAAA
Liv.Pro.	*Lives of the Prophets*	
Livre du centenaire	J. Vercoutter, ed., *Livre du centenaire, 1880-1980* (MIFAO 104)	
LL	*Living Light*	
LLAVT	E. Vogt, *Lexicon Linguae aramaicae Veteris Testamenti documentis antiquis illustratum*	
L.Morts	*Livre des morts (Book of the Dead)*	LdM
LMS	*Littérature, médecine et société*	
LNV	*Litterae numismaticae Vindobonenses*	
LOAPL	*Langues orientales anciennes, philologie et linguistique*	
Logos	*Logos: Rivista di filosofia*	
London, U.C.	*University College* London	U.C.; U.C.L.
Lost Tr.	*The Lost Tribes*	
LP	*Late Period*	
LpBer	*Berichte über die Verhandlungen der Königlichen Sächsischen Gesellschaft der Wissenschaften zu Leipzig*	
LPGL	G.W.H. Lampe, *A Patristic Greek Lexicon*	
l.p.h.	conventional translation of Egyptian *ꜥnḫ wḏꜣ snb* "life, prosperity/soundness, health" and related verbal forms	l.s.h.
LQ	*Lutheran Quarterly*	
LR	H. Gauthier, *Le Livre des rois d'Egypte* (MIFAO 17-21)	
LR	*Lutherische Rundschau*	
LRL	J. Černý, *Late-Ramesside Letters* (BAe 9)	
LS	*Louvain Studies*	
LS	*Numbering of Mastabas in Saqqara according to Lepsius*	
LSA	*Lavori e studi di archeologia*	
LSJ	H.G. Liddell et al., *A Greek-English Lexicon*	
LSJM	H.G. Liddell et al., *Greek-English Lexicon,* rev. ed.	
LSKP	*Leipziger Studien zur klassischen Philologie*	
LSRR	*Legge e società nella repubblica romana*	
LSS	*Leipziger Semitistische Studien*	
LSTTS	*Luzac's Semitic Text and Translation Series*	
LTJ	*Lutheran Theological Journal*	
LTK	*Lexikon für Theologie und Kirche*	
LTP	*Laval théologique et philosophique*	LavTP
LTQ	*Lexington Theological Quarterly*	
LUÅ	*Lunds universitets årsskrift*	
Luc	*Lucianic recension*	
Lucentum	*Lucentum: Anales de la Universidad de Alicante, Prehistoria, arqueología e historia antigua*	
LudMag	*Ludus magistralis*	
LumVie	*Lumière et vie: Revue de formation et de réflexion théologiques*	

Abbreviation	Citation	Abbreviation alternatives
LumVit	*Lumen Vitae*	
Lustrum	*Lustrum: Internationale Forschungsberichte aus dem Bereich des Klassischenaltertums*	
LW	*Lutheran World*	
LXX	*Septuagint*	
Lychnos	*Lychnos: Annual of the Swedish History of Science Society*	
LZB	*Literarisches Zentralblatt*	
MA	*Middle Assyrian*	
MAAR	*Memoirs of the American Academy in Rome*	
Maarav	*Maarav: A journal for the study of the northwest Semitic languages and literatures*	
Ma'as.	*Ma'aserot*	
Ma'as.S.	*Ma'aser Seni*	
MAB	*Miscellanea Academica Berolinensia*	
MABL	B.J. Beitzel, ed., *The Moody Atlas of Bible Lands*	
MABol	*Memorie dell'Accademia delle scienze dell'Istituto di Bologna*	
MadrForsch	*Madrider Forschungen*	
MadrMitt	*Madrider Mitteilungen*	
MAÉA	*Mélanges d'archéologie égyptienne et assyrienne*	MdA
MAFC	*Mission archéologique française au Caire*	
MAGG	*Mitteilungen der archäologischen Gesellschaft Graz*	
Maghrib	*Maghrib: Revue annuelle pour l'archéologie, les musées, les monuments et sites et les arts et traditions populaires* Algiers	
MaghrMachr	*Maghreb-Machreq*	
Magn.	*Ignatius, Letter to the Magnesians*	Ign.Magn.
MAGW	*Mitteilungen der Anthropologischen Gesellschaft in Wien*	
MAHCL	*Mémoires de l'Académie d'histoire de la culture de Leningrad*	
Maia	*Maia: Rivista di letterature classiche*	
MAIBL	*Mémoires de (l'Institut Royal de France) l'Académie des Inscriptions et Belles-Lettres*	
MainzZeits	*Mainzer Zeitschrift: Mittelrheinisches Jahrbuch für Archäologie, Geschichte und Kunst*	
MaisDieu	*Maison-Dieu*	
Mak.	*Makkot*	
Maks.	*Maksirin = Masqin*	
MAKW	*Mitteilungen der Altertumskommission für Westfalen*	
MAL	*Middle Assyrian Laws*	
MAL	*Monografie di archeologia libica*	
Mal	*Malachi*	
MALinc	*Memorie dell'Accademia nazionale dei Lincei*	
MAMA	*Monumenta Asiae Minoris antiqua*	
MAMil	*Memorie dell'Istituto lombardo, Accademia di scienze e lettere* Milan	
Man	*Man: A Monthly Record of Anthropological Science*	
Man	*Manuscripta* St. Louis (MO)	Manuscripta
MANap	*Memorie dell'Accademia di archeologia, lettere e belle arti di Napoli*	
MANE	*Monographs on the Ancient Near East*	
Mannus	*Mannus: Zeitschrift für Vorgeschichte*	
Mansrea	*Mansrea* Madrid	
Manuscripta	*Manuscripta* St. Louis (MO)	Man
MAO	*Monografie archivu orientalního*	
MAOG	*Mitteilungen der Altorientalischen Gesellschaft*	
Mar Mon div	A. Mariette, *Monuments divers recueillis en Egypte et en Nubie*	Mariette, Mon.Div.
MARB	*Mémoires de l'Académie Royale de Belgique*	
MarbWPr	*Marburger Winckelmann-Programm*	
MARHist	*Mémoires de l'Académie roumaine, section historique*	
Marianum	*Marianum* Rome	
Mariette, Dend.	A. Mariette, *Dendérah: Description générale du grand temple de cette ville*	Mariette, Dend.
Mariette, Mon.Div.	A. Mariette, *Monuments divers recueillis en Egypte et en Nubie*	Mar Mon div
MARLitt	*Mémoires de l'Académie roumaine, section littérautre*	
MARom	*Memorie della Pontificia Accademia romana di archeologia*	
Marsanes	*Marsanes (NHC XI, 1)*	
MARSc	*Mémoires de l'Académie roumaine, section scientifique*	
MarSt	*Marian Studies*	
Marsyas	*Marsyas: Studies in the History of Art*	
Mart.Bart.	*Martyrdom of Bartholomew*	
Mart.Is.	*Martyrdom of Isaiah*	
Mart.Mt.	*Martyrdom of Matthew*	
Mart.Paul	*Martyrdom of Paul*	
Mart.Pet.	*Martyrdom of Peter*	
Mart.Pet.Paul	*Martyrdom of Peter and Paul*	
Mart.Phil.	*Martyrdom of Philip*	
Mart.Pol.	*Martyrdom of Polycarp*	
MAS	*Matériaux arabes et sudarabiques: recherches en cour*	

Abbreviation	Citation	Abbreviation alternatives
Mas	*Masada texts*	
MÄS	*Münchener Ägyptologische Studien*	
MÄSB	*Mitteilungen aus der Ägyptischen Sammlung* (Staatlichen (Königliche) Museen zu Berlin)	
MASCA	*Museum Applied Science Center for Archaeology* (University Museum, University of Pennsylvania,)	
MASCA Journal	*Journal of the Museum Applied Science Center for Archaeology*	
MASE	*Memoir of the Archaeological Survey of Egypt*	ASE
Maspero, Ét.Myth.	G. Maspero, *Études de mythologie et d'archéologie égyptiennes* (BE 1, 2, 7, 8, 27-29)	
MastAb	*Masters Abstracts: Abstracts of Selected Masters Theses on Microfilm*	
MAT	*Musées de l'Algérie et de la Tunisie*	
Matt	*Matthew*	
MatTids	*Matematisk Tidsskrift*	
MATur	*Memorie dell'Accademia delle scienze di Torino*	
MAU	*Monuments archéologiques en Ukraine*	
MÄU	*Münchner ägyptologische Untersuchungen*	
MAWA	*Mededelingen der (Koninklijke) Akademie van Wetenschappen te Amsterdam*	
MAWB	*Mededelingen van de Koninklijke Academie voor Wetenschappen, Letteren & schone Kunsten van België*	
May	*Mayéutica*	
MB	*Le Monde de la Bible*	MondBibl
MB	*Middle Bronze (Age)*	
MBA	Y. Aharoni and M. Avi-Yonah, *Macmillan Bible Atlas*	
MBAH	*Münsterische Beiträge zur antiken Handelsgeschichte*	
MBP; MBPF	*Münchner Beiträge zur Papyrusforschung (und antiken Rechtsgeschichte)*	
MBS	*Mémoires de la Bibliothèque de la Sorbonne*	
MC	*Miscelanea Comillas*	MiscCom
MCACO	*Mémoires de la Commission des antiquités de la Côte-d'Or*	
MCBW	R.K. Harrison, *Major Cities of the Biblical World*	
McCQ	*McCormick Quarterly*	
MCL	*Martin Classical Lectures*	
MCM	*Miscellanea classico-medievale*	
MCS	*Manchester Cuneiform Studies*	
MCSN	*Materiali e contributi per la storia della narrativa greco-latina*	
MCV	*Mélanges de la Casa Velázquez*	
MD	E.S. Drower and R. Macuch, *Mandaic Dictionary*	
MdA	*Mélanges d'archéologie égyptienne et assyrienne*	MAÉA
MDAFA	*Mémoires de la Délégation archéologique française en Afghanistan*	
MDAIA	*Mitteilungen des Deutschen Archäologischen Institutes, Athenische Abteilung*	AM
MDAID	*Mitteilungen des Deutschen Archäologischen Instituts, Abteilung Damascus*	
MDAII	*Mitteilungen des Deutschen Archäologischen Instituts, Abteilung Istanbul*	
MDAIK	*Mitteilungen des Deutschen Archäologischen Instituts, Abteilung Kairo* [To 1944: MDIK]	Mitt.Kairo
MDAIM	*Mitteilungen des Deutschen Archäologischen Instituts, Abteilung Madrid*	
MDAIR	*Mitteilungen des Deutschen Archäologischen Instituts, Römische Abteilung*	MDIR; RM
MDAV	*Mitteilungen des Deutschen Archäologen-Verbandes*	
MDATC	*Materiali e discussioni per l'analisi dei testi classici*	
MdF	*Musées de France*	MusFr
MDIK	*Mitteilungen des Deutschen Instituts für Ägyptische Altertumskunde in Kairo* [From 1944: MDAIK]	MDIK
MDIR	*Mitteilungen des Deutschen Archäologischen Instituts, Römische Abteilung*	MDAIR; RM
MDOG	*Mitteilungen der Deutschen Orientgesellschaft*	Mitt.D.O.G.
MDP	*Mémoires de la délégation française en Perse*	
ME	*Moyen Empire (Middle Kingdom)*	
MEA	*Middle Eastern Affairs*	
Meander	*Meander: miesiecznik poswiecony kulturze swiata starozytnego*	
MedAev	*Medium Aevum*	
Médamoud	F. Bisson de la Roque, *Rapport sur les fouilles de Médamoud 1925-31* (FIFAO 3-9)	
Med.Gramm.	W. Westendorf, *Grammatik der medizinischen Texte* (Grundriß der Medizin 8)	Westendorf, Med.Gramm./ GMT; GMT
MedHab	*The Epigraphic Survey: Medinet Habu* (OIP 8-9, 23, 51, 83-84, 93-94)	Medinet Habu

Abbreviation	Citation	Abbreviation alternatives
MedHum	*Medievalia et humanistica: Studies in Medieval and Renaissance Culture*	
Mediaevalia	*Mediaevalia: Journal of Medieval Studies*	
Medinet Habu	*The Epigraphic Survey: Medinet Habu* (OIP 8-9, 23, 51, 83-84, 93-94)	MedHab
MeditArch	*Mediterranean Archaeology: Australian and New Zealand Journal for the Archaeology of the Mediterranean World*	
Mediterraneus	*Mediterraneus: Annual Report of the Collegium Mediterranistarum*	
MedMusBull	*Medelhavsmuseet Bulletin*	
MedMusMem	*Medelhavsmuseet Memoirs*	
MedRom	*Medioevo romanzo*	
MedStud	*Mediaeval Studies*	
Med.Wb	H. von Deines and W. Westendorf, *Wörterbuch der medizinischen Texte* (Grundriß der Medizin 7)	Wb.med.
MEEF	*Egypt Exploration Fund Memoirs*	EEF
MEES	*Egypt Exploration Society Memoirs*	EES; EESm; EM; ExcMem
MEF	*Middle East Forum*	
MÉFRA	*Mélanges d'archéologie et d'histoire de l'École française de Rome: Antiquité*	
MÉFRM	*Mélanges de l'École française de Rome: Moyen Age, temps modernes*	
Meg.	*Megilla*	
Me'il.	*Me'ila*	
Meir	A.M. Blackman, *The Rock Tombs of Meir* (ASE 22-25, 28-29)	
MEJ	*Middle East Journal*	
Mek.	*Mekilta*	
Melch.	*Melchizedek (NHC IX,1)*	
MélIsl	*Mélanges islamologiques* [Continued by AnIsl]	MélIsl
Mél.Mar.	*Mélanges Mariette (BdE 32)*	Fs Mariette
Mél.Masp.	*Mélanges Maspero (MIFAO 66 and 67)*	Fs Maspero
MelT	*Melita Theologica*	MelT
Melto	*Melto: recherches orientales* [Continued by ParOr]	Melto
Mem.Apos.	*Memoria of Apostles*	Mem.Apos.
Mém Inst	*Mémoires publiés par les membres de l'Institut français d'archéologie orientale*	MIFAO
MémAv	*Mémorial Avicenne*	
Mém.Miss.	*Mémoires publiés par les membres de la Mission archéologique française au Caire*	Mém.Miss.
Memphis I	W.M.F. Petrie, *Memphis I (BSAE 15)*	
Memphis II	W.M.F. Petrie, *Palace of Apries (Memphis II) (BSAE 17)*	
Memphis III	W.M.F. Petrie, *Meydum and Memphis III (BSAE 18)*	
Memphis IV	W.M.F. Petrie, *Roman Portraits and Memphis IV (BSAE 20)*	
Memphis V	W.M.F. Petrie, *Tarkhan I and Memphis V (BSAE 23)*	
MémTrav	*Mémoires et travaux* (Faculté catholiques), Lille	
MENA	*Middle East and North Africa*	
Menah.	*Menahot*	
MEOL	*Mededelingen en Verhandelingen van het Vooraziatisch-Egyptisch Genootschap (Gezelschap) "Ex Oriente Lux"*	MVEOL
MercFr	*Mercure de France*	
MÉRF	*Mélanges de l'École roumaine en France*	
Merikare	*The Instructions for King Merikare*	
Meroe (1)	*Meroe: Istorija, istorija kultury, jazyk drevnego Sudana*	
Meroe (2)	*Meroe: Problemy istorii i kulturnych svjasei*	
MeroitNewsl	*Meroitic Newsletter*	MNL
MES	*Middle East Studies*	
MESAB	*Middle East Studies Association Bulletin*	
Mesopotamia (C)	*Mesopotamia: Copenhagen Studies in Assyriology*	
Mesopotamia (T)	*Mesopotamia: Rivista di archeologia, epigrafia e storia orientale antica* Turin	
MET	*Mond Excavations at Thebes*	
Meydum and Memphis III	W.M.F. Petrie, *Meydum and Memphis III (BSAE 18)*	Memphis III
MeyerK	H.A.W. Meyer, *Kritisch-exegetischer Kommentar über das Neue Testament*	
MFA	*Museum of Fine Arts* Boston	
MFOB	*Mélanges de la Faculté orientale de l'université Saint-Joseph* Beirut [Continued by MUSJ]	
MGFC	*Mitteilungen der Gesellschaft der Freunde Carnuntums*	
MGGW	*Mitteilungen der geographischen Gesellschaft in Wien*	
MGH	*Monumenta Germaniae historica*	
MGM	*Militärgeschichtliche Mitteilungen*	
MGMN	*Mitteilungen zur Geschichte der Medizin und der Naturwissenschaften*	
MGR	*Miscellanea greca e romana*	
MGWJ	*Monatsschrift für Geschichte und Wissenschaft des Judentums*	
MHA	*Memorias de historia antigua*	
MHA-Bull	*Museum Haaretz Bulletin*	

Abbreviation	Citation	Abbreviation alternatives
MHA-Yb	*Museum Haaretz Yearbook*	
MHF	*Les Monuments historiques de la France*	
MHJ	*Medizinhistorisches Journal*	
MHL	*Mitteilungen aus der historischen Literatur*	
MHLI	J. Liver, ed., *The Military History of the Land of Israel in Biblical Times*	
MHR	*Mediterranean Historical Review*	
MHS	*Monatsschrift für höhere Schulen*	
Mic	*Micah*	
Mid.	*Middot*	
MIdÉ	*Mémoires de l'Institut d'Égypte* [To 1910: Mémoires de l'Institut égyptien]	MIÉ
MIDÉO	*Mélanges de l'Institut dominicain d'études orientales du Caire*	
Midr.	*Midras*	
MIÉ	*Mémoires de l'Institut d'Égypte* [To 1910: Mémoires de l'Institut égyptien]	MIdÉ
MIÉ	*Mémoires de l'Institut égyptien* [From 1910: Mémoires de l'Institut d'Égypte]	
MIFAI	*Mémoires de l'Institut français d'archéologie de Stambul*	
MIFAO	*Mémoires publiés par les membres de l'Institut français d'archéologie orientale*	Mém Inst
MIFD	*Mémoires de l'Institut français de Damas*	
Migr	Philo, *De migratione Abrahami*	
Minerva (B)	*Minerva* Budapest	
Minerva (L)	*Minerva: International Review of Ancient Art and Archaeology* London	
Minerva (V)	*Minerva: revista de filología clásica* (Universidad de Valladolid)	
MinRev	*Minnesota Review*	
MIO	*Mitteilungen des Instituts für Orientforschung*	
MIÖG	*Mitteilungen des Instituts für österreichische Geschichtsforschung*	
Miqw.	*Miqwa'ot*	
Mird	*Khirbet Mird texts*	
MirIsl	*Mir Islama: Izdanie imperatorskogo obscestva vostokovedenija*	
MiscCom	*Miscelanea Comillas*	MC
MiscGr	*Miscellanea graeca*	
Misc Gregoriana	*Monumenti, Musei e Gallerie Pontificie, Miscellanea Gregoriana, Raccolta di scritti pubblicati nel I centenario dalla fondazione del Pont. Museo Egizio, 1839-1939*	
MiscMed	*Miscellanea mediaevalia*	
MiscNum	*Miscellanea numismatica*	
MiscSec	*Miscellanea secentesca*	
Misc.Wilb.	*Miscellanea Wilbouriana*	MW
Mitt.D.O.G.	*Mitteilungen der Deutschen Orientgesellschaft*	MDOG
Mitth Or Slg	*Mittheilungen aus den orientalischen Sammlungen*	
Mitt.Kairo	*Mitteilungen des Deutschen Archäologischen Instituts, Abteilung Kairo* [To 1944: MDIK]	MDAIK
MittWb	*Mitteilungen aus der Arbeit am Wörterbuch der Ägyptischen Sprache*	
MJBK	*Münchner Jahrbuch der bildenden Kunst*	MJbK
MK	*Middle Kingdom*	
MLJ	*Modern Language Journal*	
MLJb	*Mittellateinisches Jahrbuch*	
MLN	*Modern Language Notes*	
MM	*Middle Minoan, Mittelminoisch*	
MM	J.H. Moulton and G. Milligan, *Vocabulary of the Greek Testament Illustrated from the Papyri and other Non-Literary Sources*	
MMA	*The Metropolitan Museum of Art*	
MMA Bull.	*Bulletin of the Metropolitan Museum of Art*	BMMA
MMAEE	*Metropolitan Museum of Art, Egyptian Expedition* [Supplement to BMMA]	EEMM; MMA Eg.Exp.
MMAF	*Mémoires publiés par les membres de la Mission archéologique française au Caire*	Mém.Miss.
MMAI	*Mémoires de la Mission archéologique en Iran*	
MME	*Manuscripts of the Middle East: Journal Devoted to the Study of Handwritten Materials of the Middle East*	
MMH	*Mémoires du Musée historique*	
MMJ	*Metropolitan Museum Journal*	
MMP	*Münchner Museum für Philologie des Mittelalters und der Renaissance*	
MMS	*Metropolitan Museum Studies*	
MNFS	*Meddelelser fra Norsk forening for Sprogvidenskab*	
MNI	*Muslim News International*	
MNIR	*Mededelingen van het Nederlandsch Historisch Instituut te Rome*	
MNL	*Meroitic Newsletter*	MeroitNewsl
MNPV	*Mittheilungen und Nachrichten des Deutschen Palaestina-Vereins*	
MNTC	*Moffatt New Testament Commentary*	

Abbreviation	Citation	Abbreviation alternatives
MNyCarlsb	*Meddelelser fra Ny Carlsberg Glyptotek*	
ModChurch	*Modern Churchman*	
ModJud	*Modern Judaism*	
ModSch	*Modern Schoolman: Quarterly Journal of Philosophy*	
Mo'ed Qat.	*Mo'ed Qatan*	
MOG	*Mitteilungen zur osmanischen Geschichte*	
MÖIG	*Mitteilungen des österreichischen Instituts für Geschichtsforschung*	
MonAeg	*Monumenta Aegyptiaca*	
MonAnt	*Monumenti antichi*	
MondBibl	*Le Monde de la Bible*	MB
MondClass	*Il Mondo classico*	
MondOr	*Le Monde oriental: Archives pour l'histoire et l'ethnographie, les langues et littératures, religions et traditions de l'Europe orientale et de l'Asie*	
MÖNG	*Mitteilungen des österreichischen numismatischen Gesellschaft*	
MonGr	*Monuments grecs*	
MonIned	*Monumenti inediti* (Instituto di Corrispondenza Archeologica)	
MonPiot	*Monuments et Mémoires publiés par l'Académie des Inscriptions et Belles-Lettres* (Fondation Eugène Piot)	
MonStud	*Monastic Studies*	
Moskau GMII	*Gosudarstvennyi Muzei Izobrazitelnykh Iskusstv Imeni A S Pushkina (Pushkin Museum of Fine Arts)* Moscow	
MoyAge	*Moyen Age: revue d'histoire et de philologie*	
MPAIBL	*Mémoires présentés à l'Académie des inscriptions et belles-lettres*	
MPAT	J.A. Fitzmyer and D.J. Harrington, eds., *A Manual of Palestinian Aramaic Texts (BibOr 34)*	
MPAW	*Monatsberichte der Königlich Preußischen Akademie der Wissenschaften zu Berlin*	
MPER	*Mitteilungen aus der Papyrussammlung der Österreichischen Nationalbibliothek Erzherzog Rainer*	
MPL	*Museum philologum Londiniense*	
MRAH	*Musées Royaux d'Art et d'Histoire*	
MRasShamra	*Mission de Ras Shamra*	MRS
MRÉ	*Monographies Reine Élisabeth*	
MRFH	*Mitteilungen über römische Funde in Heddernheim*	

Abbreviation	Citation	Abbreviation alternatives
MRR	T.R.S Broughton and M.L. Patterson, eds., *The Magistrates of the Roman Republic (Philological Monographs 15)*	
MRS	*Mediaeval and Renaissance Studies*	
MRS	*Mission de Ras Shamra*	MRasShamra
MSAA	*Mémoires présentés à la Société Archéologique d'Alexandrie*	
MSAF	*Mémoires de la Société nationale des antiquaires de France*	
MSAP	*Mémoires de la Société d'anthropologie* Paris	
MScRel	*Mélanges de science religieuse*	MSR
MSD	*Materials for the Sumerian Dictionary*	
MSE	*Malaja sovetskaja entsilopedija (Small Soviet Encyclopedia)*	
MSFO	*Mémoires de la Société finno-ougrienne*	
MSGV	*Mitteilungen der Schlesischen Gesellschaft für Volkskunde*	
MSL	*Materialien zum sumerischen Lexikon*	
MSL	*Mémoires de la Société de linguistique de Paris*	MSLP
MSLCA	*Miscellanea di studi di letteratura cristiana antica*	
MSOSAfr	*Mitteilungen des Seminars für orientalische Sprachen, Afrikanische Studien*	
MSOSAs	*Mitteilungen des Seminars für orientalische Sprachen, Westasiatische Studien*	
MSR	*Mélanges de science religieuse*	MscRel
MSSW	*Münchner Studien zur Sprachwissenschaft*	
MSU	*Mitteilungen des Septuaginta-Unternehmens*	
MT	*Masoretic Text*	
MTS	*Marburger Theologische Studien*	
MTZ	*Münchener theologische Zeitschrift*	
München, ÄS	*München, Ägyptische Sammlung*	
Mur	*Wadi Murabba'at texts*	
Mus	*Le Muséon: Revue d'études orientales = Tijdschrift voor Orientalisme* Louvain	
MusAfr	*Museum africum: West African journal of classical and related studies*	
MusBelg	*Musée belge: revue de philologie classique*	
MusCrit	*Museum criticum: Quaderni dell'Istituto di filologia classica dell'Università di Bologna*	

Abbreviation	Citation	Abbreviation alternatives
Muse	*Muse: Annual of the Museum of Art and Archaeology* (University of Missouri)	
Museum (L)	*Museum: tijdschrift voor filologie en geschiednis* Leiden [Continued by ForLett]	
Museum (P)	*Museum* (UNESCO), Paris	
MusFr	*Musées de France*	MdF
MusHelv	*Museum Helveticum: revue suisse pour l'étude de l'antiquité classique*	
MUSJ	*Mélanges de l'université Saint-Joseph* [Continues MFOB]	
MusJourn	*Museums Journal*	
MuslWorld	*Muslim World: Journal Devoted to the Study of Islam and of Christian-Muslim Relationship in Past and Present*	
MusSuis	*Musées suisses*	
MusTusc	*Museum Tusculanum*	
Mut	Philo, *De mutatione nominum*	
Mutter u.Kind	A. Erman, *Zaubersprüche für Mutter und Kind*	
Muzeum	*Muzeum: Czasopismo poswiecone sprawom wychowania i szkolnictwa*	
MVAeG, MVÄG	*Mitteilungen der vorasiatisch-ägyptischen Gesellschaft* [Continues MVG]	
MVEOL	*Mededelingen en Verhandelingen van het Vooraziatisch-Egyptisch Genootschap (Gezelschap) "Ex Oriente Lux"*	MEOL
MVFG	*Mitteilungen des Vereins der Freunde des humanistischen Gymnasiums*	
MVG	*Mitteilungen der vorasiatischen Gesellschaft* [Continued by MVÄG]	
MVN	*Materiali per il vocabolario neosumerico*	
MVPW	*Mitteilungen des Vereins klassischer Philologen in Wien*	
MW	*Miscellanea Wilbouriana*	Misc.Wilb.
Myrtia	*Myrtia: Revista de Filologia clássica*	
NA	*Neo-Assyrian*	
NAA	*Narodii Azii i Afriki*	
NAArm	*Notices d'archéologie armoricaine*	
NAB	*New American Bible*	
NAC	*Numismatica e antichità classiche: quaderni ticinesi*	
Nachr.Akad. Göttingen	*Nachrichten der Akademie der Wissenschaften in Göttingen*	NAWG
NAFM	*Nuovi Annali della Facoltà di magistero*	
NAH	*Noticiario arqueológico hispánico*	
Nah	*Nahum*	
NAJN	*North American Journal of Numismatics* (Ancient Coin Club of America)	
NAM	*Nouvelles Archives des missions scientifiques et littéraires*	
NAMC	*Notiziaro archeologico a cura del Ministero delle colonie*	
NARCE	*Newsletter of the American Research Center in Egypt*	ARCE Newsletter
NASA	*National Aeronautics and Space Administration*	
NASB	*New American Standard Bible*	
NASLA	*Nuova Antologia di scienze, lettere ed arti*	
NastVj	*Nastavni Vjesnik* Zagreb	
NatAr	*La Nation arabe: revue mensuelle politique, littéraire, économique et sociale*	
NatGeo	*National Geographic Society*	
Nauri-Dekret	C.E. Sander-Hansen, *Historische Inschriften der 19. Dynastie, I: Das Dekret Sethos' I. von Nauri (BAe 4, 1, 13ff.)*	
NAV	*Nuovo Archivio veneto*	
Naville, Tb	É. Naville, *Das aegyptische Totenbuch der XVIII. bis XX. Dynastie*	Tb (Naville)
NAWG	*Nachrichten der Akademie der Wissenschaften in Göttingen*	Nachr.Akad. Göttingen
NB	*Neo-Babylonian*	
NB	F. Preisicke, *Namenbuch*	
NBAC	*Nuovo Bollettino di archeologia cristiana*	
NBD	J.D. Douglas and N. Hillyer, eds., *The New Bible Dictionary*	
NCBC	*New Century Bible Commentary*	
NCCHS	R.D. Fuller, ed., *New Catholic Commentary on Holy Scripture*	
NCE	M.R.P. McGuire, ed., *New Catholic Encyclopedia*	
NCH	M. Noth, *The Chronicler's History (JSOTSup 51)*	
NClBC	*New Clarendon Bible Commentary*	
NDH	M. Noth, *The Deuteronomistic History (JSOTSup 15)*	
NDIEC	G.H.K. Horsley, ed., *New Documents Illustrating Early Christianity*	
NDVS-Ist	*Naucny doklady vyssej skoly, Istoriia*	
NDVS-Phil	*Naucny doklady vyssej skoly, Filologicheskie nauki*	
NE	M. Lidzbarski, *Handbuch der nordsemitischen Epigraphik*	
NE	*Nouvel Empire (New Kingdom)*	
NEA	*Near Eastern Archaeology*	
Neapolis	*Neapolis* Naples	

Abbreviation	Citation	Abbreviation alternatives
NEB	*New English Bible*	
NEBib	*Neue Echter Bibel*	
NECN	*New England Classical Newsletter*	
Ned.	*Nedarim*	
NedTTs	*Nederlands Theologisch Tijdschrift*	NedTTs
Neferti	W. Helck, *Die Prophezeiung des Nfr.tj: pErmitage 1116 B (KÄT 1970)*	
Neg.	*Nega'im*	
Neh	*Nehemiah*	
NeosHell	*Neos Hellenomnemon*	
Neot	*Neotestamentica*	
Nestor	*Nestor: Mycenaean Bibliography*	
NETR	*The Near East School of Theology Theological Review*	
NeuAr	*Neues Archiv der Gesellschaft für ältere deutsche Geschichtskunde*	
NewSchol	*The New Scholasticism*	
Nez.	*Neziqin*	
NFM	*Nordiske Fortidsminder*	
NFT	*New Frontiers in Theology*	
NGM	*National Geographic Magazine*	
NGTT	*Nederduits Gereformeerde Teologiese Tydskrif*	
NGWG	*Nachrichten von der Gesellschaft der Wissenschaften in Göttingen*	
NHC	*Nag Hammadi Codex*	
NHI	M. Noth, *The History of Israel*	
NHJ	*Neue heidelberger Jahrbücher*	
NHL	J.M. Robinson, ed., *Nag Hammadi Library in English*	
NHS	*Nag Hammadi Studies*	
NHT	S.R. Driver, *Notes on the Hebrew Text and the Topography of the Books of Samuel*	
NICNT	*New International Commentary on the New Testament*	
NICOT	*New International Commentary on the Old Testament*	
Nid.	*Niddah*	
NIDNTT	C. Brown, ed., *New International Dictionary of New Testament Theology*	
NieuGids	*De Nieuwe Gids*	
NigClass	*Nigeria and the Classics*	
NIGTC	*New International Greek Testament Commentary*	
NIV	*New International Version*	
NJAB	*Neue Jahrbücher für antike und deutsche Bildung*	
NJB	*New Jerusalem Bible*	
NJBC	*New Jerome Bible Commentary*	
NJGP	*Neue Jahrbücher für Geologie und Paläontologie*	
NJKA	*Neue Jahrbücher für das klassische Altertum*	
NJP	*Neue Jahrbücher für Pädagogik*	
NJPP	*Neue Jahrbücher für Philologie und Pädagogik*	
NJPSV	*New Jewish Publication Society Version*	
NJW	*Neue Jahrbücher für deutsche Wissenschaft*	
NJWJ	*Neue Jahrbücher für Wissenschaft und Jugendbildung*	
NK	*New Kingdom*	
NKJV	*New King James Version*	
NKZ	*Neue kirchliche Zeitschrift*	
NLB	*Numismatisches Literaturblatt*	
NLZ	*Numismatische Literatur-Zeitung*	
NMS	*Nottingham Mediaeval Studies*	
NN	*nomen nominandum*	
NNÅ	*Nordisk Numismatisk Årsskrift*	
NNB	*Numismatisches Nachrichtenblatt*	
NNM	*Numismatic Notes and Monographs*	
NO	*Novy Orient*	
NomChron	*Nomismatika chronica*	
Nomisma	*Nomisma: Untersuchungen auf dem Gebiete der antike Münzkunde*	
Norea	*The Thought of Norea (NHC IX,2)*	
NorTT	*Norsk Teologisk Tidsskrift*	
NouvClio	*La Nouvelle Clio*	
NovT	*Novum Testamentum: International Quarterly for New Testament and Related Studies*	NovTest
NovTest-Suppl.	*Novum Testamentum Supplements*	NovTSup
NOVTG (26)	E. Nestle and K. Aland, eds., *Novum Testamentum Graece, 26th ed.*	NOVTG (26)
NovTSup	*Novum Testamentum Supplements*	NovTest-Suppl.
NovVet (B)	*Nova et vetera: Revue d'enseignement et de pédagogie* Brussels	
NovVet (F)	*Nova et vetera: Revue catholique pour la Suisse romande* Freiburg (Switzerland)	
n.p.	*nomen proprium (personal name)*	
NPM	*Neuphilologische Mitteilungen*	
NPNF	*Nicene and Post-Nicene Fathers*	
NPR	*Neue philologische Rundschau*	
NPS	*New Palaeographic Society*	
NR	*Neues Reich (New Kingdom)*	

Abbreviation	Citation	Abbreviation alternatives
NRFH	*Nueva Revista de filología hispànica*	
NRHD	*Nouvelle Revue historique de droit français et étranger* [See also RHD]	
NRS	*Nuova Rivista storica*	
NRSV	*New Revised Standard Version*	
NRT	*Nouvelle Revue théologique*	
NSA	*Notizie degli scavi di Antichità*	
NSJFS	*North Staffordshire Journal of Field Studies*	
NSSEA	*Newsletter of the Society for the Study of Egyptian Antiquities* Toronto	SSEA(N)
NTA	*New Testament Abstracts*	
NTAbh	*Neutestamentliche Abhandlungen*	
NTApocr	E. Henneke, *New Testament Apocrypha*	
NTC	B.S. Childs, *The New Testament as Canon: An Introduction*	
NTCS	*Newsletter for Targumic and Cognate Studies*	
NTD	*Das Neue Testament Deutsch*	
NTF	*Neutestamentliche Forschungen*	
NTF	*Nordisk Tidsskrift for filologi*	
NTHIP	W.G. Kümmel, *The New Testament: The History of the Investigation of Its Problems*	
NTL	*New Testament Library*	
NTM	*New Testament Message*	
NTM	*Schriftenreihe für Geschichte der Naturwissenschaften, Technik und Medizin*	SGNW
NTOA	*Novum Testamentum et Orbis Antiquus*	
NTS	*New Testament Studies*	
NTS (TN)	*Nieuw theologische Studiën* Ter Neuzen	
NTSV	*Nordisk Tidsskrift for Sprogvidenskap*	
NTT	*Nederlands Theologisch Tijdschrift*	NedTTs
NTT	*Nieuw theologisch Tijdschrift*	
NTTS	*New Testament Tools and Studies*	
NubChrist	*Nubia christiana*	
Nubie	*Nubie par divers archéologues et historiens*	
NubLett	*Nubian Letters*	
Num	*Numbers*	
NumChron	*Numismatic Chronicle*	
NumCirc	*Numismatic Circular*	
NumEp	*Numismatika i epigraphika*	
NumJourn	*Numismatic Journal*	
NumKöz	*Numismatikai Közlöny*	
NumLit	*Numismatic Literature*	
NumRev	*Numismatic Review*	
NumSfr	*Numismatika i sfragistika*	
NumStud	*Numismatic Studies*	
NumZeits	*Numismatische Zeitschrift*	
NuovCult	*Nuova cultura*	
NuovDid	*Nuovo Didaskaleion: studi di letteratura e storia cristiana antica*	
NuovIt	*Nuova Italia*	
NuovStoà	*Nuova Stoà: Rivista di studi filosofici*	
NV	*Nova et Vetera*	
NWDB	H.S. Gehman, ed., *The New Westminster Dictionary of the Bible*	
NyAk	*Nyame Akuma: Newsletter of African Archaeology*	
NYHSQB	*New-York Historical Society Quarterly Bulletin*	
NYRB	*New York Review of Books*	
NZST	*Neue Zeitschrift für systematische Theologie und Religionsphilosophie*	
OA	*Old Assyrian*	
OA	*Oriens antiquus: revista del Centro per le Antichità e la Storia dell'Arte de Vicino Oriente*	OrAnt
O.Äg., o.äg.	*Oberägypten, oberägyptisch (Upper Egypt, Upper Egyptian)*	
ÖAI	*Österreichisches Archäologisches Institut*	
OAkk	*Old Akkadian*	
ÖAW	*Österreichische Akademie der Wissenschaften*	
OB	*Old Babylonian*	
Obad	*Obadiah*	
OBO	*Orbis biblicus et orientalis*	
OBOSA	*Orbis biblicus et orientalis. Series Archaeologica*	
ÖBS	*Österreichische biblische Studien*	
OBT	*Overtures to Biblical Theology*	
OC	*One in Christ*	
OC	*Oriens Christianus: Hefte für die Kunde des christlichen Orients*	OrChr
OCA	*Orientalia christiana analecta*	
OCD	*Oxford Classical Dictionary*	
OCP	*Orientalia Christiana Periodica*	Or.Christ.Per.
Odes Sol.	*Odes of Solomon*	
ODVF	*Oversigt over det Kongelige Danske videnskabernes selskabs forhandlinger*	
OECT	S. Langdon, ed., *Oxford Editions of Cuneiform Texts*	
OED	*Oxford English Dictionary*	
ÖFVS	*Översikt av Finska vetenskapssocietetens förhandlingar*	
OG	*Old Greek*	

Abbreviation	Citation	Abbreviation alternatives
Ogam	*Ogam: Tradition celtique*	
OGI	W. Dittenberger, *Orientis Graeci Inscriptiones Selectae*	OGIS
Ohol.	*Oholot*	
OI	*Oriental Institute* (University of Chicago)	Orinst
OIC	*Oriental Institute Communications*	Chic.O.I.C.
OIM	*Oriental Institute Museum*	
OIP	*Oriental Institute Publications*	
OIR	*The Oriental Institute Annual Report*	
OJA	*Oxford Journal of Archaeology*	
ÖJh	*Jahreshefte des österreichischen archäologischen Instituts in Wien*	JÖAI
OK	*Old Kingdom*	
OL	*Old Latin*	
OLA	*Orientalia Lovaniensia Analecta*	
OLP	*Orientalia Lovaniensia Periodica*	
OlympForsch	*Olympische Forschungen*	
Olynthos	*Excavations at Olynthos*	
OLZ	*Orientalistische Literaturzeitung*	
oMichaelides	H. Goedicke and E.F. Wente, *Ostraka Michaelides*	
OMRO	*Oudheidkundige Mededelingen uit het Rijksmuseum van Oudheden te Leiden*	
ÖMSO	*Österreichische Monatsschrift für den Orient*	
Onomast.	Eusebius, *Onomasticon*	
OP	*Occasional Papers on the Near East*	
Op	*Opuscula (minor works)*	
Op	Philo, *De opificio mundi*	
OpArch	*Opuscula archaeologica*	
OpAth	*Opuscula atheniensia*	
OpCourt	*Open Court: Monthly Magazine Devoted to the Science of Religion, the Religion of Science and the Extension of Religious Parliament Idea*	
OpPhil	*Opuscula philologica*	
OpRom	*Opuscula romana*	
Or	*Orientalia*	
Or	*Orla*	
OrAnt	*Oriens antiquus: revista del Centro per le Antichità e la Storia dell'Arte de Vicino Oriente*	OA
OrAr	*Orientalisches Archiv*	
OrBibliogr	*Orientalische Bibliographie*	
OrBibLov	*Orientalia et biblica lovaniensia*	
OrChr	*Oriens Christianus: Hefte für die Kunde des christlichen Orients*	OC
Or.Christ.Per.	*Orientalia Christiana Periodica*	OCP
Orient (H)	*Orient* Hamburg	
Orient (P)	*Orient* Paris	
Orient (T)	*Oriento: Bulletin of the Society for Near Eastern Studies in Japan* Tokyo	Orient (T)
Orig.World	*On the Origin of the World (NHC II,5; XIII,2)*	Orig.World
Orinst	*Oriental Institute* (University of Chicago)	OI
ORLR	*Der Obergermanische-rätische Limes des Römerreiches*	
OrMod	*Oriente moderno: rivista mensile d'informazione e di studi per la diffusione della conoscenza dell'Oriente, sopra tutto musulmano*	
OrOcc	*Oriens et Occidens* Stuttgart	
OrOcc	*Orient und Occident* Göttingen	
OrphFav	*Orpheus-Favonius* Bucarest [See also RevClas]	
OrSu	*Orientalia Suecana*	OrSuec
OrSyr	*L'Orient syrien*	
o.s.	*old series*	
OSAP	*Oxford Studies in Ancient Philosophy*	
OstkStud	*Ostkirchliche Studien*	OstStud
Ostr.u.Pap.	S. Allam, *Urkunden zum Rechtsleben im alten Ägypten* I*: Hieratische Ostraka und Papyri aus der Ramessidenzeit*	
OstStud	*Ostkirchliche Studien*	OstkStud
OT	*Old Testament*	
OTA	*Old Testament Abstracts*	
OTE	*Old Testament Essays*	
OTG	A.E. Brooke, N. McLean and H.St.J. Thackeray, eds., *The Old Testament in Greek according to the Text of Codex Vaticanus*	
OTG	*Old Testament Guides*	
ÖTK	*Ökumenischer Taschenbuch-Kommentar*	
OTL	*Old Testament Library*	
OTM	*Old Testament Message*	
OTP	J.H. Charlesworth, ed., *Old Testament Pseudepigrapha*	
OTS	*Oudtestamentische Studiën*	
Ouadi es-Sebouâ	H. Gauthier, *Le temple de Ouadi es-Sebouâ (TemplImm.)*	
OWAN	*Old World Archaeology Newsletter*	
P	*Priestly source*	
p	*papyrus designation e.g. pWilbour = Wilbour Papyrus*	
p	*Pesher (commentary)*	
PÄ	*Probleme der Ägyptologie*	ProbÄg
PAA	*Praktika tes Akademias Athenon*	
PAAA	*Proceedings of the American Academy of Arts and Sciences*	

Abbreviation	Citation	Abbreviation alternatives
PAAH	*Praktika tes en Athenais Archaiologikes Hetaireias*	
PAAJR	*Proceedings of the American Academy for Jewish Research*	
PAAS	*Proceedings of the American Antiquarian Society*	
PACA	*Proceedings of the African Classical Association*	
PACPA	*Proceedings of the American Catholic Philosophical Association*	
PAE	*Problèmes d'archéologie et d'ethnologie*	
PAGKARPEIA	*PAGKARPEIA: Mélanges Henri Grégoire*	Fs Grégoire
Paideia	*Paideia: rivista letteraria di informazione bibliografica*	
Pal.	*Palestinian*	
PalCl	*Palestra del Clero*	
PalJb	*Palästina-Jahrbuch*	PJ
PalLat	*Palaeographia latina*	
PalSbor	*Palestinsky Sbornik*	PS
Pal.Tgs.	*Palestinian Targums*	
PamKult	*Pam'atniki kul'turi* Moscow	
Pap.	*Papyrus, Papyri*	
PAPA	*Proceedings of the American Philological Association*	
PapDisc	S.I. Groll, Sarah and H.E. Stein, eds., *Papers for Discussion: Presented by the Department of Egyptology, Hebrew University, Jerusalem*	
PAPS	*Proceedings of the American Philological Society*	
Paraph.Shem	*Paraphrase of Shem (NHC VII,1)*	
ParId	*La Parola e le Idee: rivista internazionale di varia cultura e di informazione bibliografica*	
ParOr	*Parole de l'Orient*	
ParPass	*La Parola del passato: Rivista di studi antichi*	PP
PAS	*Proceedings of the Aristotelian Society*	
PASA	*Papers of the American School of Classical Studies at Athens*	
PastBon	*Pastor Bonus*	
PastPres	*Past and Present: Journal of historical studies*	
PatrOr	*Patrologia Orientalis*	PO
PBA	*Proceedings of the British Academy*	
PBH	*Patma-banasirakan handes* Erevan (Armenia)	
PBS	*Publications of the Babylonian Section*	
PBSEA	*Publications of the British School of Egyptian Archaeology*	

Abbreviation	Citation	Abbreviation alternatives
PBSR	*Papers of the British School at Rome*	
PCA	*Proceedings of the Classical Association* London	
PCAS	*Proceedings of the Classical Association of Scotland*	
PCB	M. Black and H.H. Rowley, eds., *Peake's Commentary on the Bible*	
PCPS	*Proceedings of the Cambridge Philological Society*	
PD	J.-P. Lauer and P. Lacau, *Pyramide à degrés (Fouilles Saqq.)*	
P.E.	Eusebius, *Praeparatio evangelica*	Praep.Evang.
Peet, Cemeteries	É. Naville, T.E. Peet and W.L.S. Loat, *The Cemeteries of Abydos (EEF 33-35)*	
PEFA	*Palestine Exploration Fund Annual*	PEF-Ann
PEFQS	*Palestine Exploration Fund: Quarterly Statement* [Continued by PEQ]	
PEGLAMBS	*Proceedings of the Eastern Great Lakes and Midwest Biblical Societies* [Continues PEGLBS]	
PEGLBS	*Proceedings of the Eastern Great Lakes Biblical Society* [Continued by PEGLAMBS]	
PÉLA	*Publications de l'École des lettres d'Alger*	
PÉLO	*Publications de l'École des langues orientales vivantes*	
Penn.Mus.Journ.	*The Museum Journal* (University of Pennsylvania.)	
PensPol	*Il Pensiero politico: rivista di storia delle idee politiche e sociali*	
Pen.Univ.Mus.Bull.	*The Pennsylvania University Museum Bulletin*	
PEQ	*Palestine Exploration Quarterly* [Continues BBSAJ, and PEFQS]	
Pers	*Persian*	
PerspPh	*Perspektiven der Philosophie: Neues Jahrbuch*	
Pesah.	*Pesahim*	
Pesiq.R.	*Pesiqta Rabbati*	
Pesiq.Rab Kah.	*Pesiqta de Rab Kahana*	
Petosiris	G. Lefebvre, *Le tombeau de Petosiris*	
Petrie, RT	W.M.F. Petrie, *The Royal Tombs of the First Dynasty (EEF 18, 21)*	RT
PFLA	*Publications de la Faculté des lettres d'Alger*	
PG	J.-P. Migne, *Patrologia graeca*	
PGM	*Papyri Graecae Magicae*	

Abbreviation	Citation	Abbreviation alternatives
PGM	*Petermanns geographische Mitteilungen*	
PharmHist	*Pharmacy in History*	
Ph.E.Poet	*Philo the Epic Poet*	
PhEW	*Philosophy East and West*	
PhFor	*Philosophical Forum* (Boston University)	
Phil	*Philippians*	
Philae	G. Bénédite, *Description et histoire de l'île de Philae (MMAF 13)*	
Philae I	H. Junker, *Der große Pylon des Tempels der Isis in Philä (DÖAW, Sonderbd)*	
Philae II	H. Junker and E. Winter, *Das Geburtshaus des Tempels der Isis in Philä (DÖAW, Sonderbd)*	
PhilClass	*Philologia classica: Mezhvuzovskii nauchnyi sbornik* St. Petersburg	
Phil.-hist.Kl.	*Philosophisch-historische Klasse*	
Philosophia (A)	*Philosophia: Epeteris tou Kentrou ereunes tes hellenikes philos.* Athens	
Philosophia (B)	*Philosophia* (Societas "Philosophia"), Belgrade	
PhilQuart	*Philological Quarterly*	
PhilStud	*Philologische Studiën*	
PhilWoch	*Philologische Wochenschrift*	PhW
PhJh	*Philosophisches Jahrbuch*	
Phld.	*Ignatius, Letter to the Philadelphians*	Ign.Phld
PhLit	*Philosophischer Literaturanzeiger*	PLA
Phlm	*Philemon*	
PhNat	*Philosophia naturalis*	
PHOE	G. von Rad, *Problem of the Hexateuch and Other Essays*	
Phoen	*Phoenician*	
Phoenix (L)	*Phoenix: Bulletin uitgegeven door het Vooraziatisch-Egyptisch Genootschap "EX ORIENTE LUX"* Leiden	Phoenix
Phoenix (T)	*Phoenix: Journal of the Classical Association of Canada* Toronto	
PhönWest	H.G. Neimeyer, ed., *Phönizier im Westen (Madrider Beiträge 8)*	
Photo FÉRÉ	*Photo Fondation égyptologique Reine Élisabeth*	
PhQuart	*Philosophical Quarterly*	
PhRev	*Philosophical Review*	
PhRh	*Philosophy and Rhetoric*	
PhRunds	*Philosophische Rundschau: Eine Zeitschrift für philosophische Kritik*	
PhW	*Philologische Wochenschrift*	PhilWoch

Abbreviation	Citation	Abbreviation alternatives
PI	J. Pedersen, *Israel: Its Life and Culture*	
PIA	*Palestinian Institute of Archaeology of Birzeit University*	
PIA	*Proceedings of the Royal Irish Academy*	PRIA
Pianchi	*Die Siegesinschrift des Pianchi (in Urk. III, 1 ff.)*	
PIASH	*Proceedings of the Israel Academy of Sciences and Humanities*	
PIBA	*Proceedings of the Irish Biblical Association*	
Piehl, Inscr.	K. Piehl, *Inscriptions hiéroglyphiques recueillies en Europe et en Egypte*	Piehl, Inscr.hiéro.
PIÉO	*Publications de l'Institut d'études orientales*	
PIFAO	*Publications de l'Institut français d'archéologie orientale du Caire*	
PIHANS	*Publications de l'Institut historique-archéologique néerlandais de Stamboul*	
PIHÉM	*Publications de l'Institut des hautes études marocaines*	
PIOL	*Publications de l'Institut orientaliste de Louvain*	
PIP	*Programa de Investigaciones Protohistoricas*	
PIR	*Prosopographia imperii romani*	
Pirqe R.El.	*Pirqe Rabbi Eliezer*	
PISA	*Pubblicazioni dell'Istituto di Storia Antica dell'Università di Padova*	
P.J.	*Paraleipomena Jeremiou*	
PJ	*Palästina-Jahrbuch*	PalJb
PJPES	*Proceedings of the Jewish Palestine Exploration Society*	
PKF	*Pytann'a klasycnoji filolohij* (University of Lwow)	
PL	J.-P. Migne, *Patrologia latina*	
PLA	*Philosophischer Literaturanzeiger*	PhLit
Plant	Philo, *De plantatione*	
PLA Report	*PLA Report* (Post Library Association)	
Plato Rep.	*Plato: Republic 588B-589B (NHC VI,5)*	
Platon	*Platon: Deltion tes Hetaireias hellenon philologon*	
PLCS	*Proceedings of the London Classical Society*	
pLeiden I 348	J. Borghouts, *The Magical Texts of Papyrus Leiden I 348 (OMRO 51)*	Borghouts, pLeiden I 348
PLO	*Porta linguarum orientalium*	
PLS	*Proceedings of the Linnean Society*	Proc.Linn.Soc. London

Abbreviation	Citation	Abbreviation alternatives
PM	B. Porter and R.L.B. Moss, *Topographical Bibliography of Ancient Egyptian Hieroglyphic Texts, Reliefs and Paintings*	PM
PMAAR	*Papers and Monographs of the American Academy in Rome*	
PMG	*Publications du musée Guimet*	
PMMA	*Publications of the Metropolitan Museum of Art*	
PMR	J.H. Charlesworth, *The Pseudepigrapha and Modern Research (SCS 7)*	
PMR Conférence	*Patristic, Mediaeval and Renaissance Conference*	
PN	H. Ranke, *Die altägyptischen Personennamen*	Ranke, PN
PN A	*Pottery Neolithic A*	
PN B	*Pottery Neolithic B*	
PNPI	J.K. Stark, *Personal Names in Palmyrene Inscriptions*	
PNPPI	F. Benz, *Personal Names in the Phoenician and Punic Inscriptions (StudPohl 8)*	
PNTC	*Pelican New Testament Commentaries*	
PNy Carlsb	*Publications de la Glyptothèque Ny Carlsberg*	P.Ny Carlsberg
PO	*Patrologia Orientalis*	PatrOr
POC	*Proche Orient chrétien*	
Pol.	*Ignatius, Letter to Polycarp*	Ign.Pol.
PopAr	*Popular Archaeology*	
Posener, oDeM	G. Posener, *Catalogue des ostraca hiératiques littéraires de Deir el Médineh, Nos. 1001-1675 (DFIFAO 1, 18, 20)*	
Post	Philo, *De posteritate Caini*	
POTT	D.J. Wiseman, ed., *Peoples of Old Testament Times*	
POuT	*De Prediking van het Oude Testament*	
PP	*La Parola del passato: Rivista di studi antichi*	ParPass
PPMRC	*Proceedings of the PMR Conférence: Annual Publication of the Patristic, Mediaeval and Renaissance Conference*	
PPN A	*Pre-Pottery Neolithic A*	
PPN B	*Pre-Pottery Neolithic B*	
PPR	*Philosophy and Phenomenological Research*	
PPS	*Proceedings of the Prehistoric Society*	
PPUAES	*Publications of the Princeton University Archaeological Expeditions to Syria*	
PPYE	*Publications of the Pennsylvania-Yale Expedition to Egypt*	
Praem	Philo, *De praemiis et poeniis*	
Praep.Evang.	Eusebius, *Praeparatio evangelica*	P.E.
PraFil	*Prace filologiczne*	
PrähistZeits	*Prähistorische Zeitschrift*	
Pr.Azar	*Prayer of Azariah*	
Pre.Pet.	*Preaching of Peter*	
Prel.Rep.	*Preliminary Report*	
PreußJb	*Preußische Jahrbücher*	
PRGS	*Proceedings of the Royal Geographical Society and monthly record of geography*	
PRIA	*Proceedings of the Royal Irish Academy*	PIA
Principat	W. Haase, ed., *Principat: Siebzehnter Band: Religion (Heidentum: Römische Götterkulte Orientalische Kulte in der römischen Welt)*	
Prism	A.C. Piepkorn, *Historical Prism Inscriptions of Ashurbanipal (AS 5)*	
Pr.Jac.	*Prayer of Jacob*	
Pr.Jos.	*Prayer of Joseph*	
Pr.Man	*Prayer of Manasseh*	
Pr.Mos.	*Prayer of Moses*	
PRNS	*Proceedings of the Royal Numismatic Society*	
Pro	*Proyección*	
Pro Alesia	*Pro Alesia* Paris	
Pro Arte	*Pro arte: Revue internationale d'art ancien et contemporain*	
Pro Aventico	*Pro Aventico: Bulletin de l'Association Pro Aventico*	
Prob	Philo, *Probus*	
ProbÄg	*Probleme der Ägyptologie*	PÄ
Probleme	*Probleme der koptischen Literatur*	
Procl	*Proclamation Commentaries*	
Proc.Linn.Soc.London	*Proceedings of the Linnean Society*	PLS
Proof	*Prooftexts: A Journal of Jewish Literary History*	Proof
PrOr	*Przeglad Orientalistyczny*	PrzegOr
Prospettiva	*Prospettiva: Rivista d'arte antica e moderna*	
Proteus	*Proteus: Rivista di filosofia*	
Prot.Jas.	*Protevangelium of James*	
Prov	*Proverbs*	
ProvHist	*Provence historique*	
Provid I-II	Philo, *De providentia I-II*	
Pr.Paul	*Prayer of the Apostle Paul (NHC I,1)*	
PRS	*Perspectives in Religious Studies*	
Pr.Thanks.	*The Prayer of Thanksgiving (NHC VI,7)*	
PRU	C.F.-A. Schaeffer, ed., *Le Palais Royal d'Ugarit (MRS 7, 6, 9, 11, 23)*	

Abbreviation	Citation	Abbreviation alternatives
PrzegArch	*Przeglad archeologiczny*	
PrzegHist	*Przeglad historyczny*	
PrzegKlas	*Przeglad klasyczny*	
PrzegOr	*Przeglad Orientalistyczny*	PrOr
PS	*Palestinsky Sbornik*	PalSbor
Ps(s)	*Psalm(s)*	
Ps-Abd.	*Apostolic History of Pseudo-Abdias*	
PSAL	*Proceedings of the Society of Antiquaries of London*	
PSAM	*Publications du Service des antiquités du Maroc*	
PSArabStud	*Proceedings of the Seminar for Arabian Studies*	
PSAS	*Proceedings of the Society of Antiquaries of Scotland*	
PSB	*Princeton Seminary Bulletin*	
PSBA	*Proceedings of the Society of Biblical Archaeology*	
Ps-Clem.	*Pseudo-Clementines*	
PSÉL	*Publications de la Société égyptologique* (University of Leningrad)	
Ps-Eup.	*Pseudo-Eupolemus*	
Ps-Hec.	*Pseudo-Hecataeus*	
PSI	*Papiri greci e latini: Pubblicazioni della Società Italiana per la recerce dei papiri greci e latini in Egitto*	
PSM	*Pagine di storia della medicina: Bollettino bimestrale dell'Istituto di storia della medicina dell'Università di Roma*	
Ps-Mt.	*Gospel of Pseudo-Matthew*	
PSN	*Petronian Society Newsletter*	
Ps-Orph.	*Pseudo-Orpheus*	
PSP	*Philologikos Syllogos Parnassos: Epeteris*	
Ps-Philo	*Pseudo-Philo*	
Ps-Phoc.	*Pseudo-Phocylides*	
Pss.Sol.	*Psalms of Solomon*	
PSt	*Process Studies*	
PSTJ	*Perkins (School of Theology) Journal*	
PT	*Perspectiva Teológica*	
PTA	*Papyrologische Texte und Abhandlungen*	
PTF	*Philologiae turcicae fundamenta*	
PThS	*Pretoria Theological Studies*	
PTMS	*Pittsburgh Theological Monograph Series*	
Ptol.	*Ptolemaic, ptolémaïque, ptolemäisch*	
PTT	*Private Tombs at Thebes*	
PTU	F. Gröndahl, *Die Personennamen der Texte aus Ugarit (StudPohl 1)*	
PUMB	*Pennsylvania University Museum Bulletin*	
Pun	*Punic*	
PUSC	*Pubblicazioni della Università cattolica del Sacro Cuore*	
Puteoli	*Puteoli: Studi di storia antica*	
PVS	*Proceedings of the Virgil Society*	
PVTG	*Pseudepigrapha Veteris Testamenti graece*	
PW	A.F. von Pauly and G. Wissowa, *Real-Encyclopädie der classischen Altertumswissenschaft*	RE; RealEnc
PWCJS	*Proceedings of the World Congress of Jewish Studies*	
PWSup	A.F. von Pauly and G. Wissowa, *Supplement t, Real-Encyclopädie der classischen Altertumswissenschaft*	
Pyr.	K. Sethe, *Die altägyptischen Pyramidentexte*	
Pyr., Übers.	K. Sethe, *Übersetzung und Kommentar zu den altägyptischen Pyramidentexten*	
Q	*Qumran texts (e.g. 4QTestim)*	
Q	*Quelle (source)*	
Qad	*Qadmoniot: Quarterly for the Antiquity of Eretz-Israel and Bible Lands*	
QAL	*Quaderni di archeologia della Libia*	
Qantara	*Qantara: Magazine de l'Institut du monde arabe*	
QAR	*Quaderni d'archeologia reggiana*	
Qau and Badari	G. Brunton, *Qau and Badari (BSAE 44-45, 50)*	
QCLBS	*Quarterly Check-List of Biblical Studies*	
QCLCS	*Quarterly Check-List of Classical Studies*	
QCLL	*Quarterly Check-List of Linguistics*	
QCLM	*Quarterly Check-List of Mediaevalia*	
QCLOS	*Quarterly Check-List of Oriental Studies*	
QCLRS	*Quarterly Check-List of Renaissance Studies*	
QCSCM	*Quaderni catanesi di studi classici e medievale*	
QCTC	*Quaderni di cultura e di tradizione classica*	
QD	*Quaestiones disputatae*	
QDAP	*Quarterly of the Department of Antiquities in Palestine* [Continued by ADAJ]	
QFC	*Quaderni di filologia classica*	
QHBT	F.M. Cross and S. Talmon, eds., *Qumran and the History of the Biblical Text*	
QIASA	*Quaderni dell' Istituto di archeologia e storia antica*	

Abbreviation	Citation	Abbreviation alternatives
Qidd.	*Qiddusin*	
QIFG	*Quaderni dell'Istituto di filologia greca*	
QIFL	*Quaderni dell'Istituto di filologia latina*	
QIFP	*Quaderni dell'Istituto di filosofia* (Università di Perugia)	
QIG	*Quaderni dell'Istituto di glottologia*	
QII	*Quarterly Index Islamicus: Current Books, articles and Papers on Islamic Studies*	
QILC	*Quaderni dell'Istituto di lingue e letterature classiche*	
QILL	*Quaderni dell'Istituto di lingua e letteratura latina*	
QITA	*Quaderni dell'Istituto di topografia antica*	
QJS	*Quarterly Journal of Speech*	
QL	*Qumran Literature*	
QLF	*Quaderni linguistici e filologici*	
QMAB	*Quaderni Del Museo Archeologico Provinciale Francesco Ribezzo di Brindisi*	
Qod.	*Qodasin*	
Qoh or Eccl	*Qoheleth or Ecclesiastes*	
QSA	*Quaderni di studi arabi*	
QSAE	*Quaderni di storia antica ed epigrafia*	
QSGMat	*Quellen und Studien zur Geschichte der Mathematik*	
QSGMed	*Quellen und Studien zur Geschichte der Medizin*	
QSGN	*Quellen und Studien zur Geschichte der Naturwissenschaften*	
QTLCG	*Quaderni triestini per il lessico della lirica corale greca*	
QTTA	*Quaderni triestini sul teatro antico*	
Quad	*Quaderni (notes)*	
QuadAc	*Quaderni di Acme*	
QuadCrit	*Quaderni della critica*	
QuadMed	*Quaderni medievali*	
QuadSem	*Quaderni di semitistica*	
QuadUm	*Quaderni dell' umanesimo*	
Quaes Ex I-II	Philo, *Quaestiones et solutiones in Exodum I-II*	
Quaes Gen I-IV	Philo, *Quaestiones et solutiones in Genesin I-IV*	
QUCC	*Quaderni urbinati di cultura classica*	
Quellen und Forschungen	L. Borchardt, ed., *Quellen und Forschungen zur Zeitbestimmung der ägyptischen Geschichte*	
Ques.Ezra	*Questions of Ezra*	
Quod Det	Philo, *Quod deterius potiori insidiari soleat*	
Quod Deus	Philo, *Quod deus immutabilis sit*	
Quod Omn	Philo, *Quod omnis probus liber sit*	
QV	*Queens' Valley = Valley of the Queens*	
R	Rawlinson, H.C., *Cuneiform Inscriptions of Western Asia*	R
R.	*Reihe (series)*	R.
r.	*rechts (right)*	r.
RA	*Revue archéologique* Paris	RA; RAr; RArch; Rev.arch.; RevArch
RA	*Revue d'assyriologie et d'archéologie orientale*	RA; RAAO
RA	Soden, Wolfram von and Dietz O. Edzard, eds., *Reallexikon der Assyriologie*	RA; RLA
RAA	*Répertoire d'art et d'archéologie*	RAA
RAAD	*Revue de l'Académie arabe de Damas*	RAAD
RAAM	*Revue de l'art ancien et moderne* [See also BAAM]	RAAM
RAAO	*Revue d'assyriologie et d'archéologie orientale*	RA; RAAO
RAAP	Mathieu, Bernard, *Recommandations aux auteurs et abréviations des périodiques pour les publications de l'Institut français d'archéologie orientale du Caire*	RAAP
RAAsiat	*Revue des arts asiatiques: Annales du musée Guimet*	RAAsiat
RAB	*Rendiconti dell'Accademia delle scienze dell'Istituto di Bologna*	RAB
RAB	Rogerson, J., *Atlas of the Bible*	RAB
Rab.	*Rabbah (following abbreviation for Biblical book: Gen. Rab. = Genesis Rabbah)*	Rab.
RAC	*Reallexikon für Antike und Christentum*	RAC; RLAC
RAC (P)	*Rassegna di Antichità classica* Palermo	RAC (P)
RACF	*Revue archéologique du Centre de la France*	RACF
RAChr	*Revue de l'art chrétien*	RAChr
RAComo	*Rivista archeologica dell'antica provincia e diocesi di Como*	RAComo
RACrist	*Rivista di archeologia cristiana*	RACrist; RivArCr
RAD	Gardiner, Alan H., *Ramesside Administrative Documents*	RAD
RAE	*Revue d'art et d'esthétique*	RAE
RAECE	*Revue archéologique de l'Est et du Centre-Est*	RAECE
Raggi	*Raggi: Zeitschrift für Kunstgeschichte und Archäologie*	Raggi
RAGR	*Rivista bimestrale di Antichità greche e romane*	RAGR

Abbreviation	Citation	Abbreviation alternatives
RAHA	*Revue des archéologues et historiens d'art de Louvain*	RAHA
RAI	*Rendiconti dell'Accademia d'Italia*	RAI
RAIN	*Royal Anthropological Institute News*	RAIN
RAK	*Rozprawy Akad: Umiejetnosci w Krakowie*	RAK
RAL	*Rendiconti dell'Accademia nazionale dei Lincei*	RAL
RALB	*Revue des auteurs et des livres* Brussels	RALB
RALoir	*Revue archéologique du Loiret*	RALoir
RAM	*Revue d'ascétique et de mystique*	RAM
Ramus	*Ramus: Critical Studies in Greek and Latin Literature*	Ramus
RAN	*Rendiconti dell'Accademia di archeologia, lettere e belle arti* Naples	RAN
RANarb	*Revue archéologique de Narbonnaise*	RANarb
RANE	*Records of the Ancient Near East*	RANE
Ranke, PN	Ranke, Hermann, *Die altägyptischen Personennamen*	PN; Ranke, PN
RAP	*Revue archéologique polonaise*	RAP
RAPH	*Recherches d'archéologie, de philologie et d'histoire*	RAPH
RAPic	*Revue archéologique de Picardie*	RAPic
Rapp	*Rapports*	Rapp
RappFouilles	*Rapports des fouilles*	RappFouilles; RF
RAR	*Rendiconti della Pontificia Accademia romana di archeologia*	RAR; RPAA
RAr	*Revue archéologique* Paris	RA; RAr; RArch; Rev.arch.; RevArch
RÄR	Bonnet, Hans, *Reallexikon der ägyptischen Religionsgeschichte*	RÄR; RÄRG
RArch	*Revue archéologique* Paris	RA; RAr; RArch; Rev.arch.; RevArch
RÄRG	Bonnet, Hans, *Reallexikon der ägyptischen Religionsgeschichte*	RÄR; RÄRG
RAS	*Revue archéologique syrienne*	RAS
Rass	*Rassegna (journal)*	Rass
RassColt	*Rassegna di coltura*	RassColt
RassCult	*Rassegna di cultura*	RassCult
Rasse	*Rasse: Monatsschrift der nordischen Bewegung*	Rasse
RassF	*Rassegna di filosofia*	RassF
RassMon	*Rassegna monetaria*	RassMon
RassNum	*Rassegna numismatica*	RassNum
RasT	*Rassegna di Teologia*	RasT
RAT	*Revue Africaine de Théologie*	RAT
RAVA	*Reallexikon der Assyriologie und vorderasiatischen Archäologie*	RAVA
Raydan	*Raydan: Journal of Ancient Yemeni Antiquities and Epigraphy*	Raydan
RazFe	*Razón y Fe*	RazFe
RB	*Revue biblique* [Continues RBI]	RB; RevBibl
RBA	*Revue belge d'archéologie et d'histoire de l'art*	RBA
RBAB	*Revue des bibliothèques et archives de Belgique*	RBAB
RBén	*Revue bénédictine*	RBén; RevBén
RBI	*Revue biblique internationale* [Continues RBT, Continued by RevBibl]	RBI
RBI	*Rivista biblica italiana*	RBI
RBK	*Reallexikon zur byzantinischen Kunst*	RBK
RBN	*Revue belge de numismatique et de sigillographie*	RBN
RBPH	*Revue belge de philologie et d'histoire*	RBPH
RBR	*Ricerche Bibliche e Religiose*	RBR
RBS	*Regulae Benedicti Studia: Annuarium internationale*	RBS
RBT	*Revue biblique trimestrielle* [Continued by RBI]	RBT
RC	*Revue du Caire*	RC; RevCaire
RCB	*Revista de Cultura Biblica*	RCB
RCC	*Revue des cours et conférences*	RCC
RCCM	*Rivista di cultura classica e medievale*	RCCM
RCÉA	*Répertoire chronologique d'épigraphie arabe*	RCÉA
RCFO	*Revue des conférences françaises en Orient*	RCFO
RCGO	*Recherches sur les cultes grecs et l'Occident*	RCGO
RCHL	*Revue critique d'histoire et de littérature*	RCHL; Revue critique
RCI	*Rivista delle colonie italiane*	RCI
RCK	*The Royal Cemeteries of Kush*	RCK
RCRF	*Rei Cretaria Romanae Fautorum Acta*	RCRF
RCSF	*Rivista critica di storia della filosofia*	RCSF
RCT	Gardiner, Alan H., *The Royal Canon of Turin*	Gardiner, RCT; RCT
RCT	*Revista Catalana de Teologia*	RCT
RCUCR	*Rivista del Colegio universitario de Ciudad Real* [See also CFCR]	RCUCR
RDAC	*Report of the Department of Antiquities, Cyprus*	RDAC
RdCaire	*Revue de Caire*	RdCaire

Abbreviation	Citation	Abbreviation alternatives
RdÉ	*Revue d'égyptologie*	RdÉ; Rev.d'Ég.
RDIMO	*Revue de droit international pour le Moyen Orient*	RDIMO
RDM	*Revue des Deux Mondes*	RDM
RdM	Schröder, C.M., ed., *Die Religionen der Menschheit*	RdM
RduL	*Revue du Louvre et des musées de France*	La Revue du Louvre; RduL; RevLouvre; RLMF
RE	Hauck, A., ed., *Realencyklopädie für protestantische Theologie und Kirche*	RE
RE	Pauly, August Friedrich von and Georg Wissowa, *Real-Encyclopädie der classischen Altertumswissenschaft*	PW; RE; RealEnc
RÉA	*Revue de l'Égypte ancienne* [Continues RevÉg, Continued by RdÉ]	RÉA; RÉgA
RÉA	*Revue des études anciennes*	RÉA; RÉtAnc
RealEnc	Pauly, August Friedrich von and Georg Wissowa, *Real-Encyclopädie der classischen Altertumswissenschaft*	PW; RE; RealEnc
RÉAnd	*Revue des études andalouse = Dirâsât Andalusiyya*	RÉAnd
RÉArm	*Revue des études arméniennes*	RÉArm
RÉAug	*Revue des études augustiniennes* [See also RechAug]	RÉAug
REB	*Revista Eclesiástica Brasileira*	REB
RÉB	*Revue des études byzantines* [Continues ÉtudByz]	RÉB
REC	*Revista de estudios clásicos*	REC
RecConstantine	*Recueil des notices et mémoires de la Société archéologique du département de Constantine*	RecConstantine
Rec.de Trav.	*Recueil de travaux relatifs à la philologie et à l'archéologie égyptiennes et assyriennes*	Rec.de Trav.; RecTrav; RT
Rec.dM	Brugsch, Heinrich, *Recueil de monuments égyptiens*	Brugsch, Rec.; Rec.dM; RecdM
RecdM	Brugsch, Heinrich, *Recueil de monuments égyptiens*	Brugsch, Rec.; Rec.dM; RecdM
Rech	*Recherche(s)*	Rech
RechAug	*Recherches augustiniennes*	RechAug
RechBib	*Recherches bibliques*	RechBib
Recherche	*Recherche* (Institut de coopération intellectuelle) [Continues BOIA]	Recherche
Recherches	*Recherches* (Université Saint-Joseph), Beirut	Recherches
RechPap	*Recherches de papyrologie*	RechPap
RechPh	*Recherches philosophiques*	RechPh
RechTrav	*Recherches et travaux*	RechTrav
RÉCors	*Revue des études corses*	RÉCors
RecTrav	*Recueil de travaux relatifs à la philologie et à l'archéologie égyptiennes et assyriennes*	Rec.de Trav.; RecTrav; RT
Redford, Eighteenth Dyn.	Redford, Donald B., *History and Chronology of the Eighteenth Dynasty of Egypt*	Redford, Eighteenth Dyn.
RÉDI	*Revue égyptienne de droit international*	RÉDI
RefRev	*Reformed Review*	RefRev
RefTR	*Reformed Theological Review*	RefTR
Reg.	*Register*	Reg.
RÉG	*Revue des études grecques*	RÉG
RÉgA	*Revue de l'Égypte ancienne* [Continues RevÉg, Continued by RdÉ]	RÉA; RÉgA
RÉH	*Revue des études historiques*	RÉH
RÉHom	*Revue des études homériques* [See also Acropole]	RÉHom
RÉI	*Revue des études islamiques*	RÉI
RÉIE	*Revue des études indo-européennes*	RÉIE
Reisner, Giza	Reisner, George A., *History of the Giza Necropolis*	Reisner, Giza
Reisner, Tomb Development	Reisner, George A., *The Development of the Egyptian Tomb down to the Accession of Cheops*	Reisner, Tomb Development
RÉJ	*Revue des études juives*	RÉJ
RÉL	*Revue des études latines*	RÉL
RelArts	*Religion and the Arts*	RelArts
RelCiv	*Religioni e civiltà: Studi e materiali di storia delle religioni*	RelCiv
RelCult	*Religión y cultura*	RelCult
Religio	*Religio: Rivista di studi religiosi*	Religio
Religion	*Religion: Journal of Religion and Religions* London	Religion; RelLond
RELing	*Revista española de linguistica*	RELing
RelLeb	*Religion und Leben*	RelLeb
RelLond	*Religion: Journal of Religion and Religions* London	Religion; RelLond
RelNY	*Religion* New York	RelNY
RÉLO	*Revue de l'Organisation internationale pour l'étude des langues anciennes par ordinateur*	RÉLO
RelOr	*Relations d'Orient*	RelOr
RelS	*Religious Studies* (University of Cambridge)	RelS; RelStud
RelSoc	*Religion and Society*	RelSoc
RelSRev	*Religious Studies Review*	RelSRev
RelStud	*Religious Studies* (University of Cambridge)	RelS; RelStud
RÉM	*Repertoire d'épigraphie méroïtique*	RÉM
RemAfr	*Remarques africaines*	RemAfr
Renovatio	*Renovatio* Bonn	Renovatio
RenQuart	*Renaissance Quarterly*	RenQuart
REP	*Revue de l'enseignement philosophique*	REP

Abbreviation	Citation	Abbreviation alternatives
Rep	*Report*	Rep
RÉS	*Repertoire d'éprigraphie sémitique*	RÉS
RÉS	*Revue des études sémitiques*	RÉS
ResABib	*Die Reste der altlateinische Bibel*	ResABib
RÉSB	*Revue des études sémitiques et Babyloniaca*	RÉSB
RÉSEE	*Revue des études sud-est-européennes*	RÉSEE
ResQ	*Restoration Quarterly*	ResQ
RET	*Revista española de teología*	RET
RÉtAnc	*Revue des études anciennes*	RÉA; RÉtAnc
RETP	*Revue d'ethnographie et des traditions populaires*	RETP
Rev	*Revelation*	Rev
Rev	*Review, Revue, Revista*	Rev
RevAfr	*Revue africaine*	RevAfr
RevAlg	*Revue algérienne*	RevAlg
RevAnthr	*Revue d'anthropologie*	RevAnthr
Rev.arch.	*Revue archéologique* Paris	RA; RAr; RArch; Rev.arch.; RevArch
RevArch	*Revue archéologique* Paris	RA; RAr; RArch; Rev.arch.; RevArch
RevArch (Pr)	*Revue archéologique* Prague	RevArch (Pr)
RevArchéom	*Revue d'archéométrie: bulletin de liason du Groupe des méthodes physiques et chimiques de l'archéologie*	RevArchéom
RevArq	*Revista di arqueologia*	RevArq
RevArts	*Revue des arts* [Continues BMF]	RevArts
RevBén	*Revue bénédictine*	RBén; RevBén
RevBibl	*Revue biblique* [Continues RBI]	RB; RevBibl
RevBibl (BA)	*Revista Biblica* Buenos Aires	RevBibl (BA); RevistB
RevBl	*Revue bleue*	RevBl
RevCaire	*Revue du Caire*	RC; RevCaire
RevCat	*Revista catolica*	RevCat
RevCelt	*Revue celtique*	RevCelt
RevClas	*Revista clasica* Bucarest [See also OrphFav]	RevClas
Rev.d'Ég.	*Revue d'égyptologie*	RdÉ; Rev.d'Ég.
RevÉg	*Revue égyptologique* [Continued by RÉgA]	RevÉg; RevÉgyptol
RevÉgyptol	*Revue égyptologique* [Continued by RÉgA]	RevÉg; RevÉgyptol
Rev.Eg.Anc.	*Revue d'Egypte ancienne*	Rev.Eg.Anc.
RevÉp	*Revue épigraphique*	RevÉp
RevEthn	*Revue d'ethnographie*	RevEthn
RevExp	*Review and Expositor*	RevExp
Rev.Ezra	*Revelation of Ezra*	Rev.Ezra

Abbreviation	Citation	Abbreviation alternatives
RevF (BA)	*Revista de filosofía* Buenos Aires	RevF (BA)
RevF (LP)	*Revista de filosofia* La Plata	RevF (LP)
RevF (M)	*Revista de filosofía* Madrid	RevF (M)
RevHist	*Revue historique*	RevHist; RH
RevHist (SP)	*Revista de historia* São Paulo (Brazil)	RevHist (SP)
Rev.hist.eccl.	*Revue d'histoire ecclésiatique*	Rev.hist.eccl.; RHE
RevistB	*Revista Biblica* Buenos Aires	RevBibl (BA); RevistB
RevistEspir	*Revista de Espritualidad*	RevistEspir
RevLet (A)	*Revista de letras* (Universidade Estadual Paulista), Assiz (Brazil)	RevLet (A)
RevLet (SP)	*Revista de letras* (Universidade Estadual Paulista), São Paulo (Brazil)	RevLet (SP)
RevLouvre	*Revue du Louvre et des musées de France*	La Revue du Louvre; RduL; RevLouvre; RLMF
RevMet	*Review of Metaphysics*	RevMet
RevNord	*Revue du Nord*	RevNord
RevNum	*Revue numismatique*	RevNum
RevPar	*Revue de Paris*	RevPar
RevPhil	*Revue de philologie, de littérature et d'histoire anciennes*	RevPhil; RPLHA
RevPhilos	*Revue philosophique*	RevPhilos
RevQ	*Revue de Qumran*	RevQ; RevQum
RevQum	*Revue de Qumran*	RevQ; RevQum
RevRéf	*Revue Réformée*	RevRéf
RevRel	*Review for Religious*	RevRel
RevRel	*Review of Religion*	RevRel; RR
RevSém	*Revue sémitique d'épigraphie et d'histoire ancienne*	RevSém; RSÉHA
Rev.Steph.	*Revelation of Stephen*	Rev.Steph.
RevSynt	*Revue de synthèse*	RevSynt
RevTh	*Revue de théologie*	RevTh
Revue critique	*Revue critique d'histoire et de littérature*	RCHL; Revue critique
RevUniv	*Revue universitaire*	RevUniv
Rez.	*Rezension (review)*	Rez.
RF	*Rapports des fouilles*	RappFouilles; RF
RFA	*Revue de la Franco-Ancienne*	RFA
RFC	*Rivista di filologia classica*	RFC
RFE	*Revista di filología española*	RFE
RFH	*Revista di filología hispánica*	RFH
RFIC	*Rivista di filologia e d'istruzione classica*	RFIC
RFL	*Revue franco-libanaise*	RFL
RFM	*Revue franco-macédonienne*	RFM
RFN	*Rivista di filosofia neoscholastica*	RFN

Abbreviation	Citation	Abbreviation alternatives
RGD	*Revue générale du droit*	RGD
RGF	*Römisch-germanische Forschungen*	RGF
RGG	*Die Religion in Geschichte und Gegenwart: Handwörterbuch für Theologie und Religionswissenschaft*	RGG
RGI	*Rivista geografica italiana*	RGI
RGKB	*Römisch-germanisches Korrespondenzblatt*	RGKB
RGKF	*Römisch-germanische Kommission des archäologischen Institut* Frankfurt	RGKF
RGL	*Revue de géographie de Lyon*	RGL
RGM	*Revue de géographie du Maroc (Notes marocaines)*	RGM
RGRW	*Religions in the Graeco-Roman World* [Continues ÉPRO]	RGRW
RGTC	Röllig, W., ed., *Répertoire géographique des textes cunéiformes (BTAVO B7)*	RGTC
RGZM	*Römisch-germanisches Zentralmuseum*	RGZM
RH	*Revue historique*	RevHist; RH
RHA	*Revue hittite et asianique*	RHA
RHC	*Revue d'histoire comparée*	RHC
RHCM	*Revue d'histoire et de civilisation du Maghreb*	RHCM
RHD	*Revue historique de droit français et étranger*	RHD
RHE	*Revue d'histoire ecclésiatique*	Rev.hist.eccl.; RHE
RheinMus	*Rheinisches Museum*	RheinMus
RHÉS	*Revue d'histoire économique et sociale*	RHÉS
rhet.	*rhetorisch (rhetorical)*	rhet.
Rhetorica	*Rhetorica: International Society for the History of Rhetoric*	Rhetorica
Rhetorik	*Rhetorik: ein internationales Jahrbuch*	Rhetorik
RHJ	*Rechtshistorisches Journal*	RHJ
RHLR	*Revue d'histoire et de littérature religieuses*	RHLR
RHM	*Römische historische Mitteilungen*	RHM
RHMaghr	*Revue d'histoire maghrébine*	RHMaghr
RHP	*Revue d'histoire de la philosophie*	RHP
RHPharm	*Revue d'histoire de la pharmacie*	RHPharm
RHPR	*Revue d'histoire et de philosophie religieuses*	RHPR
RHR	*Revue de l'histoire des religions*	RHR
RHS	*Revue de l'histoire des sciences et de leurs applications*	RHS
RHSCP	*Revue d'histoire du sport et de la culture physique*	RHSCP
RHSEE	*Revue historique du Sud-Est européen*	RHSEE
RHSpir	*Revue d'histoire de la spiritualité*	RHSpir
RHT	*Revue d'histoire des textes* [Continues BIRHT]	RHT
RHV	*Revue historique vaudoise*	RHV
RI	Kitchen, Kenneth A., *Ramesside Inscriptions*	Kitchen, Ram.Inscr.; KRI; RI
RIA	*Rivista del Istituto nazionale di archeologia e storia dell'arte*	RIA
RIAF	*Rivista pentru istorie, arheologie si filologie*	RIAF
RIBLA	*Revue de l'Institut des belles-lettres arabes* Tunis	RIBLA
RIC	Mattingly, H., ed., *The Roman Imperial Coinage*	RIC
RIC (2)	Sutherland, C.H.V. and R.A.G. Carson, eds., *The Roman Imperial Coinage, 2d ed.*	RIC (2)
RicF	*Ricerche filosofiche*	RicF
Ricke, Bemerkungen AR	Ricke, Herbert, *Bemerkungen zur ägyptischen Baukunst des Alten Reiches (BeiträgeBf 4 & 5, 1)*	Ricke, Bemerkungen AR
Ricke, Userkaf-SH	Ricke, Herbert, *Das Sonnenheiligtum des Königs Userkaf (BeiträgeBf 7 & 8)*	Ricke, Userkaf-SH
RicLing	*Ricerche linguistiche*	RicLing
RicMed	*Ricerche medievali*	RicMed
Ric-Rel	*Ricerche religiose: revista di studi religiosi*	Ric-Rel
RID	*Rivista italiana del Dramma*	RID
RIDA	*Revue internationale des droits de l'Antiquité*	RIDA
RIE	*Revue internationale de l'enseignement*	RIE
RIÉB	*Revue internationale des études balkaniques*	RIÉB
RIEM	*Revista del Instituto egipcio de estudios islámicos en Madrid*	RIEM
RIGI	*Rivista indo-greco-italica di filologia, lingua, Antichità*	RIGI
RIHAO	*Revista del Instituto de Historia Antigua Oriental*	RIHAO
RIL	*Rendiconti dell'Istituto Lombardo*	RIL
RILC	*Rassegna italiana di lingue e letterature classiche*	RILC
RIMA	*Revue de l'Institut des manuscrits arabes*	RIMA
RIN	*Rivista italiana di numismatica e scienze affini*	RIN
Rinascimento	*Rinascimento: rivista dell'Istituto nazionale di studi sul Rinascimento (1961-)*	Rinascimento

Abbreviation	Citation	Abbreviation alternatives
Rinascita	*La Rinascita: rivista dell'Istituto nazionale di studi sul Rinascimento (1950-1960)*	Rinascita
RIO	*Revue internationale d'onomastique*	RIO
RIP	*Revue internationale de philosophie*	RIP
RIPB	*Revue de l'instruction publique en Belgique*	RIPB
RIR	*Revista istorica romana*	RIR
RIS	*Revue informatique et statistique dans les sciences humaines*	RIS
Riscontri	*Riscontri: Rivista trimestrale di cultura e di attualità*	Riscontri
RISG	*Rivista italiana di scienze giuridiche*	RISG
RISR	*Rassegna d'informazione dell'Istituto di studi romani*	RISR
Riv.	*Rivista (journal)*	Riv.
RivArch	*Rivista di archeologia*	RivArch
RivArCr	*Rivista di archeologia cristiana*	RACrist; RivArCr
RivB	*Rivista biblica* (Associazione biblica italiana)	RivB; RivBibl
RivBibl	*Rivista biblica* (Associazione biblica italiana)	RivB; RivBibl
RivCol	*Rivista delle colonie*	RivCol
RivDalm	*Rivista dalmatica*	RivDalm
RivF (B)	*Rivista di filosofia* Bologna	RivF (B)
RivF (T)	*Rivista di filosofia* Turin	RivF (T)
RivIt	*Rivista d'Italia*	RivIt
RivPed	*Rivista pedagogica*	RivPed
RivRel	*Rivista delle religioni*	RivRel
RivTrip	*Rivista della Tripolitania*	RivTrip
RK	*Realkatalog der Ägyptologie*	RK; RKÄ
RKÄ	*Realkatalog der Ägyptologie*	RK; RKÄ
RKI	*Report of the Keio Institute of Cultural and Linguistic Studies*	RKI
RKW	*Repertorium für Kunstwissenschaft*	RKW
RLA	*Revue de législation ancienne et moderne française et étrangère*	RLA
RLA	Soden, Wolfram von and Dietz O. Edzard, eds., *Reallexikon der Assyriologie*	RA; RLA
RLAC	*Reallexikon für Antike und Christentum*	RAC; RLAC
RLAF	*Revista latinoamericana de filosofia*	RLAF
RLMF	*Revue du Louvre et des musées de France*	La Revue du Louvre; RduL; RevLouvre; RLMF
RLÖ	*Der Römische Limes in Österreich*	RLÖ
RLR	*Revue de linguistique romane*	RLR
RLT	*Revista Latinoamericana de Teologia*	RLT

Abbreviation	Citation	Abbreviation alternatives
RM	*Mitteilungen des Deutschen Archäologischen Instituts, Römische Abteilung*	MDAIR; MDIR; RM
RMÂL	*Revue du moyen âge latin*	RMÂL
RMÉ	*Revue du monde égyptien*	RMÉ
RMÉA	*Revue mensuelle de l'École d'anthropologie*	RMÉA
RMétMor	*Revue de métaphysique et de morale*	RMétMor
RMM	*Revue du monde musulman*	RMM
RMMM	*Revue du monde musulman et de la Méditerranée*	RMMM
RMMO	*Revue médicale du Moyen Orient*	RMMO
RMNW	*Rocznik Museum Narodowego w Warszawie*	RMNW
RMP	*Rheinisches Museum für Philologie*	RMP
RNP	*Revue néoscholastique de philosophie*	RNP
RNT	*Regenesburger Neues Testament*	RNT
ro	*recto (front)*	ro; Rto
ROAC	*Revue de l'Orient, de l'Algérie et des colonies*	ROAC
ROB	*Rijksdienst voor het oudheidkundig Bodemonderzoek*	ROB
Robichon-Varille, Temple Amenhotep, Fils de Hapou	Robichon, Clément and Alexandre Varille, *Le temple du scribe royal Amenhotep, fils de Hapou (FIFAO 11)*	Robichon-Varille, Temple Amenhotep, Fils de Hapou
ROC	*Revue de l'Orient chrétien*	ROC
RockArtRes	*Rock Art Research*	RockArtRes
RocTKan	*Roczniki Teologiczno-Kanoniczne*	RocTKan
RoczHum	*Roczniki humanistyczne 3 : filologia klasyczna*	RoczHum
RoczOr	*Rocznik orientalistyczny*	RoczOr
ROL	*Revue de l'Orient latin*	ROL
Rom	*Romans*	Rom
Rom.	*Ignatius, Letter to the Romans*	Ign.Rom.; Rom.
röm.	*römisch (Roman)*	röm.
Roma	*Roma: rivista di studi e di vita Romana*	Roma
Romana	*Romana: rivista degli Istituti di cultura italiana all'estero*	Romana
Romania	*Romania* Paris	Romania
Romanitas	*Romanitas: Revista de cultura romana*	Romanitas
RomBarb	*Romanobarbarica: contributi allo studio dei rapporti culturali tra mondo latino e mondo barbarico*	RomBarb
RomForsch	*Romanische Forschungen: Organ für romanische Sprachen, Volks-und Literaturen*	RomForsch
RomGens	*Romana gens*	RomGens

Abbreviation	Citation	Abbreviation alternatives
ROMM	*Revue de l'Occident musulman et de la Méditerranée*	ROMM
RomOr	*Roma e l'Oriente*	RomOr
RömÖst	*Römisches Österreich: Jahresschrift der Österreichischen Gesellschaft für Archäologie*	RömÖst
RomRev	*Romanic Review*	RomRev
RomTell	*Romana tellus*	RomTell
Roscher, Lex.Myth.	Roscher, Wilhelm H., *Lexikon der griechischen und römischen Mythologie*	Roscher, Lex.Myth.
Roš Hš.	*Roš Haššana*	Roš Hš.
ROTT	von Rad, G., *Old Testament Theology*	ROTT
Rowe, Scarabs	Rowe, Alan, *A Catalogue of Egyptian Scarabs, Scaraboids, Seals and Amulets in the Palestine Archaeological Museum*	Rowe, Scarabs
RP	*Revue de philologie*	RP
RPA	*Revue de philosophie ancienne*	RPA
RPAA	*Rendiconti della Pontificia Accademia romana di archeologia*	RAR; RPAA
RPFÉ	*Revue philosophique de la France et de l'étranger*	RPFÉ
RPL	*Revue philosophique de Louvain*	RPL
RPLHA	*Revue de philologie, de littérature et d'histoire anciennes*	RevPhil; RPLHA
RPLitt	*Res publica litterarum: Studies in the Classical Tradition*	RPLitt
RPLL	*Recherches de philologie et de linguistique* Louvain	RPLL
RPTMS	*Robb de Peyster Tytus Memorial Series (PMMA)*	RPTMS
RQ	*Römische Quartalschrift für christliche Altertumskunde und für Kirchengeschichte*	RQ; RQCA
RQCA	*Römische Quartalschrift für christliche Altertumskunde und für Kirchengeschichte*	RQ; RQCA
RQH	*Revue des questions historiques*	RQH
RQS	*Revue des questions scientifiques*	RQS
RR	*Review of Religion*	RevRel; RR
RS	*Ras Shamra*	RS
Rs.	*Rückseite (verso)*	Rs.
RSA	*Rivista storica dell'Antichità*	RSA
RSA (M)	*Rivista di storia antica* Messina	RSA (M)
RSAA	*Revue suisse d'art et d'archéologie*	RSAA
RSAC	*Recherches suisses d'archéologie copte*	RSAC
RSAConst	*Recueil des notices et mémoires de la Société archéologique de Constantine* (Société archéologique, historique et géographique de la wilaya de Constantine)	RSAConst
RSAP	*Ricerche di storiografia antica* Pisa	RSAP
RSBN	*Rivista di studi bizantini e neoellenici*	RSBN
RSBS	*Rivista di studi bizantini e slavi*	RSBS
RSC	*Rivista di studi classici*	RSC
RSCI	*Rivista di storia della chiesa in Italia*	RSCI
RSDI	*Rivista di storia del diritto italiano*	RSDI
RSE	*Rassegna di Studi Etiopici*	RSE
RSÉHA	*Revue sémitique d'épigraphie et d'histoire ancienne*	RevSém; RSÉHA
RSF	*Rassegna di scienze filosofiche*	RSF
RSF	*Rivista di Studi Fenici*	RSF; RSFen
RSFen	*Rivista di Studi Fenici*	RSF; RSFen
RSFR	*Rivista di studi filosofici e religiosi*	RSFR
RSH	*Revue de synthèse historique*	RSH
RSHum	*Revue des sciences humaines*	RSHum
RSI	*Rivista storica italiana*	RSI
RSJB	*Revue de la Société Jean Bodin*	RSJB
RSLig	*Rivista di studi liguri*	RSLig
RSLR	*Rivista di storia e letteratura religiosa*	RSLR
RSM	*Rivista delle scienze mediche e naturali*	RSM
RSN	*Revue suisse de numismatique*	RSN
RSO	*Rivista degli Studi Orientali*	RSO
RSP	*Rivista di studi Pompeiani*	RSP
RSPAT	*Recueil de la Société de préhistoire et d'archéologie de Tébessa*	RSPAT
RSPT	*Revue des sciences philosophiques et théologiques*	RSPT
RSR	*Recherches de science religieuse*	RSR
RSR (S)	*Revue des sciences religieuses* Strasbourg	RSR (S)
RSRF	*Rivista di studi religiosi* Florence	RSRF
RSRR	*Ricerche di storia religiosa* Rome	RSRR
RSS	*Rassegna storica Salernitana*	RSS
RSSM	*Rivista di storia delle scienze mediche e naturali*	RSSM
RST	*Religious Studies and Theology*	RST
RST	*Rivista storica ticinese*	RST
RSV	*Revised Standard Version*	RSV
RT	Petrie, William M. Flinders, *The Royal Tombs of the First Dynasty (EEF 18, 21)*	Petrie, RT; RT
RT	*Recueil de travaux relatifs à la philologie et à l'archéologie égyptiennes et assyriennes*	Rec.de Trav.; RecTrav; RT
RTAM	*Recherches de théologie ancienne et médiévale*	RTAM

Abbreviation	Citation	Abbreviation alternatives
RTL	*Revue théologique de Louvain* [See also CRTL]	RTL
Rto	*recto (front)*	ro; Rto
RTP	*Revue de théologie et de philosophie* [See also CRTP]	RTP
RTQR	*Revue de théologie et des questions religieuses*	RTQR
RTR	*Revista tinerimea romana*	RTR
RUB	*Revue de l'université de Bruxelles*	RUB
RUM	*Revue des universités du Midi*	RUM
Runds	*Rundschau (newsletter)*	Runds
RUO	*Revue de l'université d'Ottawa*	RUO
RUS	*Rundbrief Una Sancta* [Continued by Una Sancta]	RUS
RV	*Revised Version*	RV
RVB	*Rheinische Vierteljahrsblätter*	RVB
RVF	*Revista venezolana de filosofia*	RVF
RVG	Ebert, Max, *Reallexikon der Vorgeschichte*	Ebert, RL; RVG
RVV	*Religionsgeschichtliche Versuche und Vorarbeiten*	RVV
RVWB	*Rheinische Vorzeit in Wort und Bild*	RVWB
RWF	*Rozprawy Wydzialu filologicznego polskiej*	RWF
Ry	Ryckmans, G., *Inscriptions sudarabes I-XVII. Mus 40-72*	Ry
S + no.	*Number of a grave in Saqqara*	
SA	*Sudhoffs Archiv: Zeitschrift für Wissenschaftsgeschichte*	SudAr; ZWG
SA.	*Sonderabdruck (special publication)*	
SaalbJb	*Saalburg-Jahrbuch: Bericht des Saalburg-Museums*	
SAAS	*State archives of Assyria studies*	
Šabb.	*Šabbat*	
SAC	*Studies in Ancient Chronology*	
SacDoc	*Sacra Doctrina*	
SacEr	*Sacris Erudiri: Jaarboek voor Godsdienstwetenschappen*	SacrErud
SAColl	*Sussex Archaeological Collections*	
Sacr	Philo, *De sacrificiis Abelis et Caini*	
SacrErud	*Sacris Erudiri: Jaarboek voor Godsdienstwetenschappen*	SacEr
SADA	*Scientific American Discovering Archaeology*	
SAÉ	*Service des antiquités de l'Égypte*	
Saeculum, WG	*Saeculum, Weltgeschichte*	
SAGM	*Sudhoffs Archiv für Geschichte der Medizin und Naturwissenschaft*	
SAHG	A. Falkenstein and W. von Soden, *Sumerische und akkadische Hymnen und Gebete*	
SAJS	*South African Journal of Science*	
SAK	*Studien zur Altägyptischen Kultur*	
SAL	*Studies in Arabic Literature*	
Sal	*Salesianum* Rome	
Salman	*Salmanticensis* Salamanca	
SAMN	*Society for Ancient Medicine Newsletter*	
SamOstr	*Samaria Ostracon/Ostraca*	
Sam.Pent.	*Samaritan Pentateuch*	
SAMPN	*Society for Ancient Medicine and Pharmacy Newsletter*	
Sam.Tg.	*Samaritan Targum*	
SANE	*Sources from the Ancient Near East*	
SANH	*Somerset Archaeology and Natural History: Proceedings of the Somerset Archaeology and Natural History Society*	
Sanh.	*Sanhedrin*	
SANT	*Studien zum Alten und Neuen Testament*	StANT
SAO	*Studia et acta orientalia*	
SAOC	*Studies in Ancient Oriental Civilisation*	
Sap	*Sapienza: Rivista internazionale di filosofia e di teologia dei Domenicani d'Italia*	
SAQ	*Sammlung ausgewählter kirchen-und dogmengeschichtlicher Quellenschriften*	
SAQ	*South Atlantic Quarterly*	
SardMon	*Archaeological Exploration of Sardis, Monograph*	
SardRep	*Archaeological Exploration of Sardis, Report*	
SAS	*Sudan Antiquities Service Occasional Papers*	SASOP
SASAÉ	*Supplément aux ASAE, Cahier*	ASAÉ-Suppl.; CASAÉ
SASMP	*Sudan Antiquities Service Museum Pamphlet*	
SASOP	*Sudan Antiquities Service Occasional Papers*	SAS
SAStobi	*Studies in the Antiquities of Stobi*	
SAT	H.Gunkel, *Die Schriften des Alten Testaments in Auswahl*	
Sauneron, oDeM	S. Sauneron, *Catalogue des ostraca hiératiques non littéraires de Deir el Médineh, Nos. 550-623 (DFIFAO 13)*	
SAWB	*Sitzungsberichte der deutschen Akademie der Wissenschaften* Berlin [Continues SPAW]	SDAW

Abbreviation	Citation	Abbreviation alternatives
SAWH	*Sitzungsberichte der Heidelberger Akademie der Wissenschaften*	SHAW
SAWM	*Sitzungsberichten der (königlichen) bayerischen Akademie der Wissenschaften* Munich	SBAW
SAWW	*Sitzungsberichte der Akademie der Wissenschaften in Wien* [From 1950 SÖAW]	
SB	F. Preisicke, *Sammelbuch griechischer Urkunden aus Ägypten*	SGUÄ
SB	*Sources bibliques*	
SBA	*Studies in Biblical Archaeology*	
SBAW	*Sitzungsberichten der (königlichen) bayerischen Akademie der Wissenschaften* Munich	SAWM
SBB	*Studien zum Buch- und Bibliothekswesen*	
SBB	*Stuttgarter biblische Beiträge*	
SBF	*Studium Biblicum Franciscanum*	
SBF	*Liber Annuus* (Studium Biblicum Franciscanum)	LAnn; LASBF; LibAnn
SBibB	*Studies in Bibliography and Booklore*	
SBJ	*La sainte bible de Jérusalem*	
SBK	*Schriften der Balkankommission*	
SBLABS	*Society of Biblical Literature Archaeology and Biblical Studies*	
SBLAS	*Society of Biblical Literature Aramaic Studies*	
SBLASP	*Society of Biblical Literature Abstracts and Seminar Papers*	
SBLBAC	*Society of Biblical Literature The Bible in American Culture*	
SBLBMI	*Society of Biblical Literature The Bible and Its Modern Interpreters*	
SBLBSNA	*Society of Biblical Literature Biblical Scholarship in North America*	
SBLDS	*Society of Biblical Literature Dissertation Series*	
SBLMasS	*Society of' Biblical Literature Masoretic Studies*	
SBLMS	*Society of Biblical Literature Monograph Series*	
SBLNTGF	*Society of Biblical Literature: The New Testament in the Greek Fathers*	
SBLRBS	*Society of Biblical Literature: Resources for Biblical Study*	
SBLSBS	*Society of Biblical Literature: Sources for Biblical Study*	
SBLSCS	*Society of Biblical Literature: Septuagint and Cognate Studies*	
SBLSP	*Society of Biblical Literature: Seminar Papers*	
SBLSS	*Society of Biblical Literature: Seminar Studies*	

Abbreviation	Citation	Abbreviation alternatives
SBLTT	*Society of Biblical Literature: Texts and Translations*	
SBLWAW	*Society of Biblical Literature: Writings of the Ancient World*	
SBM	*Stuttgarter biblische Monographien*	
SBN	*Studi bizantini e neoellenici*	
SBÖAW	*Sitzungsberichte der Österreichischen Akademie der Wissenschaften* [To 1950 SAWW]	SÖAW
SborF	*Sbornik filosofické*	
SborFil	*Sbornik filologicky*	
SBS	*Stuttgarter Bibelstudien*	
SBT	*Studia biblica et theologica*	StudBT
SBT	*Studies in Biblical Theology*	
Sc	*Sources chrétiennes*	SourcChr
SCCNH	D.I. Owen and M.A. Morrison, eds., *Studies on the Civilization and Culture of Nuzi and the Hurrians*	
SCE	*Swedish Cyprus Expedition*	
ScEccl	*Sciences ecclésiastiques* [Continued by ScEspr]	
ScEs	*Science et Esprit* [Continues ScEccl]	ScEspr
ScheMed	*Schede medievali*	
Schiffbrüchiger	*The Shipwrecked Sailor* (Middle Egyptian story)	
SCHNT	*Studia ad corpus hellenisticum novi testamenti*	
Scholastik	*Scholastik: Vierteljahresschrift für Theologie und Philosophie*	
Scholia	*Scholia* [Other name of Eskolot]	
SCI	*Scripta classica israelica: Yearbook of the Israel Society for the Promotion of Classical Studies*	
SCIV	*Studii si cercetari de istorie veche*	
SCJ	*Studies in Contemporary Judaism*	
SCO	*Studi classici e orientali*	
SCR	*Studies in Comparative Religion*	
Scr	*Scripture*	
ScrB	*Scripture Bulletin*	
ScrC	*Scripture in Church*	
ScrCiv	*Scrittura e civiltà*	
ScRel	*Sciences religieuses: Revue canadienne*	
ScrHier	*Scripta Hierosolymitana*	
Scrip	*Scriptorium: revue internationale des études relatives aux manuscrits*	Scriptorium
Scritti O.Montevecchi	E. Bresciani, ed., *Scritti in onore di Orsolina Montevecchi*	Fs Orsolina Montevecchi.
Scritti Rosellini	*Scritti dedicati alla memoria di Ippolito Rosellini*	Fs Rosellini, Scritti
ScrPhil	*Scripta philologa*	

Abbreviation	Citation	Abbreviation alternatives
ScrT	*Scripta Theologica*	
SCS	*Septuagint and Cognate Studies*	
ScuolC	*La Scuola Cattolica*	ScuolCatt
SD	*Studies and Documents*	
SDAIK	*Sonderschrift des Deutschen Archäologischen Instituts, Abteilung Kairo*	
SDAW	*Sitzungsberichte der deutschen Akademie der Wissenschaften* Berlin [Continues SPAW]	SAWB
SDB	H.B.Hackett, *Smith's Dictionary of the Bible*	
SDB	*Supplement au Dictionnaire de la Bible* [Supplement to DB]	
SDHI	*Studia et documenta historiae et iuris*	
SDOG	*Sendschrift der Deutschen Orientgesellschaft*	
SDSD	*Studi e documenti di storia e diritto*	
SE	*Studia Evangelica I-III (TU 73, 87-88)*	
SEÅ	*Svensk Exegetisk Årsbok*	
SEAP	*Studi di egittologia e di Antichità puniche*	
Šeb.	*Šebi'it*	
Šebu.	*Šebu'ot*	
SecCent	*The Second Century: Journal of Early Christian Studies*	SecondCent
Sec.Gos.Mk.	*Secret Gospel of Mark*	
Sedment	W.M.F. Petrie and G. Brunton, *Sedment I and II (BSAE 34-35)*	
Sef	*Sefarad: Revista del Instituto Arias Montana de Estudios Hebraicos y Oriente Proximo*	Sefarad
SEG	J.J.E. Hondius, ed., *Supplementum Epigraphicum Graecum*	
Seia	*Seia: quaderni dell'Istituto di storia antica*	
SEL	*Studi Epigrafici e linguistici sul Vicino Oriente antico*	
Sem	*Semitica* Paris	
Sem.	*Semahot*	
SémBibl	*Sémiotique et Bible*	SémiotBib
Semeia-Stud.	*Semeia Studies*	
Semeia-Suppl.	*Semeia Supplements*	
SemHefte	*Semantische Hefte*	
SémiotBib	*Sémiotique et Bible*	SémBibl
SemKond	*Seminarium Kondakovianum*	
Sent.Sextus	*Sentences of Sextus (NHC XII,1)*	
Šeqal.	*Šeqalim*	
SER	*Swedish Excavations and Researches*	
Seux	J.M. Seux, *Epithètes Royales Akkadiennes et Sumériennes*	
SGKAO	*Schriften zur Geschichte und Kultur des alten Orients*	
SGKIO	*Studien zur Geschichte und Kultur des islamischen Orients*	
SGL	A. Falkenstein, *Sumerische Götterlieder*	
SGNW	*Schriftenreihe für Geschichte der Naturwissenschaften, Technik und Medizin*	NTM
SGP	*Studi geografici sul paesaggio*	
SGRR	*Studies in Greek and Roman Religion*	
SGUÄ	F. Preisicke, *Sammelbuch griechischer Urkunden aus Ägypten*	SB
SGV	*Sammlung gemeinverständlicher Vorträge und Schriften aus dem Gebiet der Theologie und Religionsgeschichte*	
SHAW	*Sitzungsberichte der Heidelberger Akademie der Wissenschaften*	SAWH
Sheikh Saïd	N. de G. Davies, *The Rock Tombs of Sheikh Saïd* (ASE 10)	
Shep.Herm.	*Shepherd of Hermas*	
SHIB	R.M. Grant and D. Tracy, *A Short History of the Interpretation of the Bible*	
SHPS	*Studies in History and Philosophy of Science*	
SHR	*Studies in the History of Religions*	
SHT	*Studies in Historical Theology*	
SHT	*Svensk humanistik Tidsskrift*	
Sib.Or.	*Sibylline Oracles*	
SicArch	*Sicilia archeologica*	
SicGymn	*Siculorum Gymnasium: Rassegna semestrale della Facoltà di Lettere e Filosofia dell'Università di Catania*	
SICV	H. Zilliacus, ed., *Sylloge inscriptionum Christianorum veterum musei Vaticani* (AIRF 1/1-2.)	
SIDA	*Scripta Instituti Donneriana Aboensis*	
SIDJC	*Service International de Documentation Judéo-chrétienne*	
Sieglin Exp.	*Veröffentlichungen der Ernst von Sieglin Expedition in Ägypten*	
SIF	*Studi internazionale di filosofia*	
SIFC	*Studi italiani di filologia classica*	
SIFII	*Studi italiani di filologia indo-iranica*	
SIG	W. Dittenberger, *Sylloge inscriptionum graecarum*	
SII	*Studies in Islam: Quarterly Journal of the Indian Institute of Islamic Studies* New Delhi	StudIsl (ND)
SIL	*Studi italiani di linguistica teorica ed applicata*	

Abbreviation	Citation	Abbreviation alternatives
Sileno	*Sileno: Rivista di studi classici e cristiani*	
SIM	*Sérapéum Inventaire Mariette (Designations of the Serapeum stelae in the Louvre)*	
Sinuhe	*The Tale of Sinuhe* (Middle Egyptian story)	
Sir	*Ecclesiasticus or Wisdom of Jesus Ben-Sira*	
SIRIS	Vidman, Ladislav, *Sylloge inscriptionum religionis Isiacae et Serapiacae*	
Siût	F.Ll. Griffith, *The Inscriptions of Siût and Dêr Rifeh*	
SJ	*Studia Judaica*	
SJE	*Scandinavian Joint Expedition to Sudanese Nubia*	
SJLA	*Studies in Judaism in Late Antiquity*	
SJOT	*Scandinavian Journal of the Old Testament*	
SJT	*Scandinavian Journal of Theology*	
SJT	*Scottish Journal of Theology*	
SKGG	*Schriften der Königsberger Gelehrten Gesellschaft*	
SkrAth	*Skrifter utgivna av Svenska Institutet i Athen*	
SkrifK	*Skrif en Kerk*	
SkrLund	*Skrifter utgivna av Vetenskaps-Societeten i Lund*	
SkrRom	*Skrifter utgivna av Svenska Institutet i Rom*	
SkrUppsala	*Skrifter utgivna av Kungliga Humanistiska vetenskapssamfundet i Uppsala*	
SLAG	*Schriften der Luther-Agricola-Gesellschaft*	
SlavOr	*Slavia orientalis*	
SLJT	*Saint Luke's Journal of Theology*	
SlovArch	*Slovenská archeológia*	
SLS	*Society for Libyan Studies, Annual Report*	
SMA	*Studies in Mediterranean Archaeology*	
SMAN	*Studi e materiali di archeologia e numismatica*	
SMAP	*Studies in Mediterranean Archaeology, Pocketbook*	
SMB	*Schweizer Münzblätter*	
SMC	*Studies in Medieval Culture*	
SMEA	*Studi Micenei ed Egeo-Anatolici*	
SMGB	*Studien und Mitteilungen zur Geschichte des Benediktinerordens*	
SMGR	*Studien zu den Militärgrenzen Roms*	
SMS	*Syro-Mesopotamian Studies*	
SMSR	*Studi e materiali di storia delle religioni*	
Smyrn.	*Ignatius, Letter to the Smyrnaeans*	Ign.Smyrn
SNG	*Sylloge nummorum graecorum*	
SNR	*Schweizerische numismatische Rundschau*	
SNR	*Sudan Notes and Records*	SNRec
SNT	*Studien zum Neuen Testament*	
SNTSMS	*Society for New Testament Studies Monograph Series*	
SNTU	*Studien zum Neuen Testament und seiner Umwelt*	
SNVAO	*Skrifter utgitt av det Norske Videnshaps-Akademi i Oslo*	
SO	*Symbolae osloenses*	SymbOsl
SÖAW	*Sitzungsberichte der Österreichischen Akademie der Wissenschaften* [To 1950 SAWW]	SBÖAW
Sobr	Philo, *De sobrietate*	
S.'Olam Rab.	*Seder 'Olam Rabbah*	
Somn I-II	Philo, *De somniis I-II*	
SonB	*Soncino Books of the Bible*	
SoobErm	*Soobscenija Gosudarstvennogo Ermitaza*	
SoobPouchk	*Soobscenija: Communications du musée d'art Pouchkine*	
Sop.	*Soperim*	
Soph.Jes.Chr.	*Sophia of Jesus Christ* (NHC III,4)	
SophPer	*Sophia perennis: Bulletin of the Imperial Iranian Academy of Philosophy*	
SOTSBooklist	*Society for Old Testament Study Booklist*	
SOTSMS	*Society for Old Testament Study Monograph Series*	
Sou	*Soundings*	
SourcChr	*Sources chrétiennes*	
Sources	*Sources travaux historiques*	
SourcesOr	*Sources Orientales*	SourcOr
SovArch	*Sovetskaja archeologija*	
SovEtn	*Sovetskaja etnografija*	
SovJaz	*Sovetskoe jazikoznanie*	
SovVost	*Sovetskoe vostokojedenie*	
SP	*Studia papyrologica: Revista española de papirología*	SPap; StudPap
SPASR	*Supplementary Paper of the American School of Classical Studies in Rome*	
SPAW	*Sitzungsberichte der Preußischen Akademie der Wissenschaften* [From 1948 = SDAW]	
SPB	*Studia postbiblica*	
Spec Leg I-IV	Philo, *De specialibus legibus I-IV*	
SpeechMon	*Speech Monographs*	
SPFB	*Sbornik prací Filosofické fakulty Brnenske university*	

Abbreviation	Citation	Abbreviation alternatives
SPhil	*Studia Philonica*	StPhilon; StudPhilon
SPIB	*Scripta Pontificii Instituti Biblici*	
SPP	*Studien zur Palaeographie und Papyruskunde*	StudPal
SPPosn	*Symbolae philologorum posnanensium*	
SPS	*Studia philologica salmanticensia*	
SpT	*Spirituality Today*	
SpZt	*Spätzeit (Late Period)*	
SQAW	*Schriften und Quellen der alten Welt*	
SR	*Studies in Religion = Sciences religieuses*	StudRel
SRIC	*Studi e ricerche dell'Istituto di studi storici* Cagliari	
SRIF	*Studi e ricerche dell'Istituto di storia* Florence	
SRIG	*Studi e ricerche dell'Istituto di civiltà classica, cristiana, medievale* Genoa	
SRIL	*Studi e ricerche dell'Istituto di latino*	
SS	*Studi semitici*	
SSAC	*Studi storici per l'Antichità classica*	
SSAOI	*Sacra Scriptura Antiquitatibus Orienialibus Illustrata*	
SSAW	*Sitzungsberichte der Sächsischen Akademie der Wissenschaften zu Leipzig*	
SSBK	*Studien zur spätantiken und byzantinischen Kunst*	
SSEA	*Society for the Study of Egyptian Antiquities*	
SSEA(J)	*Journal of the Society for the Study of Egyptian Antiquities* Toronto	JSSEA; SSEAJ
SSEA(N)	*Newsletter of the Society for the Study of Egyptian Antiquities* Toronto	NSSEA
SSGW	*Sitzungsberichte der Sächsischen Gesellschaft der Wissenschaften*	
SSL	*Studi e saggi linguistici*	
SSLL	*Studies in Semitic Languages and Linguistics*	
SSN	*Studia Semitica Neerlandica*	
SSR	*Studi storico-religiosi*	
SSS	*Semitic Study Series*	
ST	*Studia theologica*	StTh
ST	*Suhrkamp Taschenbuch*	
STÅ	*Svensk teologisk årsskrift*	
StädelJb	*Städel-Jahrbuch*	
StadtrChr	P. Lampe, *Die stadtrömischen Christen in den ersten beiden Jahrhunderten* (WUNT 2/18)	
StANT	*Studien zum Alten und Neuen Testament*	SANT
StBo	*Studien zu den Bogazköy-Texten*	StBT; StudBog
StDI	*Studia et Documenta ad Iura Orientis Antiqui Pertinenti*	
STDJ	*Studies on the Texts of the Desert of Judah*	
StEb	*Studi Eblaiti*	
StEc	*Studi Ecumenici*	
Steles Seth	*Three Steles of Seth* (NHC VII,5)	
Step Pyramid	C.M. Firth and J.E. Quibell, *The Step Pyramid (Excav.Saqq.)*	
StFS	*Studia Francisci Scholten*	
StG	*Studium generale: Zeitschrift für die Einheit der Wissenschaften im Zusammenhang ihrer Begriffsbildungen und Forschungsmethoden*	StudGener
StimZeit	*Stimmen der Zeit*	SZ
STK	*Svensk teologisk kvartalskrift*	
STL	*Studia theologica Ludensia*	
StLtg	*Studia Liturgica*	
StMiss	*Studia Missionalia*	
StOr	*Studia Orientalia* Helsinki	StudOr; Stud Or (H)
StOvet	*Studium Ovetense*	StOvet
StPat	*Studia patavina*	StudPat
StPatr	*Studia Patristica*	StudPatr
StPhilon	*Studia Philonica*	SPhil; StudPhilon
Str	*Stromata*	
Strabo	H.L. Jones, ed., *Geography of Strabo, Books I-XVII*	
Str-B	H.L. Strack and P. Billerbeck, *Kommentar zum NT aus Talmud und Midrasch*	
StStor	*Storia della storiografia*	
STT	O.R. Gurney et al., eds., *The Sultantepe Tablets* (Occasional Publications of the British School of Archaeology at Ankara 3, 7)	
StTh	*Studia theologica*	ST
STU	*Schweizerische theologische Umschau*	
StudAeg (B)	*Studia Aegyptiaca* Budapest	
StudAeg (R)	*Studia Aegyptiaca* Rome	
StudAlb	*Studia albanica*	
StudAnt	*Studi di Antichità*	
StudArch	*Studia archaeologica*	
StudBib	*Studia biblica*	
StudBiz	*Studi bizantini*	
StudBog	*Studien zu den Bogazköy-Texten*	StBo; StBT
StudBT	*Studia biblica et theologica*	SBT
StudCath	*Studia catholica*	
StudCatt	*Studi cattolici*	
StudClas	*Studii clasice*	

Abbreviation	Citation	Abbreviation alternatives
StudEbl	*Studia eblaiti*	
StudEtr	*Studi etruschi*	
StudFil	*Studime filologjike*	
StudGen	*Studi genuensi*	
StudGener	*Studium generale: Zeitschrift für die Einheit der Wissenschaften im Zusammenhang ihrer Begriffsbildungen und Forschungsmethoden*	StG
StudGor	*Studi goriziani: rivista a cura della Biblioteca governativa di Gorizia*	
StudHell	*Studia hellenistica*	Stud.Hellen.
StudHist	*Studime historike*	
Studi Rosellini	*Studi in memoria di Ippolito Rosellini nel primo centenario della morte*	Fs Rosellini, Studi
Studia Naster II	*Studia Paulo Naster Oblata II: Orientalia Antiqua*	Fs Naster
Studien Westendorf	*Studien zu Sprache und Religion Ägyptens: Zu Ehren von Wolfhart Westendorf überreicht von seinen Freunden und Schülern*	Fs Westendorf
Studien zur alt-ägyp.Keramik	Do. Arnold, ed., *Studien zur altägyptischen Keramik*	
Studies Hughes	*Studies in Honor of George R. Hughes* (SAOC 39)	Fs Hughes
Studies Polotsky (1964)	*Studies in Egyptology and Linguistics in Honour of Hans Jacob Polotsky* (1964)	Fs Polotsky (1964)
Studies Polotsky (1981)	*Studies presented to Hans Jakob Polotsky* (1981)	Fs Polotsky (1981)
Studies Williams	*Studies in Philology in Honour of Ronald James Williams*	Fs Williams
Studies Wilson	*Studies in Honour of John A. Wilson* (SAOC 35)	Fs Wilson
StudIr	*Studia iranica*	
StudIsl (ND)	*Studies in Islam: Quarterly Journal of the Indian Institute of Islamic Studies* (New Delhi)	SII
StudIsl (P)	*Studia islamica* (Paris)	
StudLang	*Studies in Language: International journal sponsored by the foundation "Foundations of Language"*	
StudLing	*Studia linguistica: revue de linguistique générale et comparée*	
StudMagr	*Studi magrebini*	
StudMat	*Studi e materiali* (Soprintendenza ai beni archeologici per la Toscana)	
StudMed	*Studi medievali*	
StudMisc	*Studi miscellanei*	
StudMon	*Studia monastica*	
StudNeot	*Studia neotestamentica, Studia*	
StudOliv	*Studia Oliveriana*	
StudOr	*Studia Orientalia* (Helsinki)	StOr; StudOr (H)
StudOr (R)	*Studi orientali* (Rome)	StudOr (R)
StudOv	*Studium ovetense: Revista del Centro Superior de Estudios Eclesiasticos "La Asuncion"* (Oviedo)	
StudPal	*Studien zur Palaeographie und Papyruskunde*	SPP
StudPap	*Studia papyrologica: Revista española de papirología*	SP; SPap
StudPat	*Studia patavina*	StPat
StudPatr	*Studia Patristica*	StPatr
StudPhil	*Studies in Philology*	
StudPhilon	*Studia Philonica*	SPhil; StPhilon
StudPhoen	*Studia Phoenicia*	
StudPic	*Studia picena*	
StudPohl	*Studia Pohl*	
StudPun	*Studia Punica*	
StudRel	*Studies in Religion = Sciences religieuses*	SR
StudRom	*Studi romani: rivista di archeologia è storia*	
StudRomagn	*Studi romagnoli*	
StudSal	*Studi salentini*	
StudSard	*Studi sardi*	
StudStor	*Studi storici: rivista trimestrale dell'Istituto Gramsci*	
StudTest	*Studi e testi*	
StudTh	*Studia theologica: Scandinavian Journal of Theology*	
StudZam	*Studia zamorensia*	
STV	*Studia theologica varsaviensia*	
Stylus	*Stylus: Cuaderno de filologia*	
SubGron	*Subseciva Groningana*	
SudAr	*Sudhoffs Archiv: Zeitschrift für Wissenschaftsgeschichte*	SA; ZWG
SuissCont	*Suisse contemporaine*	
SuissPrim	*Suisse primitive = Ur-Schweiz*	
Sukk.	*Sukka*	
SUL	*Per lo studio e l'uso del latino*	
Sum	*Sumerian*	
Sundries Säve-Söderbergh	*Sundries in Honour of Torgny Säve-Söderbergh* (Boreas 13)	Fs Säve-Söderbergh
SUNT	*Studien zur Umwelt des Neuen Testaments*	SUNT
SupItal	*Supplementa Italica*	
Suppl.	*Supplement*	
SurvBibliogr	*Surveys and Bibliographies*	
Sus	*Susanna*	
SUSFL	*Studi urbinati di storia, filosofia e letteratura*	
SUSGE	*Studi urbinati di scienze giuridiche ed economiche*	
SVF	J. von Arnim, ed., *Stoicorum veterum fragmenta*	
SVTP	*Studia in Veteris Testamenti pseudepigrapha*	

Abbreviation	Citation	Abbreviation alternatives
SVTQ	*St. Vladimir's Theological Quarterly*	
SW	*Southwest, Südwesten*	
SWBA	*Social World of Biblical Antiquity*	
SWJT	*Southwestern Journal of Theology*	
SWP	*Survey of Western Palestine*	
SWP 1	C.R. Conder and H.H. Kitchener, *Survey of Western Palestine: Galilee*	
SWP 2	C.R. Conder and H.H. Kitchener, *Survey of Western Palestine: Samaria*	
SWP 3	C.R. Conder and H.H. Kitchener, *Survey of Western Palestine: Judaea*	
SWP 4	E.H. Palmer, *Survey of Western Palestine: Arabic and English Name Lists*	
SWP 5	C. Wilson and C. Warren, *Survey of Western Palestine: Special Papers*	
SWP 6	C. Wilson and C. Warren, *Survey of Western Palestine: Jerusalem*	
SWP 7	H.B. Tristram, *Survey of Western Palestine: The Fauna and Flora of Palestine*	
SymbArct	*Symbolae arctoae* (Societas Philologica Christianiensis)	
SymbOsl	*Symbolae osloenses*	SO
SymBU	*Symbolae biblicae upsalienses*	
Symposium international sur la Nubie	*Actes du symposium international sur la Nubie organisé par l'Institut d'Egypte…*	
Syr	*Syria: Revue d'Art Oriental et d'Archéologie*	Syria
Syr, syr	*Syriac, Syrian, syrisch*	
SyrMA	*Syrie et monde arabe*	
Syr.Men.	*Syriac Menander*	
SZ	*Stimmen der Zeit*	StimZeit
SZG	*Schweizerische Zeitschrift für Geschichte*	SZG
T.12P.	*Testaments of the Twelve Patriarchs*	
TA	*Tel Aviv: Journal of the Tel Aviv University Institute of Archaeology*	TA
Ta'an.	*Ta'anit*	
T.Ab.	*Testament of Abraham*	
T.Adam	*Testament of Adam*	
TÄB	*Tübinger Ägyptologische Beiträge*	
TAD	*Türk Arkeoloji Dergisi*	
TAD	B. Porten and A. Yardeni, *Textbook of Aramaic Documents from Ancient Egypt*	
TAD A	B. Porten and A. Yardeni, *Textbook of Aramaic Documents from Ancient Egypt* 1: *Letters*	
TAD B	B. Porten and A. Yardeni, *Textbook of Aramaic Documents from Ancient Egypt* 2: *Contracts*	
TAD C	B. Porten and A. Yardeni, *Textbook of Aramaic Documents from Ancient Egypt* 3: *Literature and Lists*	
TAD D	B. Porten and A. Yardeni, *Textbook of Aramaic Documents from Ancient Egypt* 4: *Fragments and Inscriptions*	
TAÉI	*Textes arabes et études islamiques*	
TAik	*Teologinen Aikakauskirja*	
Talm.	*Talmud*	
TAM	*Tituli Asiae Minoris*	
Tamuda	*Hespéris Tamuda* [Continues Hespéris]	HespTam
TAPA	*Transactions of the American Philological Association*	
TAPhS	*Transactions of the American Philosophical Society*	TAPS
T.Ash.	*Testament of Asher*	
TAVO	*Tübinger Atlas des Vorderen Orients*	
Tb	K.R. Lepsius, *Das Todtenbuch der Ägypter nach dem hieroglyphischen Papyrus in Turin*	Tb (Lepsius)
Tb (Allen)	T.G. Allen, *The Egyptian Book of the Dead* (OIP 82)	Allen, BD
Tb (Barguet)	P. Barguet, *Le Livre des morts des anciens égyptiens*	
Tb (Budge)	E.A.W. Budge, *Book of the Dead: The Chapters of Coming Forth by Day*	Budge, BD
Tb (Hornung)	E. Hornung, Erik, *Das Totenbuch der Ägypter* (Bibliothek der Alten Welt)	
Tb (Naville)	É. Naville, *Das aegyptische Totenbuch der XVIII. bis XX. Dynastie*	Naville, Tb
TBC	*Torch Bible Commentary*	
TBei	*Theologische Beiträge*	
T.Benj.	*Testament of Benjamin*	
TBG	*Tijdschrift van het bataviaasch Genootschap van Kunsten en Wetenschappen*	
TBl	*Theologische Blätter*	ThBl
TBT	*The Bible Today*	BToday
TBü	*Theologische Bücherei*	
TCGNT	B.M. Metzger, *A Textual Commentary on the Greek New Testament*	
TCL	*Textes cunéiforms du Musée du Louvre*	
TCLA	*Travaux du Cercle linguistique d'Aix-en-Provence*	
TCLP	*Travaux du Cercle linguistique de Prague*	

Abbreviation	Citation	Abbreviation alternatives
TCS	*Texts from Cuneiform Sources*	
TCS 1	E. Sollberger, *Business and Administrative Correspondence Under the Kings of Ur*	
TCS 2	R.D. Biggs, *ŠÀ.ZI.GA: Ancient Mesopotamian Potency Incantations*	
TCS 3	Å. Sjöberg, E. Bergmann and G. Gragg, *The Collection of the Sumerian Temple Hymns*	
TCS 4	E. Leichty, *The Omen Series šumma izbu*	
TCS 5	A.K. Grayson, *Assyrian and Babylonian Chronicles*	
TCWA	*Transactions of the Cumberland and Westmorland Antiquarian and Archaeological Society*	
TD	*Theology Digest*	
T.Dan.	*Testament of Daniel*	
TDNT	G. Kittel and G. Friedrich, eds., *Theological Dictionary of the New Testament*	
TE	*Theologica Evangelica*	
Teach.Silv.	*Teachings of Silvanus* (NHC VII,4)	
TechnCult	*Techniques et culture*	
TechnolCult	*Technology and Culture*	
TED	*Tarih Enstitüsü Dergisi*	
Tem.	*Temura*	
Temples Immergés	*Les temples immergés de la Nubie*	TemplImm.
TempsRéfl.	*Le Temps de la réflexion*	
Ter	*Teresianum*	
Ter	*Terumot*	
TerrIsl	*En Terre d'Islam: la revue française du monde Musulman*	
Test	*Testimonianze*	
Testim.Truth	*Testimony of Truth* (NHC IX,3)	
TetzKen	*Tetzugaku Kenkyu*	
TextsS	*Texts and Studies*	
TextUnt	*Texte und Untersuchungen zur Geschichte der altchristlichen Literatur*	TU; TUGACL
TF	*Theologische Forschung*	
T.Gad	*Testament of Gad*	
TGE	*Trudy Gosudarstvennyj Ermitaz*	
Tg.Esth.I	*First Targum of Esther*	
Tg.Esth.II	*Second Targum of Esther*	
TGF	*Tragicorum graecorum fragmenta*	
TGI	K. Galling, *Textbuch zur Geschichte Israels*	
Tg.Isa.	*Targum of Isaiah*	
Tg.Ket.	*Targum of the Writings*	
TGl	*Theologie und Glaube*	ThGl
Tg.Neb.	*Targum of the Prophets*	
Tg.Neof.	*Targum Neofiti I*	
Tg.Onq.	*Targum Onqelos*	
Tg.Ps.-J.	*Targum Pseudo-Jonathan*	
Tg.Yer.I	*Targum Yerušalmi I*	
Tg.Yer.II	*Targum Yerušalmi II*	
Thal.	*Thallus*	
ThArb	*Theologische Arbeiten*	
THAT	E. Jenni and C. Westermann, eds., *Theologisches Handwörterbuch zum Alten Testament*	
THB	*Trierer Heimatbuch*	
ThBl	*Theologische Blätter*	TBl
ThEd	*Theological Educator*	
ThEH	*Theologische Existenz Heute*	
Them	*Themelios*	
Theod.	*Theodotus*	
Thera	*Excavations at Thera*	
THeth	*Texte der Hethiter*	
T.Hez.	*Testament of Hezekiah*	
ThGeg	*Theologie der Gegenwart*	
ThGl	*Theologie und Glaube*	TGl
ThH	*Theologie historique*	
ThJb	*Theologische Jahrbücher*	
THKNT	*Theologischer Handkommentar zum Neuen Testament*	
ThLZ	*Theologische Literaturzeitung*	TLZ
Thom.Cont.	*Book of Thomas the Contender* (NHC II,7)	
ThPh	*Theologie und Philosophie*	TP
ThQuart	*Theologische Quartalschrift*	TQ
ThRev	*Theologische Revue*	TRev
ThRunds	*Theologische Rundschau*	TRu
ThSe	*Theologie und Seelsorge*	
ThStud	*Theological Studies*	TS
ThStud	*Theologische Studien*	
Thund.	*The Thunder: Perfect Mind* (NHC VI,2)	
ThV	*Theologische Versuche*	
ThViat	*Theologia Viatorum*	
ThZeits	*Theologische Zeitschrift*	TZ
Tids	*Tidsskrift (journal)*	
TidsKonst	*Tidsskrift för Konstvetenskap*	
TidsMat	*Nyt Tidsskrift for Matematik*	
TIE	*Trudy Instituta etnografij*	
TijdGesch	*Tijdschrift voor Geschiedenis*	
TîjdPh	*Tijdschrift voor Philosophie*	
TijdRecht	*Tijdschrift voor rechtsgeschiedenis = Revue d'histoire du droit = Legal history review*	
TijdTheol	*Tijdschrift voor Theologie*	TvT
TIRS	*Travaux de l'Institut de recherches sahariennes*	
T.Isaac	*Testament of Isaac*	
T.Iss.	*Testament of Issachar*	
Tituli	*Tituli* (Rome)	
TJ	*Trinity Journal*	TrinJourn

Abbreviation	Citation	Abbreviation alternatives
T.Jac.	*Testament of Jacob*	
T.Job	*Testament of Job*	
T.Jos.	*Testament of Joseph*	
TJT	*Toronto Journal of Theology*	
T.Jud.	*Testament of Judah*	
TLB	*Theologisches Literaturblatt*	
T.Levi	*Testament of Levi*	
TLG	*Thesaurus linguae graecae*	
TLL	*Thesaurus linguae latinae*	
TLS	*The Times Literary Supplement*	
TLZ	*Theologische Literaturzeitung*	ThLZ
TMAI	*Trabajos del Museo Arqueologico de Ibiza*	
TMÉE	*Travaux du musée d'État de l'Ermitage* [Other name of TGE]	
TMO	*Travaux de la Maison de l'Orient*	
T.Mos.	*Testament of Moses*	
TMP	*Thèses des rapports présentés à la session scientifique consacrée au bilan des travaux du musée Pouchkine*	
T.Naph.	*Testament of Naphtali*	
TNB	*The New Blackfriars*	
TNL	*Travaux neuchâtelois de linguistique*	
TNTC	*Tyndale New Testament Commentary*	
Tob	*Tobit*	
Tôd	F. Bisson de la Roque, *Tôd 1934-36* (FIFAO 17)	
Tohar.	*Toharot*	
TOMS.E	*Triade Exploration's Opus Magnum Series in the field of Egyptology*	
TOO	*La Tour de l'Orle d'Or*	
Topoi (D)	*Topoi: An International Review of Philosophy* (Dordrecht)	
Topoi (L)	*Topoi orient-occident* (Lyon)	
TOTC	*Tyndale Old Testament Commentary*	
TP	*Theologie und Philosophie*	ThPh
TPAPA	*Transactions and Proceedings of the American Philological Association*	
TPNAH	J.D. Fowler, *Theophoric Personal Names in Ancient Hebrew* (JSOTSup 49)	
TPPI	J.J. Clère and J. Vandier, *Textes de la première periode intermédiaire et de la XIème dynastie*	
TPQ	*Theologisch-Praktische Quartalschrift*	
TPS	*Transactions of the Philological Society*	
TQ	*Theologische Quartalschrift*	ThQuart
TR	P. Lacau, *Textes Religieux Égyptiens*	
TrabPrehist	*Trabajos de Prehistoria*	
Trad	*Tradition*	
Trall.	*Ignatius, Letter to the Trallians*	Ign.Trall.
Trans.Int.Cong.Or.	*Transactions of the International Congress of Orientalists*	
Trans.Roy.Soc.Lit.	*Transactions of the Royal Society of Literature of the United Kingdom*	TRSL
Trans SBA	*Transactions of the Society of Biblical Archaeology*	TSBA
TravMém (L)	*Travaux et mémoires* (Université de Limoges)	
TravMém (P)	*Travaux et mémoires* (Centre de recherche d'histoire et civilisation de Byzance), Paris	
TRE	*Theologische Realenzyklopädie*	
Treat.Res.	*Treatise on Resurrection* (NHC I,4)	
Treat.Seth	*Second Treatise of the Great Seth* (NHC VII,2)	
Treat.Shem	*Treatise of Shem*	
TrésMon	*Trésors monétaires*	
T.Reu.	*Testament of Reuben*	
TRev	*Theologische Revue*	ThRev
TRIA	*Transactions of the Royal Irish Academy*	
Triadon	O. von Lemm, *Das Triadon*	
TRIBA	*Transactions of the Royal Institute of British Architects*	
TrierZeits	*Trierer Zeitschrift für Geschichte und Kunst des Trierer Landes und seiner Nachbargebiete*	
Trim.Prot.	*Trimorphic Protennoia* (NHC XIII,1)	
TrinJourn	*Trinity Journal*	TJ
Tri.Trac.	*Tripartite Tractate* (NHC I,5)	
TRSL	*Transactions of the Royal Society of Literature of the United Kingdom*	Trans.Roy.Soc.Lit
TRu	*Theologische Rundschau*	ThRunds
Trudy	*Gosudarstvennyi Ermitazh: Trudy Otdela Vostoka* (St. Petersburg)	
TrWPr	*Trierer Winckelmannsprogramme*	
TS	*Theological Studies*	ThStud
TSBA	*Transactions of the Society of Biblical Archaeology*	Trans SBA
T.Sim.	*Testament of Simeon*	
TSK	*Theologische Studien und Kritiken: Zeitschrift für gesamte Gebiet der Theologie*	
T.Sol.	*Testament of Solomon*	
TSSI	J.C.L. Gibson, *Textbook of Syrian Semitic Inscriptions*	
TT	*Teologisk Tidsskrift*	TTids
TT	*Theban Tomb no.*	

Abbreviation	Citation	Abbreviation alternatives
TTAE	*Türk Tarih: arkeologya ve etnografya dergisi*	
TTAO	*Textes et traductions d'auteurs orientaux*	
TTids	*Teologisk Tidsskrift*	TT
TTKi	*Tidsskrift for Teologie og Kirke*	
TTKY	*Türk Tarih Kurumu Kongresi Yayínlari*	
TToday	*Theology Today*	
TTS	*The Theban Tombs Series*	
TTS	*Trierer Theologische Studien*	
TTSO	*Tut^cankhamun's Tomb Series* (Oxford)	
TTZ	*Trierer theologische Zeitschrift*	
TU	*Texte und Untersuchungen zur Geschichte der altchristlichen Literatur*	TextUnt; TUGACL
TUAT	O. Kaiser, ed., *Texte aus der Umwelt des Alten Testaments*	
Tübingen, ÄS	*Ägyptische Sammlung* (Tübingen)	
TUGACL	*Texte und Untersuchungen zur Geschichte der altchristlichen Literatur*	TextUnt; TU
Turin Cat.	A. Fabretti et al., *Regio Museo di Torino: antichità egizie* (Catalogo generale dei Musei di Antiquità e degli oggetti d'arte raccolti nelle gallerie e biblioteche del Regno, ser. 1, 1-2)	CGT; Turin CG
TurkAnz	*Turkologischer Anzeiger*	
TV	*Teologia y Vida*	
TvT	*Tijdschrift voor Theologie*	TijdTheol
TWAT	G.J. Botterweck et al., eds., *Theologisches Wörterbuch zum Alten Testament*	
TWNT	G. Kittel, and G. Friedrich, eds., *Theologisches Wörterbuch zum Neuen Testament*	
Tyche-Suppl.	*Tyche Supplement* [Supplement to Tyche]	
Tylor-Griffith, *Paheri*	J.J. Tylor and F.Ll. Griffith, *The Tomb of Paheri at El Kab* (EEF 11)	
TynBul	*Tyndale Bulletin*	TyndBull
T.Yom	*Tebul Yom*	
TZ	*Theologische Zeitschrift*	ThZeits
T.Zeb.	*Testament of Zebulun*	
U.Äg., u.äg.	Unterägypten (Lower Egypt)	
UBSGNT	*United Bible Societies Greek New Testament*	
U.C.L.	University College London	London, U.C.; U.C.
UCLAM	*University of California at Los Angeles, Monograph*	
UCLAP	*University of California at Los Angeles, Occasional Paper*	
UCOP	*University of Cambridge Oriental Publications*	
UCPA	*University of California Publications in Archaeology*	
UCPCP	*University of California Publications in Classical Philology*	
UCPNES	*University of California Publications in Near Eastern Studies*	
UCPSP	*University of California Publications in Semitic Philology*	
U.E.	Upper Egypt	
UET	*Ur Excavations: Texts*	
UF	*Ugarit-Forschungen: Internationales Jarhbuch für die Altertumskunde Syrien-Palästinas*	Ugarit-Forschungen; UgForsch
Ug	Ugaritic	
UGA	*Urgeschichtlicher Anzeiger*	
UGAÄ	*Untersuchungen zur Geschichte und Altertumskunde Ägyptens*	Unters.
UgForsch	*Ugarit-Forschungen: Internationales Jarhbuch für die Altertumskunde Syrien-Palästinas*	UF; Ugarit-Forschungen
UGHAfr	*UNESCO General History of Africa*	
ÜgS	M. Noth, *Überlieferungsgeschichtliche Studien*	
UMB	*University (of Pennsylvania) Museum Bulletin*	UPMB
UMichS	*University of Michigan Studies*	
UMissS	*University of Missouri Studies*	
Una Sancta	*Una Sancta: Zeitschrift für ökumenische Begegnung*	
UngJb	*Ungarische Jahrbücher*	
UngRunds	*Ungarische Rundschau*	
UNT	*Untersuchungen zum Neuen Testament*	
Unters.	*Untersuchungen zur Geschichte und Altertumskunde Ägyptens*	UGAÄ
UntForsch	*Aus Unterricht und Forschung*	
UPMB	*University (of Pennsylvania) Museum Bulletin*	UMB
UPMJ	*University of Pennsylvania Museum Journal*	
UPZ	Wilcken, Ulrich, *Urkunden der Ptolemäerzeit*	
Uq.	*Uqsin*	
URAÄ	*Urkunden zum Rechtsleben im Alten Ägypten*	
Urk.	K. Sethe, *Urkunden des aegyptischen Altertums*	
US	*Una Sancta*	
USQR	*Union Seminary Quarterly Review*	
UT	C.H. Gordon, *Ugaritic Textbook* (AnOr 38. suppl)	
UTSR	*Union Theological Seminary Review*	
UUÅ	*Uppsala Universitets Årsskrift*	
VA	*Varia aegyptiaca*	VarAeg

Abbreviation	Citation	Abbreviation alternatives
VAB	*Verhandelingen van de koninklijke Akademie van België*	
VAB	*Vorderasiatische Bibliothek*	
VAHD	*Vjesnik za arheologiju i historiju Dalmatinsku*	
Val.Exp.	*A Valentintan Exposition* (NHC XI,2)	
VAMZ	*Vjesnik Arheoloskog muzeja u Zagrebu.*	
Vandier-d'Abbadie, oDeM	J. Vandier d'Abbadie, *Catalogue des ostraca figurées de Deir el Médineh* (DFIFAO 2)	
VarAeg	*Varia aegyptiaca*	VA
VAT	*Vorderasiatische Abteilung, Thontafelsammlung, Staatliche Museen zu Berlin*	
VAWA	*Verhandelingen der (Koninklijke)Akademie van Wetenschappen te Amsterdam*	
VBW	*Vorträge der Bibliothek Warburg*	
VC	*Vigilae christianae: Review of Early Christian Life and Language*	VigChr; VigChrist
VCaro	*Verbum Caro: Revue théologique et ecclésiastique*	VerbCar
VD	*Verbum Domini: Commentarii de re biblica*	VerbDom
VDI	*Vestnik Drevnei Istorii* Moscow	
VE	*Vox Evangilica*	
VerbCar	*Verbum Caro: Revue théologique et ecclésiastique*	VCaro
VerbDom	*Verbum Domini: Commentarii de re biblica*	
VergGeg	*Vergangenheit und Gegenwart: Zeitschrift für den Geschichtsunterricht und staatsbürgerliche Erziehung*	
VerkForsch	*Verkündigung und Forschung. Beihefte zu "Evangelische Theologie"*	VF
VetChr	*Vetera christianorum*	
VetTest	*Vetus Testamentum: Quarterly published by the International Organization of Old Testament Scholars*	VT
VetTest-Suppl.	*Vetus Testamentum Supplements* [Supplement to VetTest]	VTSup; VTSuppl
VF	*Verkündigung und Forschung. Beihefte zu "Evangelische Theologie"*	VerkForsch
Vg	Vulgate	
VGJ	*Vorgeschichtliches Jahrbuch*	
VHAD	*Viestnik Hrvatskoga arheoloskoga drustva*	
VHV	*Verhandlungen des historischen Vereins für Oberpfalz und Regensburg*	
VicOr	*Vicino Oriente: Annuario dell' Istituto di Studi del Vicino Oriente dell' Università di Roma*	
Vid	*Vidyajyoti*	
VIDM	*Voprosy istorii drevnego mira i srednikh vekov*	
VigChr	*Vigilae christianae: Review of Early Christian Life and Language*	VC; VigChrist
VIO	*Veröffentlichung der Institut für Orientforschung* (Deutsche Akademie der Wissenschaften zu Berlin)	
Virt	Philo, *De virtutibus*	
Vis.Ezra	*Vision of Ezra*	
Vis.Is.	*Vision of Isaiah*	
Vis.Paul	*Vision of Paul*	
VisRel	*Visible Religion: Annual for Religious Iconography*	
Vita	*Vita Adae et Evae*	
Vita C	Eusebius, *Vita Constantini*	
Vita Cont	Philo, *De vita contemplativa*	
Vita Mos I-II	Philo, *De vita Mosis I-II*	
VitLat	*Vita latina*	
VitPens	*Vita e Pensiero*	
VizOb	*Vizantiskoe Obozrenie*	
VKF	*Voprosy klassiçeskoj filologii*	
VKGNT	K. Aland, ed., *Vollständige Konkordanz zum griechischen Neuen Testament*	
VL	*Vetus Latina*	
VLUF	*Vestnik Leningradskogo Universiteta, Filosofiia*	
VLUIst	*Vestnik Leningradskogo Universiteta, Istoriia*	
VMAW	*Verslagen en Mededelingen der Koninklijk Akademie van Wetenschappen*	
VMMK	*A Vezprém Megyei Museumok Kozleményei*	
VMUF	*Vestnik Moskovskogo Universiteta, Filosofiia*	
VMUFil	*Vestnik Moskovskogo Universiteta, Filologia*	
VMUIst	*Vestnik Moskovskogo Universiteta, Istoriia*	
VoiceTurt	*The Voice of the Turtle* (Ancient Coin Club of America)	
Vopr	*Voprosy*	
VoprF	*Voprosy filosofii*	
VoprFil	*Voprosy filologii*	
VoprIst	*Voprosy istorii*	
VoprJaz	*Voprosy jazykoznanija*	
Vorsokr.	H. Diels, ed., *Fragmente der Vorsokrater*	

Abbreviation	Citation	Abbreviation alternatives
Vortr.Marburg	*Vorträge der orientalistischen Tagung von Marburg, Fachgruppe Ägyptologie*	
VoxLat	*Vox latina*	
VoxRom	*Vox romanica: Annales helvetici explorandis linguis romanicis destinati*	
VoxTh	*Vox theologica*	
Voyageurs	*Voyageurs occidentaux en Égypte*	
VR	*Vox Reformata*	
VS	*Vorderasiatische Schriftdenkmäler der königlichen Museen zu Berlin*	
V sessija	*V Vsesojuznaja sessija po drevnemu vostoku*	
v.Soden, AkkHwb	W. von Soden, *Akkadisches Handwörterbuch*	AHW
VSpir	*Vie spirituelle*	
VSS	*Videnskapsselskapet Skrifter*	
VSSF	*Videnskapsselskapet Skrifter, Forhandlinger*	
VSWG	*Vierteljahresschrift für Sozial- und Wirtschaftsgeschichte*	
VT	*Vetus Testamentum: Quarterly published by the International Organization of Old Testament Scholars*	VetTest
VTM	*Villes et tribus du Maroc*	
VTSup	*Vetus Testamentum Supplements* [Supplement to VetTest]	VetTest-Suppl.; VTSuppl
VVDP	*Verhandlungen der Versammlung deutscher Philologen und Schulmänner*	
WA	J.K.F. Knaake, ed., *Weimar Ausgabe = Martin Luthers Werke: Kritische Gesamtausgabe*	
WAC	*World Archaeological Congress*	
WAT	*Wagenbachs Taschenbücherei*	
WB	F. Preisigke, *Wörterbuch der griechischen Papyrusurkunden*	
Wb	A. Erman, and H. Grapow, eds., *Wörterbuch der ägyptischen Sprache*	
Wb Belegst.	A. Erman, and H. Grapow, eds., *Wörterbuch der ägyptischen Sprache, Die Belegstellen*	
WBC	*World Bible Commentary*	
WBFA	*Wiener Blätter für die Freunde der Antike*	
WBKL	*Wiener Beiträge zur Kulturgeschichte und Linguistik*	
WbMyth	H.W. Haussig, ed., *Wörterbuch der Mythologie*	
WC	*Westminster Commentaries*	
WD	*Wort und Dienst* (Bielefeld)	
WDB	*Westminster Dictionary of the Bible*	
WdO	*Die Welt des Orients: Wissenschaftliche Beiträge zur Kunde des Morgenlandes*	WeltOr; WO
WDZ	*Westdeutsche Zeitschrift für Geschichte und Kunst*	
Wehr	H. Wehr, *Dictionary of Modern Written Arabic*	
WeltGesch	*Die Welt als Geschichte: Zeitschrift für Universalgeschichte*	
WeltIsl	*Die Welt des Islams: internationale Zeitschrift für die Entwicklungsgeschichte des Islams, besonders in der Gegenwart*	
WeltOr	*Die Welt des Orients: Wissenschaftliche Beiträge zur Kunde des Morgenlandes*	WdO; WO
Westendorf, *Med.Gramm.*	W. Westendorf, *Grammatik der medizinischen Texte* (Grundriß der Medizin 8)	
WF	*Wege der Forschung*	
WGI	J. Wellhausen, *Geschichte Israels* [See also WPGI, and WPHI]	
WHAB	*Westminster Historical Atlas of the Bible*	
WHB	*Wiener humanistische Blätter*	
Whitaker	R.E. Whitaker, *A Concordance of the Ugaritic Literature*	
WHJP	*World History of the Jewish People*	
Wien Anz.	*Österreichische Akademie der Wissenschaften, Anzeiger* (Vienna)	
WienJh	*Wiener Jahreshefte*	
WienStud	*Wiener Studien: Zeitschrift fur klassische philologie und Patristik*	
WilbMon	*Wilbour Monographs*	WM
Wild, *Ti*	H. Wild, *Le tombeau de Ti* (MIFAO 65)	
Wis	*Wisdom of Solomon*	
WissGlaub	*Wissen und Glauben*	
WJA	*Würzburger Jahrbücher für die Altertumswissenschaft*	WürzJb
WJKG	*Wiener Jahrbuch für Kunstgeschichte*	
WKP	*Wochenschrift für klassische Philologie*	
WLSGF	C.L. Meyers, and M. O'Connor, eds., *The Word of the Lord Shall Go Forth: Essays in Honor of David Noel Freedman*	Fs Freedman
WM	*Wilbour Monographs*	WilbMon
WMANT	*Wissenschaftliche Monographien zum Alten und Neuen Testament*	
WMBH	*Wissenschaftliche Mitteilungen aus Bosnien und Hercegowina*	

Abbreviation	Citation	Abbreviation alternatives
WO	*Die Welt des Orients: Wissenschaftliche Beiträge zur Kunde des Morgenlandes*	WdO; WeltOr
WoAr	*World Archaeology*	WorldArch
Wor	*Worship* (Collegeville, MN)	Wor
WordWorld	*Word & World* (St. Paul, MN)	WW
WorldArch	*World Archaeology*	WoAr
WörtSach	*Wörter und Sachen*	
WPGI	J. Wellhausen, *Prolegomena zur Geschichte Israels*	
WPHI	J. Wellhausen, *Prolegomena to the History of Israel*	
WPZ	*Wiener prähistorische Zeitschrift*	
Wresz., *Atlas*	W. Wreszinski, *Atlas zur altägyptischen Kulturgeschichte*	
WS	*World and Spira*	
WSÄ	*Wissenschaftliche Schriftenreihe Ägyptologie*	
WTJ	*Westminster Theological Journal*	
WTM	J. Levy, *Wörterbuch über die Talmudim und Midraschim*	
WTS	E. Littmann, and M. Höfner, *Wörterbuch der Tigre-Sprache*	
WuD	*Wort und Dienst* (Bielefeld)	WD
WUNT	*Wissenschaftliche Untersuchungen zum Neuen Testament*	
WürzJb	*Würzburger Jahrbücher für die Altertumswissenschaft*	WJA
WUS	J. Aistleitner, *Wörterbuch der ugaritischen Sprache* (BSAW 106/3)	
WUS	*Washington University Studies*	
WuW	*Wissenschaft und Weisheit*	
WVDOG	*Wissenschaftliche Veröffentlichungen der Deutschen Orientgesellschaft*	
WVPM	*Wissenschaftliche Veröffentlichung(en) des Pelizaeus-Museums zu Hildesheim*	
WW	*Word & World* (St. Paul, MN)	WordWorld
WZ	*Wissenschaftliche Zeitschrift*	
WZB	*Wissenschaftliche Zeitschrift der Humboldt-Universität* (Berlin)	
WZG	*Wissenschaftliche Zeitschrift der Ernst-Moritz-Arndt-Universität* (Greifswald)	
WZH	*Wissenschaftliche Zeitschrift der Martin-Luther-Universität* Halle-Wittenberg	WZMLU
WZJ	*Wissenschaftliche Zeitschrift der Friedrich-Schille-Universität* Jena	
WZKM	*Wiener Zeitschrift für die Kunde des Morgenlandes*	
WZKSO	*Wiener Zeitschrift für die Kunde Süd und Ostasiens*	
WZL	*Wissenschaftliche Zeitschrift der Karl-Marx-Universität* (Leipzig)	

Abbreviation	Citation	Abbreviation alternatives
WZMLU	*Wissenschaftliche Zeitschrift der Martin-Luther-Universität* (Halle-Wittenberg)	WZH
WZR	*Wissenschaftliche Zeitschrift der Wilhelm-Pieck-Universität* (Rostock)	
WZV	*Wiener Zeitschrift für Volkskunde*	
Yad.	*Yadayim*	
YAJ	*Yorkshire Archaeological Journal*	
Yal.	*Yalqut*	
YarmNum	*Yarmuk Numismatics*	
YCS	*Yale Classical Studies*	
Yebam.	*Yebamot*	
Yediot	*Yediot* [Continues BIES, Continued by Qadmoniot]	
Yem.Tg.	*Yemenite Targum*	
YES	*Yale Egyptological Studies*	
YGC	W.F. Albright, *Yahweh and the Gods of Canaan*	
YJS	*Yale Judaica Series*	
YNER	*Yale Near Eastern Researches*	
YOS	*Yale Oriental Series*	
YULG	*Yale University Library Gazette*	
YWA	*The Year's Work in Archaeology*	
YWCS	*The Year's Work in Classical Studies*	
ZA	*Zeitschrift für Assyriologie und verwandte Gebiete*	ZAVG
ZAH	*Zeitschrift für Althebräistik*	
ZAK	*Zeitschrift für schweizerische Archäologie und Kunstgeschichte*	
ZÄK	*Zeitschrift für Ästhetik und allgemeine Kunstwissenschaft*	
ZAL	*Zeitschrift für arabische Linguistik*	
ZÄS	*Zeitschrift für Ägyptische Sprache und Altertumskunde*	ÄZ
ZASS	*Zentralasiatische Studien des Seminars für Sprach- und Kulturwissenschaft Zentralasiens der Universität Bonn*	
ZATW	*Zeitschrift für die Alttestamentliche Wissenschaft*	ZAW
ZAVA	*Zeitschrift für Assyriologie und vorderasiatische Archäologie*	
ZAVG	*Zeitschrift für Assyriologie und verwandte Gebiete*	ZA
ZAW	*Zeitschrift für die Alttestamentliche Wissenschaft*	ZATW
ZB	*Zürcher Bibelkommentare*	
ZBB	*Zentralblatt für Bibliothekswesen*	
ZBK	*Zeitschrift für bildende Kunst*	
ZCK	*Zeitschrift für christliche Kunst*	
ZCP	*Zeitschrift für celtische Philologie*	
ZDA	*Zeitschrift für deutsches Altertum*	
ZDMG	*Zeitschrift der Deutschen Morgenländischen Gesellschaft*	

Abbreviation	Citation	Abbreviation alternatives
ZDPV	*Zeitschrift des Deutschen Palästina-Vereins*	
ZE	*Zeitschrift für Ethnologie*	ZeitEthn
Zebah.	*Zebahim*	
Zech	*Zechariah*	
ZEE	*Zeitschrift für evangelische Ethik*	
ZeitArch	*Zeitschrift für Archäologie*	
ZeitBalk	*Zeitschrift für Balkonologie*	
ZeitEthn	*Zeitschrift für Ethnologie*	ZE
ZeitNum	*Zeitschrift für Numismatik*	
ZeitPsy	*Zeitschrift für Psychologie*	
ZeitSemiot	*Zeitschrift für Semiotik*	
ZeitSemit	*Zeitschrift für Semitistik*	
ZeitVölk	*Zeiten und Völker*	
Zeph	*Zephaniah*	
Zer.	*Zera'im*	
ZFDF	*Zeitschrift für freie deutsche Forschung*	
ZGAIW	*Zeitschrift für Geschichte der arabisch-islamischen Wissenschaften*	
ZGE	*Zeitschrift der Gesellschaft für Erdkunde*	
ZGO	*Zeitschrift für die Geschichte des Oberrheins*	
ZGW	*Zeitschrift für das Gymnasialwesen*	
ZHT	*Zeitschrift für historische Theologie*	
ZiAn	*Ziva antika*	ZivAnt
ZJKF	*Zprávy jednoty klasickych filologu*	
ZKF	*Zeitschrift für Keilschriftforschung und verwandte Gebiete*	
ZKG	*Zeitschrift für Kunstgeschichte*	
ZKirchG	*Zeitschrift für Kirchengeschichte*	
ZKT	*Zeitschrift für katholische Theologie*	
ZKV	*Zopiski Kollegii Vostokovedov = Mémoires du Comité des orientalistes*	
ZMK	*Zeitschrift für Missionskunde und Religionswissenschaft*	ZMR
ZMNP	*Žurnal Ministertsvo Narodnogo Prosvescenija*	
ZMR	*Zeitschrift für Missionskunde und Religionswissenschaft*	ZMK
ZNF	*Zeitschrift für Namenforschung* [Continues ZONF]	
ZNTW	*Zeitschrift für neutestamentliche Wissenschaft*	Zs.f.nt.Wiss.
ZNW	*Zeitschrift für die neutestamentliche Wissenschaft*	

Abbreviation	Citation	Abbreviation alternatives
ZÖG	*Zeitschrift für die österreichischen Gymnasien*	
ZÖM	*Zeitschrift für die österreichischen Mittelschulen*	
ZONF	*Zeitschrift für Ortsnamenforschung* [Continued by ZNF]	
Zost.	*Zostrianos* (NHC VIII,1)	
ZPE	*Zeitschrift für Papyrologie und Epigraphik*	
ZPF	*Zeitschrift für philosophische Forschung*	
ZPKT	*Zeitschrift für Philosophie und Katholische Theologie*	
ZRG	*Zeitschrift für Religions- und Geistesgeschichte*	ZRGG
ZRK	*Zeitschrift für Rassenkunde*	
ZRP	*Zeitschrift für romanische Philologie*	
ZSF	*Zeitschrift für Sozialforschung*	
Zs.f.nt.Wiss.	*Zeitschrift für neutestamentliche Wissenschaft*	ZNTW
ZSG	*Zeitschrift für schweizerische Geschichte*	
ZSSR	*Zeitschrift der Savigny-Stiftung für Rechtsgeschichte*	
ZST	*Zeitschrift für systematische Theologie*	
ZSVG	*Zeitschrift für Semitistik und verwandte Gebiete*	
ZTK	*Zeitschrift für Theologie und Kirche*	
ZV	*Zeitschrift für Volkskunde*	ZVK
ZVB	*Zeitschrift des deutschen Vereins für Buchwesen und Schrifttum*	
ZVK	*Zeitschrift für Volkskunde*	ZV
ZVR	*Zeitschrift für Vergleichende Rechtswissenschaft*	
ZVS	*Zeitschrift für Vergleichende Sprachforschung*	
ZVV	*Zeitschrift des Vereins für Volkskunde*	
ZWF	*Zeitschrift für deutsche Wortforschung*	
ZWG	*Sudhoffs Archiv: Zeitschrift für Wissenschaftsgeschichte*	SA; SudAr
ZWT	*Zeitschrift für wissenschaftliche Theologie*	
ZwZt	Zwischenzeit (intermediate period)	
ZycMysl	*Zycie i Mysl*	

Fronted Adverbials

John Gee

Standard Theory

In the standard theory laid down by Polotsky, the purpose of the second tenses is to emphasize the adverbial adjunct.[1] The usual way to emphasize the adverbial adjunct in English translations is to front the adverbial adjunct in a cleft sentence.[2] Emphasis and fronting are thus equated on some level. Since "the emphasized adverbial adjunct as a rule (with the exception of *n*- with suffixes) occupies rear position"[3] it is incompatible with fronting, hence the need of a special verb form to emphasize it. The purpose of this article is point out a rather peculiar phenomenon that might have a bearing on Polotsky's standard theory. First, however, it will be worthwhile to see how this theory was developed.

In 1944, Polotsky published his *Études de syntaxe copte*.[4] The second study in this work was devoted to the second tense. He opened this study with the following observation: "On rencontre assez fréquemment deux phrases successives, toutes deux ayant même sujet et même verbe, mais dont la seconde possède, au surplus, un complément adverbial fortement mis en relief. Il peut s'agir ou de deux phrases principales dont la seconde apporte une précision à la première, ou bien d'une combinaison de proposition subordonnée (conditionnelle, temporelle, relative) et de phrase principale. De toute manière la seconde phrase est toujours une principale. Or, en copte, le verbe de cette seconde phrase exige régulièrement un des Temps Seconds, tandis que la première a l'un des Premiers, à moins que le type de la proposition ne réclame une forme verbale particulière où la dualité des séries n'existe pas (ⲉϥϣⲁⲛ-, ⲛⲧⲉⲣⲉϥ-, relative)."[5]

Polotsky demonstrated that the Coptic second tense originated in the Late Egyptian *iir* form.[6] Then he extended the form into Middle Egyptian.[7]

Polotsky began his study with the Coptic and Greek versions of 2 Corinthians 4:3 (Greek:

1 Among many possible places, see H.J. Polotsky, "Egyptian Tenses," *The Israel Academy of Sciences and Humanities* 2/5 (1965), 9, henceforth Polotsky, "Egyptian Tenses."
2 Polotsky, "Egyptian Tenses," 8.
3 Polotsky, "Egyptian Tenses," 8.
4 H.J. Polotsky, *Études de syntaxe copte* (Cairo, 1944), henceforth Polotsky, *Études de syntaxe copte*.
5 Polotsky, *Études de syntaxe copte*, 24.
6 Polotsky, *Études de syntaxe copte*, 69-78.
7 Polotsky, *Études de syntaxe copte*, 78-98.

εἰ δὲ καὶ ἔστιν κεκαλυμμένον τὸ εὐαγγέλιον ἡμῶν, ἐν τοῖς ἀπολλυμένοις ἔστιν κεκαλυμμένον; Sahidic: **ⲉϣϫⲉ ⲡⲉⲛⲕⲉⲉⲩⲁⲅⲅⲉⲗⲓⲟⲛ ϩⲟⲃⲥ· ⲉϥϩⲟⲃⲥ ⲛⲛⲉⲧⲛⲁⲧⲁⲕⲟ**; Bohairic: **ⲓⲥϫⲉ ⲇⲉ ϥⲉⲣⲡⲕⲉϩⲏⲡ ⲛϫⲉ ⲡⲉⲛⲉⲩⲁⲅⲅⲉⲗⲓⲟⲛ· ⲁϥϩⲏⲡ ϧⲉⲛ ⲛⲏ ⲉⲟⲛⲁⲧⲁⲕⲟ**) which he compared with French and Arabic translations (Calmet, 1730: Que si l'Évangile que nous prêchons, est encore voilé, c'est pour ceux qui périssent qu'il est voilé; Allo, 1937: Si portant il est encore voilé, notre évangile, c'est chez ceux qui se perdent qu'il est voilé).[8] He noted especially that the French translation of the passage used "la construction française *c'est . . . que . . .*"[9] and the French translation of this one passage with a cleft sentence (phrase coupée) would play a dominant role in his interpretation and translation of the second tense. Polotsky did not provide any of the English translations of this verse, which are enlightening:

"For if also our gospel is covered, or hid, in these that perish it is covered." (Wycliffe, 1384)

"Yff oure gospell be yet hid, it is hid amonge them that are lost" (Tyndale, 1526)

"But if our gospel be hid, it is hid to them that are lost" (King James Version, 1611)

"And even if our gospel is veiled, it is veiled in them that perish." (American Standard Version, 1901)

"And even if our gospel is veiled, it is veiled only to those who are perishing." (Revised Standard Version, 1952)

I have limited citations to readily available English versions before and up to a decade after Polotsky's work. None of these English translations use a cleft sentence the way the French versions did. This might suggest that in contrast to French translations, a cleft sentence might not be the most appropriate way to render the second tense into English.

Polotsky noted that the cleft sentence was used in "classical Arabic, Amharic (and other neo-Ethiopian languages), French, English."[10] He then argued that the Egyptian second tense was the equivalent of the cleft sentence in these other languages.[11] He gave two and a half pages of English citations to illustrate the use of the cleft sentence,[12] because "our lectures are heard more in this language than in French"[13] but he failed to provide references for the passages he cited. Polotsky argued that in the English cleft sentence, the clefted part was the logical predicate.[14] Polotsky and his followers would argue that the part of the sentence set off by "it is" was emphasized. A more careful look at the Shakespearian examples Polotsky used shows problems with this analysis:

"'Tis *not the king* that sends you to the Tower; / *My Lady Grey his wife*, Clarence, 'tis *she*

---

8 Polotsky, *Études de syntaxe copte*, 24-26.
9 Polotsky, *Études de syntaxe copte*, 26.
10 Polotsky, *Études de syntaxe copte*, 57.
11 Polotsky, *Études de syntaxe copte*, 58-59.
12 Polotsky, *Études de syntaxe copte*, 60-62.
13 Polotsky, *Études de syntaxe copte*, 58.
14 Polotsky, *Études de syntaxe copte*, 58-59.

/ That tempers him to this extremity."[15]

"'Tis *Joan, not we*, by whom the day is won; / for which I will divide my crown with her, / And all the priests and friars in my realm / Shall in procession sing her endless praise."[16]

"If't be *th' affliction of his love or no* / That thus he suffers for."[17]

In these Shakespearian examples, it is not for emphasis but the contrasting of two possibilities that the cleft sentence construction is used. The use of a fronting is not necessarily for emphasis. In English "the proper place in the sentence for the word or group of words that the writer desires to make most prominent is usually the end."[18] Thus the rule is to "place the emphatic words of a sentence at the end."[19] From the idea of placing a negative expression (which is emphatic by nature) first "comes the mistaken idea that they derive emphasis from their position."[20] Placing words first in a sentence is "not always in order to emphasize the words so placed, but merely to give an impressive effect to the whole."[21] The rhetorical term for unusual word order, such as fronting, is *hyperbaton*. Although fronting is well known in Egyptian,[22] hyperbaton in Egyptian is not necessarily to be equated with emphasis. The best known example of non-emphatic hyperbaton is found in Shipwrecked Sailor 104-5:

nwy.t im=f nt mḥ 8 "waves were in it, of eight cubits."

Here the preposition phrase is moved forward to interrupt the genitival construction but the rhetorical purpose does not seem to be to emphasize the prepositional phrase. If it were, according to Polotskian theory it should read **wnn nwy.t nt mḥ 8 im=f*. So whatever the situation might be in Egyptian, words to be emphasized in English should be placed in a sentence not at the beginning but at the end.

In 1957, Polotsky published his paper on the emphatic *sḏm.n=f*.[23] In this paper, he argued that although in Middle Egyptian all *sḏm.n=f* forms will look morphologically the same, the fact that Late Egyptian and Coptic show two distinct descendant forms, one of which was emphatic, that there should be an emphatic *sḏm.n=f* in Middle Egyptian.[24] Polotsky used the passive forms to argue that the emphatic *sḏm.n=f* existed; the unemphatic passive past tense being the passive *sḏm=f*, whereas the emphatic form is the *sḏm.n.tw=f*.[25] Polotsky argued "if the *sḏm.n.tw.f* is **always** 'emphatic', it follows, since the *sḏm.n.tw.f* is merely an extension of *sḏm.n.f*, that *sḏm.n.f*

---

15 William Shakespeare, *Richard III* I.i.63-65; Polotsky, *Études de syntaxe copte*, 60.

16 William Shakespeare, *1 Henry VI* I.vi.17-20; Polotsky, *Études de syntaxe copte*, 61.

17 William Shakespeare, *Hamlet* III.i.35-36; Polotsky, *Études de syntaxe copte*, 61.

18 William Strunk, Jr., and E.B. White, *The Elements of Style*, 3rd ed. (New York, 1972), 32.

19 Strunk and White, *Elements of Style*, 32.

20 H.W. Fowler and F.G. Fowler, *The King's English* (Ware, Hertfordshire, 1993), 199.

21 Fowler and Fowler, *King's English*, 199-200.

22 Many examples gathered in A.H. Gardiner, *Egyptian Grammar*, 3rd ed. (Oxford, 1957), 115-116.

23 H.J. Polotsky, "The 'Emphatic' *sḏm.n.f* form," *RdÉ* 11 (1957) 109-117, henceforth Polotsky, "The 'Emphatic' *sḏm.n.f* form."

24 Polotsky, "The 'Emphatic' *sḏm.n.f* form," 109-110.

25 Polotsky, "The 'Emphatic' *sḏm.n.f* form," 110-114.

can **sometimes** be 'emphatic'."[26] He went on to state that this result was of "no great practical importance":[27] "For practical philological work and for elementary teaching the consequences of this conclusion are negligible, because there can never be absolute certainty about any individual case."[28]

In 1965, Polotsky published his article on Egyptian tenses.[29] In this article, he claimed that the "initial position, which seems the obvious first choice, is not a suitable point from which to start our inquiry."[30] Looking at verbs in clauses of circumstance,[31] instead, Polotsky determined that these are subordinate clauses.[32] Polotsky also argued that initial verbs of motion are emphatic,[33] as are bare initial *sḏm.n=f* forms of transitive verbs,[34] because they are followed by circumstantial clauses. Polotsky expressed his "conviction that the indicative ('narrative') 'imperfective' *sḏm.f* (*mrr.f*) is a mere ghost-form which has been suffered to haunt Egyptian grammar long enough."[35]

Polotsky's student, Ariel Shisha-Halevy, collected a number of clear examples of second tenses that have no possible adverbial adjuncts to emphasize.[36] Unfortunately if, in Shisha-Halevy's terms, the second tenses were "the Sleeping Beauty among Coptic grammatical categories,"[37] Shisha-Halevy has surrounded it not with a wall of thorns but with his impenetrable prose which has prevented Egyptologists from reading or understanding his work. Shisha-Halevy also pointed out that Polotsky's arguments were circular and unsubstantiated by outside evidence, that the second tenses were not necessarily nominal, and that Polotsky failed to situate his analyses of small units in their larger context.[38]

Problematic Evidence

If Polotsky's understanding of grammar has had success, it is because in a large number of cases, it seems to work very well. Unfortunately, some cases are not explained by the standard theory. As the standard theory explains the existence of second tenses by Egyptian's inability to front adverbial expressions, the existence of fronted adverbials presents something of a problem

26 Polotsky, "The 'Emphatic' *sḏm.n.f* form," 115.
27 Polotsky, "The 'Emphatic' *sḏm.n.f* form," 114.
28 Polotsky, "The 'Emphatic' *sḏm.n.f* form," 114.
29 Polotsky, "Egyptian Tenses."
30 Polotsky, "Egyptian Tenses," 2.
31 Polotsky, "Egyptian Tenses," 2-7.
32 Polotsky, "Egyptian Tenses," 2-10.
33 Polotsky, "Egyptian Tenses," 10-16.
34 Polotsky, "Egyptian Tenses," 16-19.
35 Polotsky, "Egyptian Tenses," 23.
36 A. Shisha-Halevy, *Coptic Grammatical Categories, Structural Studies in the Syntax of Shenoutean Sahidic,* AnOr 53 (Rome, 1986), 76-79, henceforth Shisha-Halevy, *Coptic Grammatical Categories*.
37 Shisha-Halevy, *Coptic Grammatical Categories*, 62.
38 Shisha-Halevy, *Coptic Grammatical Categories*, 63-64.

for it. I will present four anomalous examples (out of many possible), that indicate the presence of the fronted adverbial: two each of fronted prepositional phrases and fronted circumstantial clauses. I begin with examples from the later stages of the language because in these stages there is less ambiguity in verbal forms.

I. What happens when the grammar contradicts the logic of the situation? A problem comes up when we have to decide with which sentence certain phrases belong. For example:

> *ir=w ḏḏy iir=w ii iw in=w s m-bꜣḥ pr-ꜥꜣ* ***n tꜣy ḥty*** *ḏ n=f pr-ꜥꜣ ꜥnḫ-ššnqy sꜣ ṯꜣy-nfr in wnm=k pꜣy=y ꜥq sḏm=k tꜣy bn.t iw bn-pw=k ii r di gm=y ḏ st bny* (P. Onch. 3/20-22)

Does the phrase *n tꜣy ḥty* "at that moment" belong at the end of the first sentence: "They ran and, bringing him before Pharaoh, they returned," or with the second sentence: "Pharaoh said to him: Onchsheshonqy son of Tjaynefer, did you eat my bread so that you could hear this evil thing without coming to let me discover that they were evil?"

If we follow the standard Polotskian grammar, then we are compelled to group this phrase with the first sentence and to translate it (with the second tense emphasizing the adverbial adjunct): "they ran and it was at that moment that they returned**,** bringing him before Pharaoh."[39] So the servants brought him back at the moment that they ran off: an absurd situation. On the other hand, if the phrase goes with the second sentence then Pharaoh asks Onchsheshonqy his question as soon as he is brought in. If we follow the sense of the story, we chose the second option, which violates the standard grammar. This is what both Glanville and Lichtheim have done in their translations.[40] So a prepositional phrase can be fronted.

II. Now consider the following phrase from the Setne story: *iw bw ir=y sḫ* "because I have always been illiterate" (P. Setne I 4/3).[41] Should this statement go with the one before or after? Grammar tells us that, as a clearly marked circumstantial clause, it should go with the sentence preceding:

> *ꜥš=y ky hpe n sḫ nw=y r pꜣ-rꜥ iw=f ḫꜥ n tꜣ p.t irm tꜣy=f psḏ.t nw=y r pꜣ iꜥḥ iw=f wbn irm nꜣ syw.w n tꜣ p.t ḏr=w irm pꜣy=w gy nw=y r nꜣ rym.w n pꜣ mty iw wn mḥ n nṯr 21 n mw tꜣy=w ri.t ḥry.t* "I read another written text and I saw the sun rising in the sky with his council of gods, I saw the moon rising with all the stars of heaven with their forms and I saw the fishes of the deep even though there were twenty-one divine cubits of water above them." (P. Setne I 4/1-3)

The concession of the circumstantial clause—"because I was always illiterate"— simply undermines the remainder of the previous statement: Ihwere read the text because she was illiterate. With the following statement, however, it makes good sense:

> *wn-nꜣw iw=y ḏ r nꜣ-nfr-kꜣ-ptḥ pꜣy=y sn ꜥꜣ nt iw sḫ nfr rmṯ-rḫ m-sš pꜣy di=f in=w wꜥ.t šꜥṯ.t*

[39] Compare H.J. Thissen, *Die Lehre des Anchscheschonqi (P. BM 10508)* (Bonn, 1984), 17.

[40] S.R.K. Glanville, *The Instructions of `Onchsheshonqy (British Museum Papyrus 10508)*, Catalogue of Demotic Papyri in the British Museum 2 (London, 1955), 11; M. Lichtheim, *Ancient Egyptian Literature* 3 (Berkeley, 1980), 162.

[41] See now, S. Goldbrunner, *Der verblendete Gelehrte* (Sommerhausen, 2006), Tf. 3.

n ḏmꜥ n-mꜣy iir-ḥr=f sẖ=f md.t nb r-wn-nꜣw pꜣ ḏmꜥ iir-ḥr=f ḏr=w di=f mḥ=f n sty wty=f s ẖr mw rẖ=f s iw-wꜣḥ=f wyt s swr=f s rẖ=f r pꜣy-wn-nꜣw iw=f n-im=f

"I should have said that Naneferkaptah, my older brother who is a good and wise scribe, placed a piece of new papyrus before himself so that he could write all the words which were on the scroll before him, and that he might set it on fire and dissolve it in water so that he might know it was dissolved so that he might drink it and know what was on it." (P. Setne I 4/3-4)

Prefaced to this sentence, the clause about Ihweret's illiteracy becomes a preface to an explanation of how she was able to read the scroll even though she was illiterate. Appended to the previous sentence, it becomes a refutation of the statement just made. The circumstantial clause goes with the following sentence, and so here again we have a fronted adverbial clause, in this case a circumstantial clause.

III. My next example is from an understudied ritual called the Ritual of expelling the angry one. It comes at the beginning of the ritual so there is no question about which sentence the adverbial clause belongs to:

ḏd-mdw
pr.n=i m iwnw ir.t-ḥr m-ḫt=i
iw ir=i pr n iwnw iw tꜣ ir.t-ḥr irm=i (*Urk.* VI 63)

Now, with the Middle Egyptian version, we think we have a straight forward analysis. By the standard theory the *sḏm=f* form is obviously a second tense, nominal, or emphatic form (whichever one wishes to call it) and the second clause is obviously the emphasized adverbial adjunct. That, however, is not how the ancient Egyptians analyzed the sentence, as is clear from the Late Egyptian translation. In Late Egyptian the nominal/emphatic/second tense is always clearly marked with the verb *iir*. In this case, however, the sentence is introduced with the particle *iw* followed by the *sḏm=f* form of the verb *pri*, and in Late Egyptian that can only mean the circumstantial past form of the verb. So the ancient Egyptians, who knew their language much better than we do, considered the verb in the Middle Egyptian version to be a circumstantial *sḏm.n=f*. This, however, is the very beginning of the ritual and the first thing said. So a circumstantial *sḏm.n=f* can stand as the initial verbal form in a sentence, which completely refutes Polotsky's arguments in his article on Egyptian Tenses. Be that as it may, this is another example of a fronted adverbial, in this case a clause with a circumstantial verbal form that can come first in a sentence. The translation must be "When I came forth from Heliopolis, when the eye of Horus was with me. . ."

Polotsky, in his article on Egyptian Tenses, does say that in many cases "literal translation would sound too unnatural to be of any use."[42] He says that "in such cases the relatively best solution is to make a subordinate clause of the initial verb-form and to turn the clause of circumstance into main sentences."[43] Polotsky's sense of the meaning and translation of such

[42] Polotsky, "Egyptian Tenses," 10.
[43] Polotsky, "Egyptian Tenses," 8.

passages is correct.

IV. For my next example, I take Chicago Hawara Papyrus I (P. OI 17481), which begins as follows:

ḥsb.t 17 ibt 2 ꜣḫ.t n Pr-ꜥꜣ Nḫt-nb=f ḏ ḫtmw-nṯr wyt ꜥnḫ-mr-wr . . . n sḥm.t psṯ

"On year 17, second month of inundation of Pharaoh Nectanebo, the god's sealer and embalmer Ankhmerwer said . . . to the woman Peset . . . (P. OI 17481, line 1).[44]

The document begins with a date followed by a simple statement with an indicative *sḏm=f.* Expressions of time frequently omit the preposition,[45] as is the case here. Here then is another example of a fronted adverbial expression. Because the second tense is clearly and unambiguously marked in Demotic, it is clear that the verb is not a second tense but rather a simple indicative *sḏm=f.* There is nothing exceptional about this document, it is simply a standard contract, and that is the point. All standard contracts begin the same way, with a fronted adverbial. One can easily produce hundreds of examples.[46] Furthermore, the same type of beginning can be found in many royal and historical documents. Again one can easily produce hundreds of examples. Gardiner preferred to see these as examples of nouns with the function of a sentence.[47] Their use, however, serves to specify the time at which the action of the main verb takes place. They thus modify the verb that follows them and are adverbial to it. That makes them part of the sentence that follows them. Fronted adverbials thus turn out to be extremely common, if not ubiquitous.

Gardiner provided three examples of fronted adverbials, two from the New Kingdom and one from the Middle Kingdom. These are worth examining as well.

V. From the Annals of Thutmosis III, we read the following:

wn.in=sn nfr ḥr ib n ḥm=f r ḫt nb.t ***m-ḫt nn*** *wḏꜣ ḥm=f r šnꜥ n wdn* (*Urk.* IV 685)

The prepositional phrase *m-ḫt nn* "after this" makes much more sense with the sentence that follows "his majesty went to the treasury of offerings" rather than the one that proceeds "they were more desirable to his majesty's mind than anything." Both Gardiner[48] and Sethe[49] have taken it so.

VI. The next example comes from CCG 34012:

iw ḥtp.n nṯr st=f wr.t ***m-ḫt nn*** *wḏꜣ nb=i r sḫꜣt it=f imn* (*Urk.* IV 836)

Here again, the prepositional phrase "after this" marks a transition to a new phase of the narrative

---

44 G.R. Hughes and R. Jasnow, *Oriental Institute Hawara Papyri: Demotic and Greek Texts from an Egyptian Family Archive in the Fayum (Fourth to Third Century B.C.)*, OIP 113 (Chicago, 1997), 9.

45 A.H. Gardiner, *Egyptian Grammar*, 67: "Indications of *time* are often expressed by a noun used absolutely, i.e. without preposition."

46 As a starting point, simply consult M. Depauw, *A Chronological Survey of Precisely Dated Demotic and Abnormal Hieratic Sources*, Version 1.0 February 2007 (Cologne and Louvain, 2008) or the older P.W. Pestman, *Chronologie égyptienne d'après les textes démotiques (332 av. J.-C. – 453 ap. J.-C.)* (Leiden, 1967).

47 Gardiner, *Egyptian Grammar*, 115 and 67-68.

48 Gardiner, *Egyptian Grammar*, 115.

49 *Urk.* IV, 685.

action and goes with the following sentence "my lord proceeded to cause his father Amun to appear" rather than with the sentence before "the god rested in his shrine."[50]

VII. Gardiner's final example comes from a letter from the Illahun archive:

mk in-g3w-n wpwty ꜥ3 ḥnꜥ=i iw 3 rdi.n=i iwt=f r int n=i smi m rḫ=k[51]

The introductory particle *mk* sets this off as a new sentence. As Gardiner recognized, *in-g3w-n* must be the prepositional phrase "through lack of."[52] Gardiner only translated the first part noting "translation dubious": "behold, through lack of a messenger here with me I have caused him to come."[53] Collier and Quirke translated: "Look, because of the lack of a messenger here with me I could hardly have sent him to bring me a report of your opinion."[54] Even Wente translated: "Because for a want of a messenger here with me, I couldn't send one to bring me back a reply with your opinion."[55] Thus all of the translators of this passage have taken this as a fronted prepositional phrase. There is nothing else it could be.

Dilemmas

This paper ends in dilemmas rather than conclusions. I have tried to argue for the existence of something rather than its interpretation, which I leave to others. Fronted adverbials not only exist in ancient Egyptian but are common. Both prepositional phrases and circumstantial clauses can be fronted. If the second tense emphasizes an adverbial adjunct, then a cleft sentence is probably not the best way to translate it into English. What to make of the existence of fronted adverbials leaves the following dilemmas: if the purpose of the second tense is to emphasize the adverbial adjunct, because fronted adverbials are impossible, then how should we interpret the second tense now that we know that fronted adverbials not only exist, but in fact are quite common? Although Polotsky's interpretation seems to work well in many cases, with the existence both of fronted adverbials and second tenses with no adverbial adjuncts to emphasize, what is left of Polotsky's interpretation of the second tenses?

Neal A. Maxwell Institute for Religious Scholarship
Brigham Young University

50 For the cultic use of *s.t-wr.t*, see P. Spencer, *The Egyptian Temple: A Lexicographical Study* (London, 1984), 108-14; P. Wilson, *A Ptolemaic Lexikon, A Lexicographical Study of the Texts in the Temple of Edfu,* OLA 78 (Louvain, 1997), 948-949.

51 P. UC 32201, verso 8-11, in F.Ll. Griffith, *Hieratic Papyri from Kahun and Gurob* (London, 1898), pl. 31; M. Collier and S. Quirke, *The UCL Lahun Papyri: Letters* (Oxford, 2002), 106-107.

52 Gardiner, *Egyptian Grammar*, 134.

53 Gardiner, *Egyptian Grammar*, 115.

54 Collier and Quirke, *The UCL Lahun Papyri: Letters*, 107.

55 E. Wente, *Letters from Ancient Egypt,* SBL Writings from the Ancient World 1 (Atlanta, 1990), 81.

Pyramid Shapes of the Twelfth Dynasty

Dieter Arnold

An architectural surprise was unearthed during the 2008 excavation season of the Metropolitan Museum of Art, New York at the pyramid of Senwosret III, Dahshur, necessitating a revision of excavation results previously (and obviously too hastily) published by the author.[1] It has been apparent since the 2005 season that contrary to earlier structures, the pyramid did not stand on a base that was more or less level with the surrounding court, but was surrounded by a step at least 2.50 m high, decorated with pairs of vertical grooves. Results from the last season showed that the exterior of this step was not only articulated with grooves, but also with 80 cm deep and 110 cm wide projections. The previously discovered grooves occupied the rear of recesses. Additional grooves, which decorated the front and sides of the projections, are only preserved in displaced fragments. The upper part of both the projections and recesses were decorated with slightly sunk, window-like squares. In other words, the pyramid foot was surrounded by a structure similar to the brick outer and stone inner enclosure walls that delimited Senwosret III's pyramid complex.

Remains of the pyramid foot were preserved on the north side of the pyramid 3-14 m east of the north chapel (Figs. 2-3) and on the east side 14-19 m north of the pyramid temple (Figs. 4-5). The actual projections were completely removed by ancient stone robbers, leaving only the double grooves of the recesses. However, clear outlines of the projections remained on the foundation platform. The surface of the rear wall on the north side of the pyramid retains two distinct colorations: the exposed surfaces of the recesses had a deeper patina than the vertical stripes that were protected by the towers. Directly in front of the pyramid foundation, we also found a great number of fragments with groove and window decoration. The location argues against the possibility that they migrated there from the area of the stone inner enclosure wall, which had the same decoration.[2]

It is remarkable that the projections were not bonded to the pyramid casing, but only rested against it and were slightly inclined. The poor construction method seems to suggest that the projections were an afterthought, but because the pyramid foundation extends 3 cubits (1.575 m) in front of the pyramid casing, such a wide step could only have been created in expectation of the projections.

If the features were regularly spaced, each side of the pyramid would have been surrounded by forty-four projections, interrupted only in the center of the east and north sides by the pyramid temple and north chapel. However, the problem of creating a corner

---

1 "Changing the shape of the pyramid of Senusret III," in *Abusir and Saqqara in the Year 2005,* eds. M. Bárta, et al. (Prague, 2006), 108-115.

2 The dimensions of both paneling systems are identical, meaning that size cannot be used to assign the fragments to either the inner enclosure wall or the pyramid foundation.

from two inclined walls must have forced an alteration.[3] The sloping walls of the first recesses next to the corner projections would have separated the corner projections from the back wall. The corner projections therefore must have been wider than the others. On the drawing in Figure 6, the recesses between the corner projections are shown filled with masonry, but we cannot determine if the designers chose this solution or if they solved the problem by distributing the resulting irregularities among the following projections and recesses. It is therefore possible that the number of projections should be reduced.

Thus far, the paneled elements have been found in situ only on the lowermost casing course on the north side of the pyramid, making an assessment of the original height of the platform difficult. When we rebuilt a 10 m long section of the stone inner enclosure wall in 2005, we chose a minimum height of 5 cubits (2.625 m),[4] a dimension that seemed to accord well with the amount of preserved wall fragments. In this reconstruction, the height of the projecting towers (2.625 m) is 2.38 times the width of a tower.[5] However, if one analyzes the dimensions and proportions of paneled walls and sarcophagi decorated with the same pattern, one arrives at a more slender proportion of tower width to height of up to 1/3.66, or excluding the more questionable evidence of the sarcophagi, up to 1/2.88.

Monument	Proportion of width to height of towers[6]
Inner enclosure wall of Senwosret III	1 : 2.38 (?)
Outer enclosure wall of Senwosret III	1 : 3.0
Sarcophagus of Senwosret III	1 : 4.89
Sarcophagus of Queen Weret II	1 : 4.6
Sarcophagus of Senet-senebetes	1 : 3.0
Sarcophagus of Menet	1 : 2.8
Sarcophagus of Amenemhat III	1 : 3.7
Sarcophagus of Aat	1 : 5.1
Sarcophagus of Tomb 7 at Illahun	1 : 3.9
Djoser enclosure wall	1 : 3.25

These proportions suggest that the paneled pyramid foot was perhaps 6 or 8 cubits (3.15 or 4.20 m) high. The higher number seems to correspond to the height of the present reconstruction of the north chapel. As a result, the north chapel would protrude from the wall but not tower over it (Fig. 7). However, a paneled pyramid foot 3.15 to 4.20 m high would have been much lower than the roof height of the pyramid temple, meaning that the upper part of the rear side of the temple was separated from the pyramid slope (Fig. 6). In order to compensate for this discrepancy, the triangular gap between the rear part of the temple and the casing must have been filled with solid masonry. The possibility that

---

3 For details, see D. Arnold, *The Pyramid Complex of Senwosret III at Dahshur: Architectural Studies,* PMMA 26 (New York, 2002), 21, fig. 1.

4 See A. Sauerbier, "Die nischengegliederte Umfassungsmauer der Pyramidenbezirke im Mittleren Reich," *Sokar* 12 (2006), 53-55; D. Arnold, "Pyramidenbezirk und Nekropole Sesostris' III. in Dahschur," *Sokar* 13 (2006), 44, fig. 8.

5 Not enough fragments of the lower part of the wall were preserved to justify a higher construction.

6 The measurements are taken from: D. Arnold, *The Pyramid Complex of Senwosret III,* 20, 23-24, pls. 5, 29, 112, 114; idem, *Der Pyramidenbezirk des Königs Amenemhet III. in Dahschur, Die Pyramide,* AV 53 (Mainz, 1987), figs. 13, 18; G. Brunton, *Lahun* I, *The Treasure,* BSAE 33 (London, 1914), pl. 22; J.-Ph. Lauer, *La pyramide à degrees: L'architecture,* Fouilles à Saqqarah 1 (Cairo, 1936), pl. 28.

the paneled wall reached the top of the approximately 7.35 m high pyramid temple is not only contradicted by the resulting, awkward proportions of the projections (1:6.7), but also by structural considerations. Since the projections were not bonded to the back wall, one can be sure that the builders would not have dared to raise 7 m high towers without interlocking the blocks.

The brick core of the pyramid does not reflect the step in the casing, but starts at ground level with a slope of 50º. The interior structure of the pyramid therefore shows that the basic concept was not to raise the pyramid on a platform, but to surround the pyramid foot with an additional layer. Although this distinction seems trifling and the resulting visual effect was the same, it is essential in order to correctly understand the innovation. The concept of an inner space enveloped by a larger unrelated outer space with a different shape was frequently used in Egyptian art and can be traced back to the First Dynasty. The "Menes" tomb of Neqada included a paneled wall that enclosed a higher core building, perhaps in the shape of a *per-nu.*[7] The same combination is also found on granite sarcophagi of the Old and Middle Kingdoms.[8] The aim was probably to express the fusion of two primeval, emblematic building forms, the burial mound and the palace wall.[9] At the same time, this encirclement was intended to magically protect a sacred space, actions that were manifested during the *sed*-festival and other occasions by the "circumambulation of the walls" or the "procession about the desert."[10]

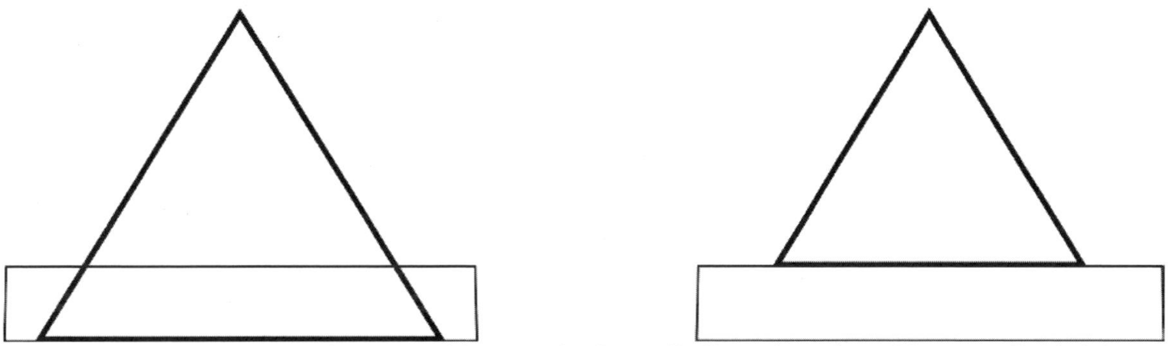

Figure 1. Structure of a pyramid on a platform (left) and enclosed by a wall (right)

A seeming forerunner of our construction is found at the pyramid of Pepi II (Fig. 8). After completion of the pyramid, the pyramid foot was surrounded by a layer of blocks 6.50 m thick but only 1.53 m high. Experts agree, however, that this layer was not part of the original plan, but added only to prevent an imminent collapse of the casing blocks.[11] The idea that the square center building of the Mentuhotep Nebhepetra temple at Deir el-Bahari actually enveloped a pyramid has been repeatedly expressed, even

7 L. Borchardt, "Das Grab des Menes," *ZÄS* 36 (1898), 87-105.

8 Old Kingdom: M. Donadoni-Rovere, *I sarcofagi egizi dalle origini alla fine dell'Antico Regno* (Rome, 1969), nos. B15, B22, B32-33, B35-36, B40, B47; Twelfth Dynasty: D. Arnold, *The Pyramid Complex of Senwosret III*, for example pls. 19, 28-29, 61.

9 See H. Ricke's discussions of the *Hügelgrab* and the *Hausgrab* in *Bemerkungen zur ägyptischen Baukunst des Alten Reiches* 1, *BÄBA* 1 (Zurich, 1944), 38-43.

10 R.K. Ritner, *The Mechanics of Ancient Egyptian Magical Practice*, SAOC 54 (Chicago, 1993), 57-63.

11 This building disaster even prompted the removal of the north chapel, see G. Jéquier, *Le monument funéraire de Pepi II* 2 (Cairo, 1938), 6-7; A. Labrousse, *L'architecture des pyramides à textes* 2, BdÉ 131 (Cairo, 2000), 78-79, figs. 149-153, pl. 34.

though the building's inner structure contradicts such a supposition.[12] Two questionable Old Kingdom examples of enveloping a core building with recesses also must be mentioned. In the late Fourth Dynasty, masons started to carve grooves into the bedrock beneath the mastaba of Khentkaues at Giza[13] and the lower part of the Mastabat el-Fara'un may also have been surrounded by paneled elements.[14]

The pyramid of Senwosret II at Illahun was not only the immediate predecessor of the Senwosret III pyramid, but, despite its unfinished state, seems to have played a significant role in pyramid development. The foot of the pyramid was surrounded by a wide trench with a V-shaped section,[15] which was in turn enclosed by a wall cased from the outside by paneled limestone slabs attached to a vertical rock core.[16] The excavators assumed that the trench was designed to absorb rain water, an explanation that is not convincing as the trench would have been quickly filled with wind-blown sand. But what was in the trench? Was it paved to create an inner court? Or could the space have been filled to the top of the enclosure wall, providing a step around the pyramid base that was cased with a paneled wall?[17] Even if there was no such step, the introduction of a trench and a paneled wall suggests that Senwosret II's architects had started to experiment with the design of the pyramid foot and with the motive of paneling.[18]

There is reason to believe that the new pyramid shape was not restricted to the pyramid of Senwosret III, but that the following pyramids continued the trend. Strong evidence indicates that the pyramid of Amenemhat III at Dahshur had such a feature. In his publication, De Morgan illustrates[19] a trench in front of the pyramid casing at the center of the structure's north side (Fig. 9).[20] The photo shows two workers standing in front of the foundation course and, a short distance behind them, five courses of casing blocks that appear to have been cracked and dislocated by earthquakes and human activity. The front of these blocks does not appear to slope, as one would expect for a pyramid with a 55° incline, but seem to be vertical. No vertical grooves or traces of the projections are visible in the photo, but one would not expect them at the place where the north chapel was originally attached to the vertical casing. Although evidence of these

---

12 D. Arnold, *Der Tempel des Königs Mentuhotep von Deir el-Bahari* 1, *Architektur und Deutung*, AV 8 (Mainz, 1974), 28-31.

13 However, the carving of niches was abandoned and the grooves covered with casing blocks, see V. Maragioglio and C. Rinaldi, *L'architettura delle piramidi menfite* 6 (Rapallo, 2000), pl.18.

14 A theory presented in H.W. Müller, "Gedanken zur Entstehung, Interpretation und Rekonstruktion ältester ägyptischer Monumentalarchitektur," in *Ägypten –Dauer und Wandel*, SDAIK 18 (1985), 21-24.

15 The publication of W.M.F. Petrie, G. Brunton, and M.A. Murray, *Lahun* 2, BSAE 33 (London, 1923), 2-3, pls. 4-9 provides only one plan at 1:1000, but no sections or detailed drawings.

16 *Ibid.* pls. 23, 51[1]. Brunton's reconstruction needs some correction. The sides of the towers normally have two vertical grooves and the wall certainly did not carry a parapet. The excavators also failed to address the question as to how the slabs could have been fastened to the rock.

17 More recent excavations did not address this question, see R.A. Frey and J.E. Knudstad, "The Re-examination of Selected Architectural Remains at El-Lahun," *JSSEA* 35 (2008), 72-79.

18 This observation supports the notion that several political and religious developments known from the reign of Senwosret III have their roots in the short reign of the preceding pharaoh Senwosret II.

19 *Fouilles à Dahchour Mars-Juin 1894* (Vienna, 1895), pl. 40.

20 The location of the trench is shown on his plan, see *Fouilles à Dahchour 1894-1895* (Vienna, 1903), pl. 16. The photo was taken May 10, 1894, before De Morgan opened at this exact spot the search tunnel that led him into the royal chamber (December 5, 1894).

features was uncovered during excavations in 1983, it was not understood at that time.[21] In particular, two limestone blocks with inclined vertical grooves were excavated that could not be explained because the inner and outer enclosure walls of the pyramid complex were both built of brick (Fig. 10).[22] The 31 cm wide grooves on the fragments from Amenemhat III suggest the towers were 1.55 m wide,[23] which is 30 % wider than the Senwosret III towers. The paneled foundation might therefore have been higher as well.

As is to be expected, the pyramid of Amenemhat III at Hawara seems to have included the same features.[24] For remains of the casing, one must examine the entrance staircase, which is located at the west end of the south side of the pyramid. The actual entrance in the casing and the upper end of the staircase has been quarried away, meaning that we see now the vertically set heads of the sloping wall blocks bridged by a ceiling block.[25] The lost upper end of the staircase led through the 4 m thick pyramid casing and, according to Petrie's sketch, placed the original entrance at ground level.[26] About 2 m east of the entrance, a masonry bulwark four courses high flanks the entrance breach (Fig. 11). The front surface is smooth, has a patina and clearly shows a vertical articulation apparently consisting of shallow grooves. These features suggest that the masonry block was not part of an underground foundation, but belonged to the aboveground front of a paneled step surrounding the foot of the pyramid.[27]

The preoccupation with paneled elements in the pyramid complex of Senwosret III (outer and inner enclosure walls, pyramid platform and sarcophagus base) is astonishing. This building form is the most conspicuous architectural feature adapted by Senwosret II and Senwosret III from the vast repertoire of Third Dynasty architectural shapes and types, which survive mainly in the Djoser complex at Saqqara.[28] Another such adaptation was the elimination of the axial approach to the pyramid complex, an integral feature of most pyramid complexes from the reigns of Snefru to Amenemhat II. Instead, the first, square phase of the pyramid complex of Senwosret III was accessed through a gate at the south end of the east wall.[29] The shift was even more pronounced in

---

21 Unaware of this important feature and discouraged by the huge masses of sand that covered the pyramid foot, we did not attempt to reach the casing. We only cleared the areas immediately around the east and west entrances of the pyramid, where no casing blocks were preserved. See D. Arnold, *Der Pyramidenbezirk*, pls. 42, 48. The reconstructions on plates 43-44 show an incorrect inclined casing.

22 *Ibid*., 67, fig. 34, pl. 31d. The blocks were even found in the debris of the casing at the northeast corner of the pyramid.

23 The grooves are 31 cm wide.

24 Except for R. Lepsius's confused excavation, *Denkmäler aus Aegypten und Aethiopien*, *Texte* 2 (Leipzig, 1904), 24-27 and Petrie's adventurous exploration of the interior of the pyramid, see *Kahun, Gurob, and Hawara* (London, 1890), 5-8, no one has examined or documented the structure of the pyramid.

25 The same arrangement is found in the king's Dahshur pyramid, compare Arnold, *Der Pyramidenbezirk*, pls. 7, 42-43.

26 It is possible that the upper part of the corridor did not continue the upward slope and dipped so far down that the entrance remained hidden below ground level, see W.M.F. Petrie, *Kahun, Gurob, and Hawara*, pl. 3.

27 This conclusion of course needs to be confirmed by an exact determination of the ancient court level and a precise documentation of the pyramid entrance and the masonry in question.

28 D. Arnold, *The Pyramid Complex of Senwosret III*, 121-122.

29 *Ibid*., plan I.

the north-south orientation of the later phase of the complex, again with the entrance at the south end of the east wall. One must admit that these later modifications of the complex may have been primarily motivated by the intention to build the south temple. Nevertheless, the outcome was a ground plan with some parallels to that of the Djoser complex and a marked contrast to the standard east-west orientation of most preceding pyramid complexes. The introduction of other archaistic architectural features such as a triple corner torus combined with a cavetto curving out from a ledge, rounded door frames and a tree-trunk ceiling pattern were also intended to revive images of the past. This resumption of already ancient forms in royal funerary architecture may be understood as a major component of the reorientation of Egyptian society, administration, burial customs and art that took place during the second half of the Twelfth Dynasty.[30]

Addenda: A visit made to Hawara by the author in September 2009 revealed that the above-described stone surface adjacent to the pyramid entrance is not the exterior surface of the pyramid. Therefore the feature cannot be used in an evaluation of the shape of Amenemhat III's pyramid.

Department of Egyptian Art
Metropolitan Museum of Art

[30] L. Gestermann, "Der politische und kulturelle Wandel unter Sesostris III.," in *Per Aspera ad Astra, Wolfgang Schenkel zum neunundfünfzigsten Geburtstag. Ein Entwurf*, eds. L. Gestermann and H. Sternberg-El Hotabi (Kassel, 1995), 31-50.

Figure 2. Pyramid of Senwosret III: Traces of projections on the foundation platform east of the north chapel (photo by author).

Figure 3. Pyramid of Senwosret III: Traces of recesses on the pyramid casing east of the north chapel (photo by author).

Figure 4. Pyramid of Senwosret III: Traces of projections on the pyramid casing north of the pyramid temple (photo by author).

Figure 5. Pyramid of Senwosret III: Traces of projections on the pyramid casing north of the pyramid temple (photo by author).

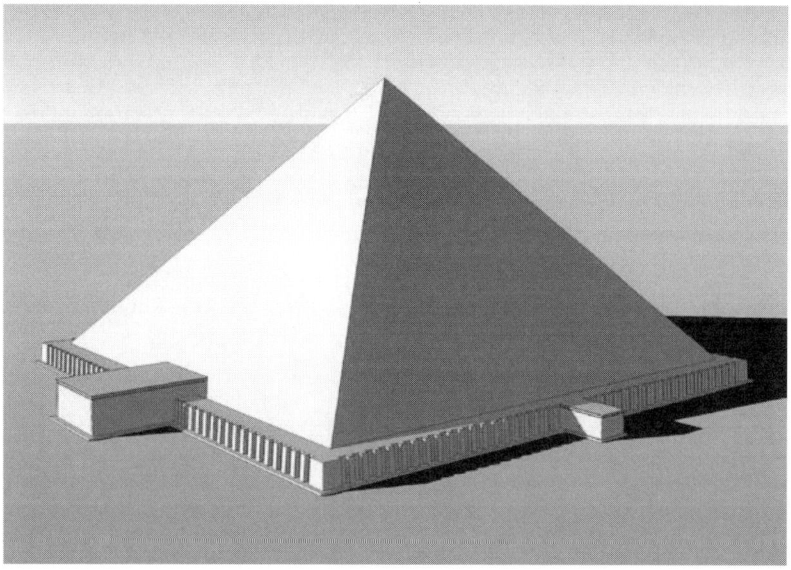

Figure 6. Pyramid of Senwosret III: Reconstruction of the pyramid, north chapel and pyramid temple (computer drawing by Scott Murphy).

Figure 7. Pyramid of Senwosret III: Reconstruction of the foot of the pyramid casing east of the north chapel (computer drawing by Scott Murphy).

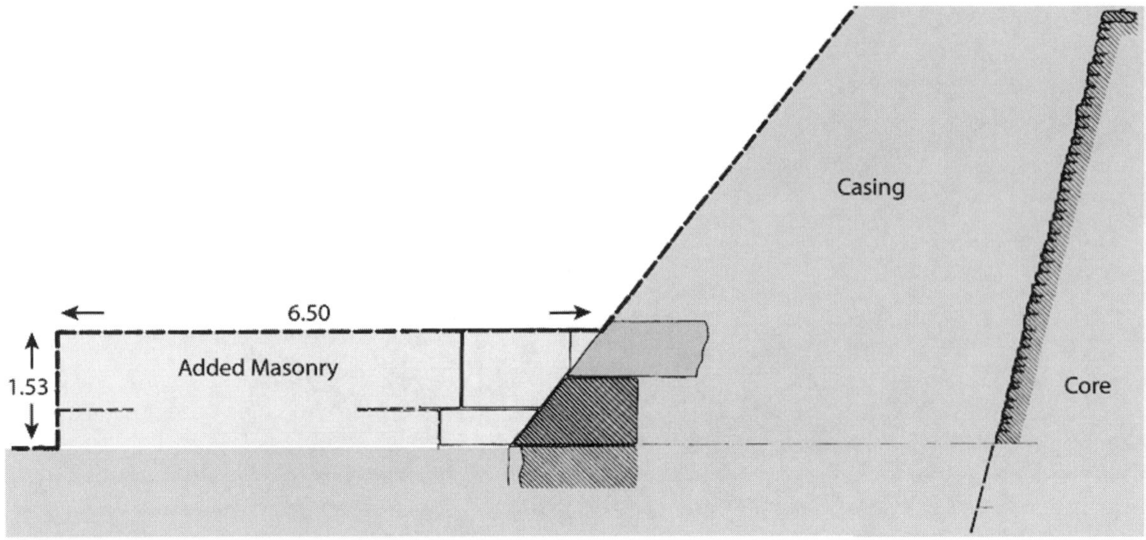

Figure 8. Pyramid of Pepi II: Added masonry around the pyramid foot (after Audran Labrousse, *L'architecture des pyramides à textes*, 2 (Cairo, 2000), pls. 181-186).

Figure 9. Pyramid of Amenemhat III at Dahshur: Casing in the center of the north side, exposed by De Morgan (Jacques De Morgan, *Fouilles à Dahchour Mars-Juin 1894* [Vienna, 1895], pl. 40).

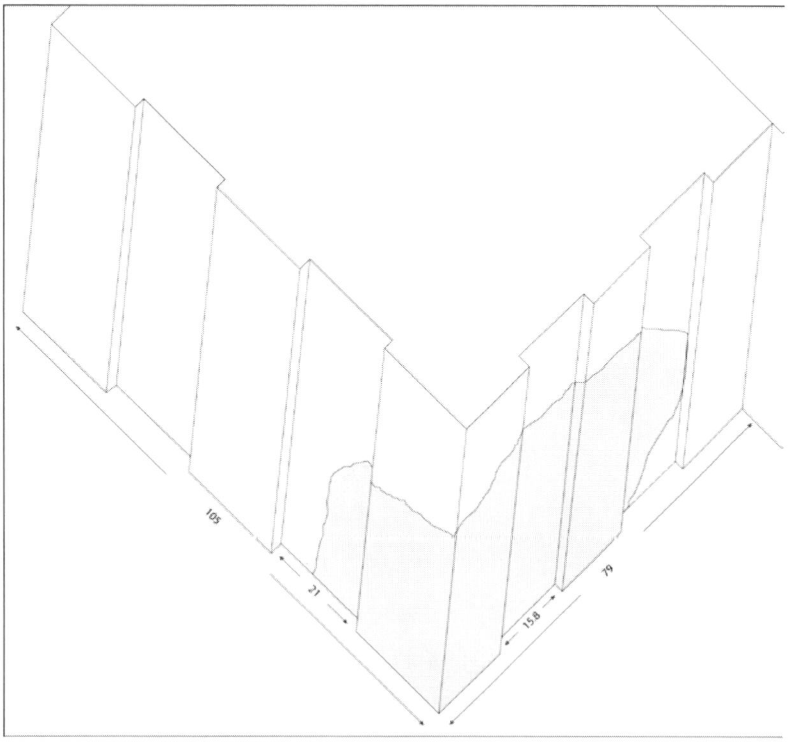

Figure 10. Pyramid of Amenemhat III at Dahshur: Fragment of a block with grooves (Dieter Arnold, *Der Pyramidenbezirk des Königs Amenemhet III. in Dahschur* [Mainz, 1987], fig. 34).

Figure 11. Pyramid of Amenemhat III at Hawara: Casing east of the pyramid entrance (photo by author).